THE Algonquin KID

By Michael Elihu Colby

Adventures Growing Up at New York's Legendary Hotel

Illustrations by Hannah Chusid and Dennis Porter

Based on the series "The Algonquin Kid"
from www.TheaterPizzazz.com

THE ALGONQUIN KID
by Michael Elihu Colby
Adventures Growing Up at New York's Legendary Hotel
Illustrations by Hannah Chusid and Dennis Porter
Based on the series "The Algonquin Kid" from www.TheaterPizzazz.com

 Published in the USA by:
BearManor Media
P O Box 71426
Albany, Georgia 31708
www.bearmanormedia.com

ISBN: 978-1-59393-792-8
Printed in the United States of America
Book design by Robbie Adkins, www.adkinsconsult.com

The Algonquin Kid with Aunt Barbara Anspach.

Table of Contents

Acknowledgments

Thanks to the following who helped me on this project and/or shared recollections of the Algonquin Hotel and Bodne Family:

Joy Abbott, Robbie Adkins, Barbara Anspach, Robert Armin, Len Baron, Elizabeth Anspach Carlson, Renee Mae Colby Chubet, David Colby, Douglas Colby, Steven Colby, Stephen Cox, Roxanna Anspach Devlin, Alice de Almeida, Carol Dunitz, Michael Feinstein, Sandra Joy Fishman, Alison Fraser, Robert Freedman, Elinor Goodman, John Guare, Ernie Harburg, Jennifer & Larry Hart II, Louise Kerz Hirschfeld, James Jennings, Leslie Howard, Michael Hurley, Rosalind Jacobs, Judson Memorial Church (Abigail Hastings, Melissa Jameson), Barry Koron, Jill Krementz, Raymond Kursar, David Leopold, Elizabeth Linning/Haigood Family, Emily Mann (ICM), Jeremy Markoe, Andie Markoe-Byrne, The Mabel Mercer Foundation (Jason Martin), Dave Menefee, Eric Myers, Dr. Ryan T. Nelson (Northwestern University), Ben Ohmart, Frederic Ohringer, Michael Parva, Linda Purl, Mike Renzi, Sandra Reynolds, Nilda I. Rivera (Museum of the City of New York), Rodgers & Hammerstein: an Imagem Company (Ted Chapin, David Loughner, Robin Walton), Howard & Ron Mandelbaum (Photofest), Eric Roberts, Steve Ross, Will Sawyer, Steve Schalchlin, Elyse Schulman, Scott Shiller, Harriet Spanier, Gary Springer, Jim Steinblatt (ASCAP), K.T. Sullivan, Gail Thacker (Gene Frankel Theatre), Jason Viarengo, Martha Nelly Wasserman, Joseph Weiss (Jule Styne, Inc.), Rita Coburn Whack (Caged Bird Legacy, LLC.), Bruce Yeko.

Special thanks: to Sandi Durell and www.TheaterPizzazz.com, the recent home of the Algonquin Kid, and to Andrea Colby, my editor and love of my life.

Dedicated to my grandparents,
Mary and Ben B. Bodne,
whose doors were always open
so I could "pend de night."

Caption: Mary and Ben B. Bodne.

Chapter 1: *Way Back When*

Algonquin early 1930s. Courtesy of the Algonquin Hotel.

There were the many talks Harpo Marx shared with my Grandpa Ben. There was the time Marilyn Monroe flashed Grandma Mary. There was the afternoon Lerner and Loewe promised a role to eight-year-old me in their new musical, *Camelot.* Through the years, I collected a trove of treasured stories, while growing up around the Algonquin Hotel, as a real-life counterpart to "Eloise of the Plaza."

New York's landmark Algonquin Hotel was bought in 1946 by my grandparents, Ben and Mary Bodne, Southern Jews atypical of the hotel's literary types and stage folk. They lived there for the rest of their lives even after selling the hotel in 1987 to a Brazilian subsidiary of a Tokyo corporation (a strange combination leading to a succession of other owners).

According to family legend, my grandparents first fell in love with the Algonquin while honeymooning there in the 1920s. They were dazzled to be hobnobbing with guests like Mary Pickford, Douglas Fairbanks Jr., Beatrice Lillie, Sinclair Lewis, and Will Rogers, whom they'd just seen in the *Ziegfeld Follies* (1924).

The Manhattan hotel already had a multifaceted history. Rather than globetrotters, horse stables once occupied the address—59 West 44th Street—where the Algonquin opened in 1902. Noted architect Goldwyn Starrett designed this 174-room, Edwardian-style hotel. The place became a Mecca for rising New York luminaries through the guidance of Frank Case, who'd worked there since its inception and who became its owner-manager in 1927. It was he who suggested that the original owner name the hotel the Algonquin (rather than "The Puritan"). A strong advocate for the Arts, Frank Case offered special rates to actors, writers, and artists. He established the Algonquin Round Table, where the likes of Dorothy Parker, George S. Kauffman, Alexander Woollcott, and Robert Benchley regularly lunched, exchanging quips and quotes that proved exceptional public relations for the hotel.

Frank Case courtesy of Hilary Morgan and Frank Case Family.

Portrait of the Algonquin Round Table by Natalie Ascencios: (bottom row, left to right): Dorothy Parker, Harold Ross, George S. Kaufman, and Heywood Broun. (top row, left to right): Robert Benchley, the Algonquin Cat, Franklin P. Adams, Robert E. Sherwood, Harpo Marx, Alexander Woollcott, Marc Connelly, and Edna Ferber. Courtesy of the Algonquin Hotel.

My grandparents came from a very different background than the urbane Frank Case. Of European Jewish ancestry, Grandpa Ben (Polish/Latvian) and Grandma Mary (Russian) also had large families in common: Grandpa had three sisters and three brothers, Grandma seven sisters and two brothers. Their homes were already like hotels. Grandpa Ben was born in Shamokin PA, but his Orthodox family eventually moved to Chattanooga, Tennessee—as unlikely as it may be to use Tennessee and

Bodne Family: Ben, Florence, Michael, Phillip, Joe, Mollie, Harry, Elizabeth, and Rose.

Torah in the same sentence. His father, Michael Bodne, after whom I'm named, was a junk dealer. His mother Mollie cooked food that reportedly tasted like junk, albeit Kosher. The family was so poor, young Ben supplemented their family income as a paperboy. Grandpa Ben claimed he first met a celebrity selling her a paper: he believed that woman, who tipped him generously, was Helen Keller.

Grandpa never finished school, though he told some funny school stories. He'd relate how, when he was in ninth grade, the teacher called in Grandpa's father for a special meeting, saying, "You have to do something about your son. He's a real Smart Alec. Last week I asked Ben, 'Who wrote *Hamlet*?,' and Ben replied, 'Well, it wasn't me!'"

To that, Grandpa's father said, "Listen, Ma'am. My Benny's a good boy. If he told you he didn't write *Hamlet*, he didn't write *Hamlet*!"

Grandpa also recounted how he quit school out of embarrassment, when he got to the eighth grade and caught up with his father. Where Grandpa Ben excelled were athletics and business. He was a champion athlete at the local YMHA, considered becoming a professional baseball player, and later became promoter for such greats as world boxing champ Marcel Cerdan. In fact, Grandpa's ultimate business decision was choosing between buying the Algonquin Hotel and the Pittsburgh Pirates.

Ben Bodne (l.) on YMHA basketball team. 1922, Knoxville, Tennessee.

Grandma Mary was born in Odessa, Russia (now part of Ukraine), the daughter of Elihu and Anastasia (a.k.a. Essie) Mazo. When she was an infant, her family hid with other Jews in an attic while Cossacks plundered their village. She started to cry, and the terrified fugitives thought they'd have to suffocate her if she continued to endanger them. Then, with precocious insight, she hushed up till it was safe for them to escape. It's said her later outspokenness was compensation for that momentary silence.

When Grandma was six months old, the Mazos—including older sister Betty—immigrated to Charleston, South Carolina, which had a sizable Jewish population. It's there that Elihu Mazo opened Mazo's Grocery ("Mazo's"), which evolved into the first Jewish deli in the South,

Essie (middle) and Elihu Mazo (far right) with friends and family at Mazo store.

serving Kosher sandwiches. Essie kept busy creating eight more children, enough to tend the deli and each other. Growing up, it was at Mazo's that Grandma cultivated her Southern hospitality, filling the knish list of Carolina's Kleiners and Feiners. It was also where she got her first taste not only of pickles but of show business. Both Elihu Mazo and his brother Dave—who owned an even bigger, if generic, grocery store—became good friends of a prominent Charlestonian, writer DuBose Heyward. Heyward was best known for his 1925 novel *Porgy*, based on life in Charleston's Cabbage Row (renamed Catfish Row). The book was later adopted into a hit play by Heyward's wife, Dorothy. DuBose would soon collaborate with George and Ira Gershwin on a musical version of the play.

Around 1934, when George Gershwin was researching in Charleston for *Porgy and Bess* (1935), the Mazo deli became one of Gershwin's favorite hangouts. He developed a strong friendship with all the Mazos. At Mazo family dinners, he'd play his newest songs on their piano. He even dated Grandma Mary's beautiful younger sister Cyd (born Sara Sadie). The Mazos had high hopes of a celebrity in the family until a courtship date when Gershwin bought Aunt Cyd a chocolate ice cream cone. She complained—she wanted vanilla. Bad move! The romance soon broke up, possibly over a flavor.

By the time Aunt Cyd was dating Gershwin, Grandpa Ben had already moved to Charleston, eventually marrying Mary Mazo. He believed there

George Gershwin courtesy of Photofest.

were greater work opportunities in Charleston, and a wider choice of Jewish women, than in Chattanooga. Grandma Mary had charms Grandpa couldn't resist: she was a dynamo and a much better cook than Mollie Bodne. Mary was also quite a dancer—her specialty, the Charleston—entering competitions including one where she befriended guest performer Ginger Rogers. Moreover, she was the first in the family accepted at a college. However, she gave up attending Baltimore's Goucher College when Grandpa Ben proposed, driving to meet her in his Model T Ford. She thought that her best option: after growing up with seven sisters, the prospect of a marrying a sporty Kosher catch seemed more appealing than four years at an all-female college. By the way, another show business connection was Grandma's cousin, Charlestonian Frances Mazo Butwin. Frances and her husband Julius wrote the original Yiddish-to-English translation of Sholem Aleichem's "Tevye's Daughters," source of *Fiddler On the Roof.* The authors of *Fiddler On the Roof*—Joseph Stein, Sheldon Harnick, and Jerry Bock—drew heavily from the Butwins' versions; an early draft of the musical even borrowed the same title as a Butwin volume, *The Old Country* (1956).[1]

After Grandpa set himself up in business, Ben and Mary worked side by side like a tag-team. While Grandpa Ben was building his fortune selling coal, then recycling oil cylinders during World War II, Grandma Mary operated his office and his trucks with enough stamina to deliver through a tsunami. Add to the work burden, Grandma tended to their two daughters, Renee* Mae (*pronounced "REE-knee") and Barbara Ann.

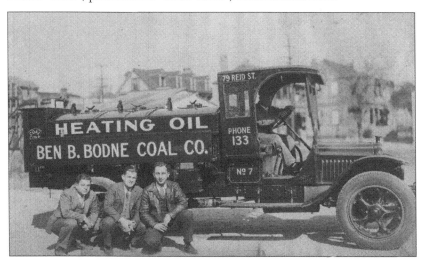

Ben Bodne (c.) at his oil company. 1933, Charleston, South Carolina.

Still, it all paid off. By 1946, Grandpa Ben had become a millionaire via various oil ventures. He had built the first independent deep-water terminal in South Carolina. His company had drummed most of the diesel fuel that went into the African campaign of World War II. The time came when he decided to parlay his fortune into a new business. There were two major choices. 1946 was the year Frank Case died and the Algonquin was up for resale, as were the Pittsburgh Pirates. The Pittsburgh Pirates would be a dream-come-true for Grandpa, who craved being part of professional sports. I suspect Grandma had a different preference than being taken out to the ballgame and selling peanuts and Crackerjack. The Algonquin was a setting where she could mingle with people like George Gershwin and Ginger Rogers. Just the kind of place where she could display the Southern hospitality she cultivated offering salami, lox, and other delicacies at her father's deli.

The choice became moot when a group headed by Bing Crosby pitched a bid on the Pittsburgh Pirates that was a homerun. Grandpa struck out, but Grandma was swinging on a star, as her husband clinched the remaining deal. The Bodnes picked up their suitcases and daughters and headed to their new address, the venerable Algonquin Hotel. Notwithstanding, there was a hitch to their new hitching post. In the aftermath of World War II, the place was in terrible disrepair, with antiquated plumbing, faded décor, and worn-out furniture—the ghost of a past golden age. Advisors had warned the Bodnes that the hotel's glamour and vitality had died with Frank Case. How could a Southern oilman and his wife restore the former glory of this cultural invalid? The daunting task ahead was just another challenge for Grandma, who'd survived the Cossacks, and Grandpa, who'd survived poverty and his mother's cooking. They somehow knew—as would be sung in the future Algonquin cabaret—"The Best Is Yet to Come." Times with Lord Olivier, Jacqueline Kennedy, Ella Fitzgerald, and countless others were in the offing. As was I, "The Algonquin Kid." But, for now, the adventure had just begun.

Mary and Ben with daughters Barbara and Renee Mae.

Chapter 2: *Algonquin Renaissance*

Algonquin Staff. Photo: Lucas Monroe-Lucas Pritchard courtesy of Museum of the City of New York.

Upon moving into the Algonquin Hotel in 1946, Grandpa Ben oversaw 160 employees, far more than he'd ever supervised before. Among them were characters as colorful as the celebrities housed at the hotel.

Renowned writer Quentin Reynolds described a few such employees in his article "The Hotel That Refused to Die" (*Esquire*, February 1950 edition). There was switchboard operator Lovilla Bush, affectionately nicknamed "Bushy," who reputedly could track down anyone from Gertrude Lawrence to Noel Coward to J. Edgar Hoover. Hotel regulars didn't even have to feed her phone numbers: she had ways and means to find anyone. Also notable was Martin the Valet (Martin Stephen Kalydjian), who worked in an office resembling that of Broadway agent, his walls filled with warmly inscribed photos of theatre luminaries. Maître d' Raul (Raul Viarengo) was a backer of plays, to whom fellow investors often turned for advice on best bets.[1] Raul was likewise a master strategist at solving daily dining dilemmas. When a guest found a fly in her salad, he popped it in his mouth, swallowed down the evidence, and exclaimed "Delicious! A raisin." Another quick solution involved Mrs. Robert Bolt, who was staying at the hotel during the

Chef Otto Schmock and Raul Viarengo courtesy of Jason Viarengo.

Broadway run of her husband's hit play, *A Man For All Seasons* (Broadway, 1961). When she tried to enter the hotel's Oak Room wearing slacks, Raul cautioned, "We have a rule against women in slacks, but if you will permit me, I will supply you with a skirt, the same kind of skirt I once made for Tallulah Bankhead." Thereupon, he draped a tablecloth around Mrs. Bolt's waist, adjusted it, added a sash he fashioned from the pink silk ribbon of a candy box, and regally ushered Mrs. Bolt to a table.[2]

As Grandpa Ben learned, personal attention—as offered to guests by the hotel staff—was the lifeblood of the hotel's longevity. Knowing names, habits, favorite rooms, and other details was essential to making visitors feel the Algonquin was a home away from home. Yet, in 1946, such cordiality couldn't sweep the hotel's state of disrepair under the moldy rug. Grandpa Ben had bought the hotel for just over a million dollars and rustled up another $300,000 for renovations. For eight months, he marshaled a covert mission to overhaul the hotel during late hours when no one would notice. According to the Quentin Reynolds' article, "He sent three hundred chairs, divans, tables, and beds to the city dump. But he replaced them with replicas of the old and no one noticed the difference. He had all of the halls and most of the rooms painted, but he stuck to the old colors."[3] Among other improvements, he replaced the antiquated kitchen equipment with optimum upgrades. In time, it was as if elves had impeccably dry-cleaned the place, so subtle yet thorough was the makeover. Grandpa said, "I was spending a fortune to make the guests more comfortable, but couldn't let them find out. Don't forget that many of them had been living off and on at the Algonquin for twenty years or more, and they wanted no changes."[4]

Grandpa had become a bona fide "Boniface," the expression for innkeeper that often described past Algonquin owner Frank Case. Grandpa proved a worthy successor. He liked to be called by the authoritative name

Grandpa Ben at hotel with visiting Mary Livingston, unidentified serviceman, and Jack Benny.

Illustration of Algonquin Lobby courtesy of the Algonquin Hotel.

Ben B. Bodne and loved using the initials B.B.B. on engravings (though privately he admitted that he never really had a middle name and the "B" in Ben B. Bodne stood for "baloney"). He was the rare hotel owner who told his steward the bills for meat and other foods weren't high enough! He wanted only the best meals at his hotel, still smarting from that salty boiled water that his mother called chicken soup.

He was a tireless worker, always looking for new ways to modernize the Algonquin while retaining its Edwardian elegance. From the 1950s through the 1970s, he made the place a paradox: an old-fashioned hotel featuring new technology. Before they became commonplace, he installed such novelties as air conditioning and smoke detectors. He supplied the maids with walkie-talkies. He also made the Algonquin the first hotel in New York to use electronic key-cards. However, he insisted on one cozy concession to the past, employing an elevator man when other hotel elevators were going automatic (Grandma Mary's strong claustrophobia probably clinched the deal).

Busy as he was, he demanded time-out during the baseball season. No one was to disturb him when a ballgame was on radio and later TV. In fact, he often had up to three televisions playing, watching baseball, football, basketball, and/or golf tournaments.

Meanwhile, the Algonquin was enjoying a Renaissance. The visitors not only included New York show people but members of the U.S. Supreme Court, international filmmakers, musicians, novelists, and, of course, everyday civilians. The hotel's three restaurants— the Rose Room, Oak Room, and Chinese Room—were hotspots for celebrity sightings.

In addition, the Blue Bar was a favorite haunt of Tennessee Williams, Norman Mailer, William Saroyan, and John Cheever. After Broadway openings, the Rose Room teemed with regulars including Ingrid Bergman, caricaturist Al Hirschfeld, Moss Hart, Kitty Carlyle, and Tallulah Bankhead (Bankhead—like Angela Lansbury—lived at the Algonquin, while still in her teens, on arriving in New York). Before openings, critics like George Jean Nathan, Walter Kerr, and H. L. Mencken would gather. Mencken called the hotel "The most comfortable hotel that I have ever found in America—and God knows I've seen a lot of them." Visiting, as well, were original "Round-Tablers" (members of the Algonquin Round Table), such as Dorothy Parker, George S. Kaufman, Marc Connelly, and various Marx Brothers. To wit, the hotel remained the stomping ground of writers from *The New Yorker* magazine, including its editor Harold Ross and his successor, William Shawn. In fact, Ross conceived *The New Yorker* there in 1925, during a poker game with illustrious writers.

Algonquin resident Enid Markey: personal photo; in Tarzan of the Apes *as the original screen "Jane" opposite Elmo Lincoln; Helen Hayes, Marga Ann Deighton, Mildred Chandler, Enid Markey, and Brandon de Wilde in the original play,* Mrs. McThing. *From the collection of Brian J. Bohnett, author of* The Remarkable Enid Markey: First Lady of the Tarzan Films *(2012).*

Tony Cichielo, the hotel's veteran Bell Captain, reported, "When I first came here, at night when you walked down the halls all you heard was typewriters. Writers seem to get inspired at 2 or 3 in the morning. These guys would have been lousy working 8 to 5."[5]

Grandma Mary basked in the glitter and the glamour. Where else could she enter the elevator alongside William Faulkner and Thornton Wilder and introduce them, saying "Don't you two boys know each other?" And what neighbors the Bodnes had! Every day was like a TV episode featuring great guest stars. Among the permanent Algonquin residents were Mr. and Mrs. James Thurber, composer Alec Wilder, and character actress Enid Markey, who was the silent screen's first Jane—opposite Elmo Lincoln's Tarzan in *Tarzan of the Apes* (1918) and *The Romance of Tarzan* (1918). Her later film and TV roles included Barney Fife's landlady on *The Andy Griffith Show* (1963) and Gomer Pyle's grandmother on *Gomer Pyle: USMC* (1966). Alongside year-round inhabitants were playwrights in temporary residence for their latest works, such as Arthur Miller (*All My Sons*, 1947), Tennessee Williams (*A Streetcar Named Desire*, 1947), and William Inge (*Picnic*, 1953).

Family friend Ted Lewis with young Elizabeth Anspach and David Colby.

As in Charleston, Grandma worked with Grandpa like a tag-team. She was the Will Rogers of hoteliers: she never met a guest she didn't like (at least, early on). She continued the hotel's tradition of personal service, catering to each guest's preferences. Ingratiating herself with the theatre crowd, she soon became the go-to person for hard-to-get theatre tickets, indulging guests and her own relatives, many who'd moved to the New York area or periodically vacationed there. Meanwhile, she and Grandpa Ben cultivated a group of stellar friends, including Joe DiMaggio, columnist Leonard Lyons, attorney/writer Louis Nizer, *Variety* editor Abel Green, and actor

Dana Andrews (whose movie, *Laura*, was partly filmed at the Algonquin). My grandparents grew particularly fond of Ted and Adah Lewis, Ted being the entertainer famous for the phrase "Is Everybody Happy?" and the hit song "Me and My Shadow." The childless Lewises would one day treat me like family.

Beyond the daily bustle, the Algonquin wasn't a typical setting for the Bodnes to oversee their two daughters. As living quarters, they had reconstructed half of the 10th floor into one homey apartment. Younger teenage daughter, Barbara Ann, attended New York's Calhoun School. My mother, Renee Mae, who was five years older

Renee Mae Bodne weds Sidney Jack Colby.

than Barbara, stayed south at the University of Georgia—until a trip to New York City, whereupon she met Sidney Jack Colby, a freshman at New York University. It was hello Sidney, goodbye Southland. They were both eighteen at the time and married by age twenty in 1948. This was not a lavish Algonquin event, but a ceremony in a rabbi's study, followed by a simple party at my grandparents' apartment. My father, Sidney, was the younger of two sons born to Dora and Irving Cohen, who owned a tuxedo and bridal gown shop in Brooklyn. Needless to say, my father wore a wedding suit worthy of Beau Brummel.

My father had changed his name from Sidney Cohen while aspiring to be a radio broadcaster. Music, especially Jazz, was his greatest joy. It seemed like a living fantasy when he visited the Algonquin and encountered musical celebrities from Ted Lewis to Rosemary Clooney, from Irving Berlin to Noel Coward, and ultimately a woman he idolized, Ella Fitzgerald.

In a photograph of their wedding day, my parents look like a gorgeous wedding cake couple. Regrettably, their marriage would become bittersweet. They were simply too young and ill prepared for years ahead. My porcelain-pretty mother, pampered all her life by my grandparents, was unable to fend for herself. Meanwhile, instead of a radio announcer, my father became a manager at the Algonquin, jumping at the opportunity offered by Grandpa Ben, even though Dad had no hotel training (but then, neither had my grandfather when he bought the place).

A proviso was for my father to first learn the ropes at the hotel, working in different departments from the kitchen onward. With his Kirk Douglas cleft and dimples, coupled with a sunny personality, my father proved quite popular as manager. Through the years—according to my father—he had to deflect flirtations from such guests as Miriam Hopkins, Rona Barrett, and Michael Redgrave. My father wasn't *that* captivated by celebrities, especially with my grandparents around.

The Colbys set up an apartment on Central Park West. My grand-mother engaged a housekeeper to keep everything tidy there. Though time would prove otherwise, the marriage seemed perfect, at least from afar. Within a few years, my mother was pregnant with the first of a new generation descended from Bodnes, Mazos, and Cohens. In 1951, I was born Michael Elihu Colby, named after Grandpa Ben's father, Michael Bodne, and Grandma's father, Elihu Mazo.

Naming children after Elihu was a tradition in the Mazo family, so beloved was this man, who often gifted groceries to the poor and needy in Charleston—regardless of background or color. Elihu's generosity was likewise exemplified during a time when Grandpa Ben was financially strapped; Elihu handed him, unprompted, an envelope full of large bills for living expenses, for which Grandpa would be ever grateful. Among Elihu Mazo's descendants, those named after him include an Elliot, Elinor,

Bethe Austin (as Ellie Ash) and Jason Graae (as Elmo Green) crossing the country, seeking a life of glamour in Tales of Tinseltown. *Photo: Elizabeth Wolynski.*

Eileen, Ellen, Eric, and several Elihus—in perhaps one of the few families where you still hear the name "Elihu." This tradition has even influenced my writing: when I co-created with Paul Katz the musical, *Tales of Tinseltown* (1985), I named the lead characters Ellie Ash and Elmo Green.

Because of his kind heart and charity, Elihu Mazo was something of a celebrity in Charleston. Upon my birth, Michael Elihu Colby immediately had another celebrity connection. Right after delivery, the first people the Bodnes phoned were Ted and Adah Lewis. I can just imagine Ted Lewis responding, "Is everybody happy?" Every year, for as long as they lived, I received a birthday card and present from "Aunt Adah and Uncle Ted." Uncle Ted Lewis even loaned me his signature top hat for a singing per-formance I gave of "Me and My Shadow" (it's no wonder that my favorite Abbott and Costello movie is 1941's *Hold That Ghost*, in which Ted Lewis was spotlighted). I was deeply blessed to know many legendary figures as a kid visiting my grandparents, and it was even better when these figures were like family.

Chapter 3: *Screaming At Agnes Moorehead and Other Adventures*

First birthday party for Michael. (Bottom) Grandma Dora Cohen, Grandpa Irving Cohen, Grandma Mary, Grandpa Ben, Mom, and Michael. (Top) Uncle Ted Cohen, Aunt Barbara Cohen, Aunt Barbara Bodne, visitors, and Dad.

Born "Michael Elihu Colby," I even had a middle name similar to "Eloise of the Plaza." Still, I didn't really live at the Algonquin until I was eighteen. Nonetheless, much of my childhood revolved around the hotel, and it's uncanny how much happening there, even during my infancy, would affect my future.

In 1951, the hotel was the hangout for stars of the Broadway hit *Don Juan In Hell*, a "heavenly" situation for my grandparents even if they didn't understand the show. Consisting of the third act of Shaw's *Man and Superman*, this production top-lined Algonquin regulars, Charles Boyer (as Don Juan), Charles Laughton, Cedric Hardwicke, and Agnes Moorehead, with whom I'd have a memorable encounter some years later.

1952 produced the Broadway success, *Mrs. McThing*, featuring such Algonquin regulars as Helen Hayes, Iggie Wolfington, and Enid Markey. Above all, it was written by Mary Chase, Pulitzer Prize winner for *Harvey* (the 1944 comedy about what looks to be a giant rabbit). Mary not only stayed at the Algonquin but would become my good friend. Indeed, as an adult, I collaborated with Mary and composer Jack Urbont on the musical

Second birthday party for Michael. (Bottom) Aunt Cyd Mazo, Elinor Weisman Goodman, Great Grandma Essie Mazo, Aunt Ethel Liberman, her sister Grandma Dora Cohen, Dad, Aunt Florence Mazo Nirenblatt, and Michael. (Back) Mom, Norman Nirenblatt, Grandpa Irving Cohen, Donald Mazo, and Harvey Weisman.

version of *Mrs. McThing*, a whimsy about witches, goofy gangsters, and a rich mother whose wishes backfire.

During my childhood, Mary would give me white chocolate bunnies, resembling her character Harvey, around Easter time. She had many merry times with my Grandma Mary, who recommended *Mrs. McThing* to everyone. Grandma made the show an especially magical experience for her niece, Elinor Weisman. Elinor, who lived in a modest Brooklyn home, felt like Cinderella as she rode beautifully attired in the Bodne Rolls-Royce to see

Mary Chase, playwright of Harvey and Mrs. McThing. Courtesy of The Robert A. Freedman Dramatic Agency, Inc.

Mrs. McThing musical (1984): Jeanne Lehman and Ray Gill; Dennis Parlato, Tommy Hollis, Gill, Gibby Brand; Lynn Eldredge; Jeanne Lehman and Bobby Cavanaugh; Cavanaugh and Danyle Heffernan. Photos: Edward Stone courtesy of Goodspeed Opera House.

Mrs. McThing alongside Grandma, who knew everyone at the show. Elinor (now Elinor Goodman) still beams discussing that night. Grandma Mary shared many such treasured evenings with family members.

The Bodnes made a custom of attending Broadway opening nights, even if Grandma sometimes fell asleep during a performance and Grandpa would say things like, "Mary, I realize I forgot something—I forgot to stay home." Still, Grandma gained a reputation for loving every show she saw, even the ones she spent in dreamland. It became a matter of good business for the Bodnes to keep up with theatre. Among the reasons, the Algonquin was the voting center for the New York Drama Critics Circle ever since the group's inception in 1935. The group's choices in 1952 coincidentally figured in my later life. The 1952 "Best Play" was John Van Druten's *I Am a Camera*—based on Christopher Isherwood's *Berlin Stories* (1945)—sources of the 1966 musical, *Cabaret*, my favorite show and the main reason I started writing musicals. The 1952 "Best Musical" was *Pal Joey* by Richard Rodgers, John O'Hara, and lyricist Lorenz Hart, whose sister-in-law and biographer Dorothy Hart would one day become my mentor.

Gig Young; James Dean (photo © bokehstock/shutterstock.com); Nancy Carroll (photo courtesy of Photofest).

In 1953, my personal Algonquin adventures began. A Hollywood star staying there became very fond of the cute two-year old who frequently visited his grandparents. While on Broadway in Edward Chodorov's *Oh Men! Oh Women!* (1953), Gig Young used to dandle me on his knee in the lobby. Young would exemplify some of the ascendant Algonquin guests whose fortunes would later tragically reverse. Born Byron Barr, he changed his name to "Gig Young," the character he played in the film, *The Gay Sisters* (1942). He would win the Oscar in 1969 for his superlative performance in *They Shoot Horses, Don't They?* When his career foundered, he killed himself and his wife.

During the early 1950s, the lobby was the hangout of another tragic figure, a struggling young actor who would die in a car crash at the age of twenty-four. James Dean circulated in the lobby seeking opportunities and cultivation, while living down the street at the less expensive Iroquois Hotel. According to the actor's biographer, David Dalton, "Jimmy used it [the Algonquin] as a baroque inkwell in which he would dip himself to refine his public image."[1] No one at the Algonquin had an inkling that this unsophisticated "hayseed" would soon become a Hollywood icon.

Witnessing the ups and downs of Algonquin celebrities was a sobering experience that gave me an invaluable perspective on the mutability of success in the Arts. If that weren't enough, Grandma Mary frightened me with cautionary tales. For instance, she told me about another guest I knew as a child: former Paramount star, Nancy Carroll. The story was that Nancy Carroll was hoping to make a comeback in a Broadway show, ironically titled *Never Too Late* (1962). She even had her face lifted to play a pregnant woman in her late 40s. Carroll was devastated when the role went instead to the fifty-one-year old Maureen O'Sullivan. Grandma recounted how

Carroll was found dead a while later, slumped over her TV set watching old movies. The upside, Grandma reminded me, was, "At least she looked years younger." I later learned that, despite what Grandma reported, Nancy Carroll did eventually do *Never Too Late*. In fact, at the time she was found dead, she was touring in it at the age of sixty-one playing a pregnant lady.[2] Still, Grandma's version of the truth did the trick, scaring me about show biz (and plastic surgery) from an early age.

Michael, Dad, Douglas, and Mom on Paine Road, Hewlett, Long Island.

However, there were brighter tales to be told. In 1954, a blessed event occurred for the Colby family. Another "Algonquin Kid" was born, the first of my two brothers, Douglas Steven Colby. The birth would mean a move from New York City to suburbia: Hewlett, Long Island. As a gift, the Bodnes bought a stately white colonial home there for the Colbys, at an address sounding a little bit ominous: 1340 Paine Road.

Relocated to Hewlett, I wasn't able to journey to the Algonquin as often. Yet, being the hotel's associate manager, my father was soon taking the hour-long drive there every working day. And, as my new brother grew older, my parents made sure we *all* visited the hotel, spending time with welcoming grandparents. I continued growing up at the Algonquin and, due to severe carsickness, on at least two occasions arrived there throwing up.

1956 was a milestone year for me. I saw my first Broadway show—a musical, of course—*L'il Abner*. One visit to this stage incarnation of Dogpatch and it was instant puppy love. 1956 was also the year something loverly was blooming in the Algonquin's Room 908, one floor below the Bodnes' apartment. Lyricist/librettist Alan Jay Lerner was in residence with a borrowed piano, while he and his composer Frederick Lowe were creating a new musical eventually titled *My Fair Lady* (1956) (Lerner's uncle was in fact a go-between in the sale of the Algonquin to my grandfather). Ultimately, the sounds of late-night creativity bothered Grandpa Ben. He was not always astute about new musicals, having walked out of a backer's audition for *Kiss Me Kate* (1948) in midsummer, grumbling it was too damn hot.

One evening, Grandpa could no longer stand the ivories tinkling in Room 908—one flight below—disturbing his sleep. He phoned the hotel operator to ask Lerner and Loewe to quiet down, complaining, "I wouldn't mind it they were writing something good, but this is just noise." It turned out Lerner and Loewe were creating the song "I Could Have Danced All Night."

The same year, the Algonquin was a setting where Leonard Bernstein, Arthur Laurents, and Jerome Robbins met to discuss the musical they were developing that became *West Side Story* (1957). At one point, they were thrown out of the hotel because "Laurents was not wearing a tie."[3] Too bad maître d' Raul couldn't wrap a tablecloth around Laurents, as he had for Tallulah Bankhead.

Though their last names sounded alike, Laurents was not to be confused with fellow playwright Jerome Lawrence, who lived at the Algonquin when in New York. With his writing partner Robert E. Lee, Jerome Lawrence had authored the Broadway classic, *Inherit the Wind* (1955). During this period, they were working on a play version of Patrick Dennis' 1955 book, *Auntie Mame: An Irreverent Escapade*, a book loaded with references to the Algonquin. In the book, which begins in 1928, Auntie Mame is a friend of Algonquin owner Frank Case and devises "a personal shopping service as a convenience to guests" there. She also takes her secretary, Agnes Gooch,

Andrew Anspach and Barbara Bodne Anspach.

on an emancipating drinking binge at the hotel. In another scene, Mame decorates the Algonquin suite of her best friend, flamboyant actress Vera Charles.[4] Jerome Lawrence and Robert E. Lee included none of these incidents in the play, *Auntie Mame* (1957). Still, when they adopted the story into the 1966 musical version, *Mame*, Auntie Mame's first scene features this exchange with Frank Case: "Goodnight Frank. See you Tuesday at the Algonquin"[5] (a great plug for the hotel). It's no wonder my grandparents were very fond of the musical and Jerome Lawrence.

Meanwhile, 1956 was a banner personal year for the Bodne family. My aunt Barbara Ann, whom I frequently called "Aunt Bobbie," married Andrew A. Anspach. A graduate of Yale and Columbia Law School, he had found great success as Director of Personnel and Labor Relations for Louis Sherry and Child's (the ice cream and restaurant chain)—that merged with the Hotel Corporation of America. Grandpa Ben was very impressed with Andrew during the romance with Barbara, telling his daughter the Algonquin could use a man like that. Barbara replied, "I'll see what I can do." In no time, Barbara and Andrew were engaged. Barbara, whose pretty, patrician features were sometimes mistaken for actress Teresa Wright, was an elegant, cultured match for Andrew. He was likewise a good match for the Algonquin. In 1957, he would succeed the retiring John Martin as the Algonquin's Managing Director. Martin, who had worked at the hotel since Frank Case owned it, was the holdover that most helped Grandpa Ben stabilize the hotel during transition years. John Martin would not be an easy act to follow. Yet Uncle Andrew was ideal. In decades ahead, Uncle Andrew would further upgrade the hotel's technology, enlarge its status as an international cultural mecca, and spearhead the esteemed re-opening of the Algonquin cabaret.

The Anspach wedding ceremony, the first I ever attended, took place in the living room of the Bodne apartment with a reception downstairs. Ever fastidious, Grandma Mary worked like the dickens to make sure the apartment looked perfect for the occasion. Sometimes perfection has a price. As the appointed hour grew near, Grandma noticed one flaw. The venetian blinds looked dusty high atop one window. "Mary!" Grandpa shouted, "No one will notice—just leave it alone." A few minutes later, there was a loud crash. Thanks to her cleaning fixation, Grandma had fallen off a chair. That's why, in photos of the wedding, Grandma had a black eye.

On a historical level, the years 1956-1957 were the tail end of McCarthyism, a.k.a. the Red Scare. During this notorious period, which began around 1950, Senator Joseph McCarthy conducted hearings at the House of Un-American Activities Committee (HUAC) naming citizens as communists and subversives (often in an irresponsible, ruinous manner). People in the Arts were largely impacted. Hollywood, the TV industry, and other businesses had blackballed most anyone who was named by HUAC, but the Broadway community bypassed the hysteria. New York theatres continued to employ talents who'd been blackballed elsewhere, and my grandparents made sure blacklist victims were welcome at the Algonquin. Arthur Miller would visit while writing *The Crucible*, his famous 1953 allegory on such witch-hunting. The hotel was neutral ground for such "named" artists as Dalton Trumbo, Ring Lardner Jr., Jules Dassin, Lillian Hellman, Jack Gilford, and Zero Mostel. The closest the hotel came to embracing any McCarthy were actor Kevin and his sister, writer Mary McCarthy. Most notably, my grandfather made the Algonquin the free-of-charge home for blacklisted radio host John Henry Faulk after CBS radio fired him in 1957. Represented by attorney Louis Nizer, Faulk's dragged-out trial finally concluded with the largest libel settlement up to that time: $3.5 million. The case became famous via Faulk's book *Fear on Trial* (1963), later presented as an Emmy-winning TV movie (1975), ironically, on CBS. John Henry Faulk remained a dear friend to my family for the rest of his life.

Another example of my grandparents' social conscience was how they made the Algonquin a haven for African-Americans from early on. Through the years, their guest list boasted Maya Angelou, Coretta King, Roy Wilkins (head of the NAACP), Thurgood Marshall, and Jazz greats like Ella Fitzgerald and Oscar Peterson. Perhaps their affinity was due to experiences in Charleston, South Carolina, where Great Grandpa Elihu Mazo was always supportive of the Black community. A slight paradox was that my grandmother followed the Southern tradition of hiring Black women to keep house and help raise children—in an affectionate if somewhat subordinating fashion. Grandma imported two such housekeepers from South Carolina, Louise Brown and Maggie Washington. Louise worked for our family from the time she was a young woman in Charleston through most of her life; Maggie died relatively young. Both women continued in the New York household of the Bodnes, then—off and on—were assigned to the Colbys. For a couple who welcomed African-American guests at the Algonquin, the Bodnes could be quite proprietary about Louise and Maggie. But, then again, my grandparents were full of contradictions, this countrified oilman raised in Tennessee, and his Charleston wife, now mingling with celebrities in very urban surroundings.

As a kid, I knew I was especially lucky when my grandparents introduced me to their array of illustrious guests—even if I didn't always know who they were. Not everyone in Hewlett got to shake hands with Fred

Harpo Marx and the Bodnes in the Rose Room.

McMurray and his wife June Haver, Julie Andrews, Burgess Meredith, and both Groucho and Harpo Marx. Harpo was particularly conspicuous. Honking first, he gave out souvenir taxi horns when he was promoting his book, *Harpo Speaks!* (1961). Moreover, he had a unique travel habit. According to fifty-year employee Harry Celentano, "I [as Bellman] checked Harpo in. He had his harp in a big crate, and we had a tough time getting it into the elevator."[6]

In 1958, I, too, made something of a spectacle of myself in the lobby. I had recently seen the TV episode "Rapunzel" on *Shirley Temple's Storybook*, starring Carol Lynley in the title role. Suddenly, the other star of the episode entered the lobby and I was flabbergasted. "There's the witch! There's the awful witch!!" I screamed for all to hear. Agnes Moorehead was none too pleased. Rather than introducing me, my grandmother hauled me away before further damage was done. I can just imagine what Moorehead's character, Endora, might have done to me, years later, on her TV series *Bewitched* (1964). Thank goodness Grandma Mary was there to protect me—at least in the lobby that day.

The Algonquin Kid meets Agnes Moorehead; Grandma Mary intercedes. Illustration: Hannah Chusid.

Chapter 4: *Dreams of Camelot*

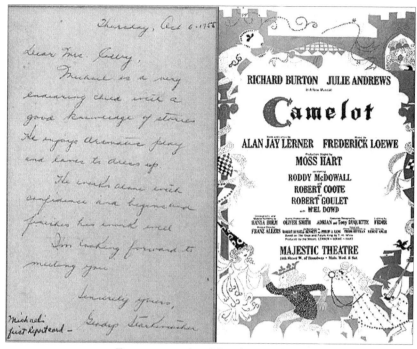

First report card and first favorite show.

Was it the Algonquin Hotel that sparked my interest in theatre? Not necessarily. It may have been nature as much as nurture. In 1955, when I was four, my first report card, from teacher Gladys Starkenweather, stated: "Michael is a very endearing child with a good knowledge of stories. He enjoys dramatic play and loves to dress up." This was before I ever attended a Broadway show.

As a kid, I was more interested in being an actor than a writer. It seemed to me that writers were people who gathered in the Blue Bar till closing, trying to outdo each other with bon mots and libations. Or they were like Norman Mailer, who knew every Algonquin waiter and bartender by name and who, in a 1958 interview there, made the comment, "I mean, a guy just wouldn't push his wife out of a window in Los Angeles—for one thing, there aren't that many *high* windows!"[1] This was two years before he drunkenly stabbed his second wife with a penknife. Fortunately she survived, and he subsequently proved the pen is mightier than the penknife.

Algonquin regulars: Norman Mailer with his second wife, Adele Morales; and Preston Sturges. Both photos courtesy of Photofest.

Moreover, I couldn't forget Grandma Mary's frightening tales about legendary writers who'd stayed at the hotel: among them, Preston Sturges, one of the sharpest writers of comedy, both on Broadway (*Strictly Dishonorable*, 1929) and then movies. Sturges died at the Algonquin in 1959. At one time, he was in such demand that he wrote seven films in four years.[2] An Oscar winner for his screenplay of *The Great McGinty* (1940), his classic films included *The Lady Eve* (1941) and *Sullivan's Travels* (1941). In 1959, Sturges' career as a writer/director had met several setbacks, capped by failed and aborted projects. However, just before his death, he was hard at work on an autobiography for Henry Holt publishers.[3] According to an article in *Vanity Fair*, "He did not give up . . . But in a jarring breach of tone that matched the ones from his films, just as things seemed to be turning around, he had a heart attack in his room at the Algonquin Hotel. Doctors tried to revive him with a shot of adrenaline, but they could not."[4]

That was not the tale Grandma told me. According to her, one night, Sturges took a break from writing and decided to go out for a Mexican dinner. He returned inebriated and sick from the food. That's when he suffered his heart attack, taking a fatal spill down the hotel's second-floor stairs. Ironically, according to reports, Sturges intended to title his autobiography *The Events Leading Up to My Death*.[5]

Frederick Loewe and Alan Jay Lerner. Photo courtesyy of Photofest.

Grandma seized on episodes like this to remind me, "It's the hotel business you should go into. You want a happier, healthier future, don't you?" But how could I dream of just assisting actors in the lobby when I was witnessing them captivating audiences in shows like *My Fair Lady*, *The Music Man* (1957), and *Gypsy* (1959)? Then came what I imagined would be my "big break"!

Alan Jay Lerner and Frederick Loewe were back at the hotel, writing the musical that would become *Camelot* (1960). By that time, Grandma often invited me weekends to "Come 'pend de night" (paraphrasing an expression I used when I was four, "Grandma, can I 'pend de night with you and Grandpa?"). I took every opportunity to accept her Southern hospitality. One day in the lobby, when Grandma had me dressed up in a cute blue suit, Frederick Loewe came over. After a few exchanges, he said, "You know, you'd be just right to play the King's page in our show."

Thunderstruck, I replied something like, "Oh, Mr. Loewe. Do you really mean it!?"

He answered, "Yes. Would you like that—to play the page?"

"Oh, that would be

Michael in Rumpelstilskin *(1960) at Camp Swago.*

incredible, Mr. Loewe! Just tell me one thing—what's a King's page?"

For months after that, I went around telling everyone I was going to play the page—that is, "King Arthur's young attendant"—in a new musical by the writers of *My Fair Lady*. Sad to say, nobody took me seriously at Woodmere Academy, the school I attended (from kindergarten through 12th Grade). I was something of an anomaly at this Long Island school: a kid with a heavy Southern accent, which I'd inherited from my grandparents and mother, whose deep Southern drawl was like a Confederate soldier refusing to surrender. Even though 90 percent of the kids at Woodmere Academy were Jewish like me, I often felt like a foreigner there. Besides being forced to take special coaching so I could speak like a "propah Lawn Guylandah," I took training to get rid of my left-handedness; the Southern accent faded, but I remain a Southpaw.

Nevertheless, my confidence reversed that summer at sleep-away Camp Swago. The Drama Counselor was so impressed that an eight-year-old camper knew about *Camelot*—and professedly "was promised a part"—he cast me in lead roles in both of our camp shows. My favorite role was the debonair King in *Rumpelstilskin*, where I got to sing most of the ballads, even though I sounded a bit like Afalfa of *The Little Rascals*. Leaving camp

Bodnes with Douglas and Michael; Grandpa Ben with Michael and Douglas.

like a seasoned pro, I was just raring to make my Broadway debut in *Camelot*. Then, instead of an advance check, I got a reality check as the fall fell: my parents told me I wasn't about to leave school in Hewlett for the road to *Camelot* and that Frederick Loewe had cast a professional child actor.

Though dreams were dashed, Grandma Mary gave me a wonderful consolation prize. On December 3, 1960, I was her date to the Broadway premiere of *Camelot* —my first opening night and most treasured until decades later when my show, *Charlotte Sweet* (1982), opened off-Broadway. Still, Grandma also used the history of *Camelot* to remind me of the pitfalls of theatre. She detailed how, during the show's development, Lerner was hospitalized with a bleeding ulcer, director Moss Hart suffered his second heart attack, and costume designer Adrian died from his *own* heart attack even before rehearsals. She stressed, "Nothing like that happens to people in the hotel business."

Camelot wasn't the only musical in 1960 with a prominent member in residence at the Algonquin. There was a charming actor at the hotel who *was* about to get his big break. Taking a special interest in him, Grandma stayed up late to phone his room and report rave opening night reviews. It was the night that Dick Van Dyke became a star in *Bye Bye Birdie* (1960). Through the years, Grandma similarly played den mother to Algonquin residents making their Broadway debuts, such as Anthony Hopkins (*Equus*, 1974) and—a decade later (1984)—Whoopi Goldberg. Grandma loved schmoozing with Whoopi Goldberg, even though the entertainer could be a bit enigmatic. According to former desk clerk Len Baron, Goldberg checked in under her real name, Caryn Johnson. When she presented Baron with her credit card, she teased, "Now you know my secret!"

While Grandma was playing hostess, Grandpa was busy establishing his own version of the Algonquin Round Table. In the Oak Room, rather than the original Rose Room location, he presided over luncheons populated by famed guests such as Joe DiMaggio, Louis Nizer, humorists Anita Loos and Harry Hershfield, and an occasional Marx Brother. On daily rounds, Leonard Lyons might likewise sit in, culling items for his *New York Post* column, "The Lyons Den."

Still, Grandpa Ben was occasionally shy about introducing himself to some the hotel's more celebrated guests. He could be like King Arthur roaming incognito among his populace. He described this fact as a guest columnist for the news service, *New York Daily Column*:

"For quite a few years I remained a stranger in my own hotel. I was just Mr. Nobody who owned the place, an ex-oil man from

South Carolina. I didn't even dream of stepping into the departed Frank Case's shoes as a sought-after pal of New York's great and near great.

"I never pushed myself—I've never been socially aggressive. I waited until they got to know me in their own good time—which is what gradually happened. James Thurber had been around five years before he even talked to me. Then one day, in mock indignation, he stormed over to me in the lobby and demanded: "What's wrong? Are you above speaking to your guests in this hotel?" We both laughed, and became good friends.

"Charles Laughton, with his awesome bearing, was another I never dared approach. One night he came in with Burgess Meredith. They got into a violent argument over some Shakespearean lines while standing at the bar. Then Laughton, in his imperious way, called me over.

"'You look fairly intelligent,' he said. 'Can you settle our little dispute?' 'Sure,' I said, beckoning to the barman. 'Give these two gentlemen a drink on the house.' That's how the ice was broken with these two worthies. Then George, our highly literate bartender, actually did resolve the fine Shakespearean point in question."[6]

Notwithstanding, Grandpa seemed in command heading his new Round Table. When my brother Douglas and I visited, Grandma often had us shake hands with members, like they were knights of a modern-day Camelot. Then she'd play mother hen again and lunch with Douglas and me at a table across from them. One afternoon, she pointed out another Algonquin notable in the corner of the room, a majestic woman whose expression will always haunt me. It was Margaret Case Harriman, who'd written books about the hotel, which her father Frank Case once owned. She looked lost in reverie, gazing at the room, her face both glowing and somewhat sorrowful. Today, as another person who once lived at the Algonquin but who's now just a visitor, I can almost imagine the kaleidoscope of feelings she experienced.

The new Algonquin Round Table only lasted a short while and never provided such immortal quotes as, say, when Dorothy Parker announced, "You can lead a horticulture but you can't make her think."[7] Yet Grandpa Ben had his own wicked wit, finding humor in everything, even Grandma's carpal tunnel syndrome. I'll never forget how he described the night Grandma's hand bothered her so much, she woke Grandpa out of a deep

Terry Moore. Photo courtesy of Photofest.

sleep. "Ben, Ben," she exclaimed. "I'm in such pain I'd jump out the bedroom window if I could only fit. Ben, what should I do? What should I do?" He answered, "Lose weight."

I must say there was one Algonquin guest, among them all, who gave me the greatest thrill when Grandma introduced her. The occasion was shortly after I'd been home ill and watched TV reruns of the movie, *Mighty Joe Young* (1949). Consequently, I was a nine-year-old with a mad crush on the film's beautiful star, Terry Moore. She was right in the lobby with her mother when Grandma introduced me. I stammered and gushed. Then, when she gave me a little kiss on the face, my cheeks blushed redder than the Rose Room. Oh, if the kids at Woodmere Academy knew I'd been kissed by a film star, let alone an Oscar nominee (for *Come Back Little Sheba*, 1952)!

With or without an active Round Table, the Algonquin remained the place-to-be for writers and playwrights, a modern-day equivalent of London's Mermaid Tavern—where the likes of Ben Johnson, John Donne, and Beaumont & Fletcher once gathered. A new influx of British up-and-comers made the Algonquin their American headquarters. In 1957, it was where John Osborne looked back in delight as *Look Back In Anger* became a Broadway smash. In 1962, it was where you'd find playwright Robert Bolt and star Paul Scofield holding the season's Tony Awards for *A Man For All Seasons*. In the early 1960s, you might pass playwright Harold Pinter, busy with *The Caretaker* (1961), actress/singer Georgia Brown about to rehearse *Oliver!* (1963), or long-time regular Noel Coward skippering his latest musical, *Sail Away* (1961). A full chapter will be devoted later to the British at the Algonquin.

There are numerous stories about Noel Coward's stays at the hotel. One such story is how he ran into writer Edna Ferber (*Show Boat*, 1927 and *Stage Door* 1936), who wore a suit resembling his own. Greeting her, Coward remarked, "You look almost like a man," to which she responded, "So do you."[8] My father told me Noel Coward's eccentricities included having eight pillows when he slept, beyond just a room with a view. What may be most surprising about Coward is that, along with his self-taught erudition, Coward was the kindliest of men: my family thought him an exceptionally magnanimous guest, quietly giving guidance and financial aid to many an actor and actress in need—which Grandma Mary reminded me was a bottomless well.

Not so suave was writer/poet Brendan Behan, who first stayed at the hotel when his drama, *The Hostage,* played Broadway in 1960. The hard-drinking Irishman, who'd been jailed for his Irish Republican Army activities, was often a boisterous presence in the lobby. Husky and unkempt, he would plow forward and say hello to Grandma, exuding the unmistakable aroma of inebriation. Grandma worried about Behan. As reported by Leonard Lyons in "The Lyons Den," Behan was about to leave the Algonquin on a freezing day, when he realized he didn't have his coat. Witnessing this, Grandma hurried upstairs fetching one of Grandpa's coats to loan. Donning the coat, the grateful Brendan Behan declared, "May you be the mother of a bishop,"[9] not recalling Grandma was Jewish and the mother of two daughters. In 1964, Behan reportedly made a similar

Brendan Behan (photo courtesy of Photofest); at Algonquin, Dad with guest Caesar Romero.

proclamation ("Bless you, sister—may you be the mother of a bishop!") to an ancient nun tending him on his deathbed.[10] Heaven knows how many other women heard those words during inapt situations.

Behan's drinking and brawling led to ill health and, eventually, his being barred from places like the Algonquin. He died in 1964 at the age of forty-one. Behan was another prime example of a show business casualty whom Grandma Mary could cite while telling me that the hotel business was much more sanguine. However, an acute counter example was evolving at the Colby household. Back in 1952, during my father Sidney's early days working at the Algonquin, he seemed to be living the American Dream. There are homey photos of Dad working side by side with Grandpa Ben. There are publicity pictures of him happily mingling with celebrity guests. The Algonquin brochures accentuate only two names as heads of the hotel, "BEN B. BODNE President" and "S. J. COLBY General Manager." Still, Grandpa Ben, spurred by a bad temper, grew increasingly difficult for my father to work with. By 1956, Dad's insecurities augmented when he began sharing managerial duties with my uncle, Andrew Anspach, who'd just married Aunt Barbara and already had a successful track record in the hotel business (unlike Dad, who started from scratch at the Algonquin). Adding fuel to the flame was a vicious circle ever since my parents moved to Long Island. My mother felt isolated while my father spent most of the day in New York City. She didn't like him coming home late. Having inherited my grandfather's temper, she increasingly fought with Dad when he got home. Then she'd phone details to Grandma Mary, who in turn vented at my father at the hotel—making it all the harder for him to work well.

The most devastating blow for Dad came in 1957, when his beloved mother, Dora Cohen, his sturdiest ally and buffer, suddenly died of a heart attack at age fifty-four. The life that Dad first envisioned as (paraphrasing *Camelot*) "happ'ly ever after-ing" was not to be. The strain between my mother and father intensified. Shortly thereafter, the smell of alcohol I'd detected on Brendan Behan became evident on Dad. Fights at home gradually grew worse. And it was impossible for me to know what to expect.

Until I was eleven or so, I had three illusions about families: I thought most were Jewish, saw shows every weekend, and fought in between. Soon enough, I'd learn that wasn't typical. But at least I had those magical weekends at the Algonquin.

1950s Algonquin brochure.

Chapter 5: *Somewhere Between Marilyn Monroe and Liz Taylor*

Marilyn Monroe. Photo courtesy of Photofest.

Grandma knew Marilyn Monroe ever since Monroe was married to Joe DiMaggio. Every now and then, they'd say hello at events. I only wish I'd been there the day when Grandma ran into Marilyn on Fifth Avenue, around the corner from the Algonquin. Marilyn was wearing a gorgeous

The Bodnes setting sail.

full-length white mink. After greeting each other, Grandma remarked, "Marilyn, that's the most beautiful mink you have on!" Marilyn replied, "You think that's something, you should see what's underneath." She pulled open the mink, and wasn't wearing anything. Not every kid can claim his grandmother was flashed by Marilyn Monroe.

Grandma's days were packed with standout moments. Actually, most of Grandma's days were spent packed, period. Anyone entering my grandparents' apartment would see suitcases packed for a trip. That's because my grandparents were always planning a trip: they loved to travel. There are photos of Grandma and Grandma boarding the New Amsterdam liner, boarding the Queen Elizabeth, and taking trips alongside such stars as Rossano Brazzi and Rock Hudson—to Grandma's obvious bliss.

Yet there was an aspect of traveling that Grandma dreaded. She hated planes and preferred to travel by ship or train. For years, she ingrained that fear in her children and grandchildren. I remember her telling my father if we all took a plane to Canada and were killed in a crash, she'd never speak to him again.

In March 1961, the Bodnes traveled three days by train to California, generously bringing along the whole Colby family. We spent a thrilling month there, mostly in Bungalow 7 of the Beverly Hills Hotel. The sizable Bungalow 7 had room for my grandparents, my immediate family, and our

The Bodnes with Mr. and Mrs. Rossano Brazzi.

Rock Hudson with Grandma.

Colbys on the set of The Twilight Zone; *Elizabeth Taylor, Richard Burton, and Taylor's sons, Michael and Christopher Wilding, on the set of* Cleopatra *(1963, photo courtesy of Photofest).*

housekeeper. It felt as if my parents, my brother Douglas, and I were living the *I Love Lucy* season (1954-1955) where the Ricardos saw the sights of Hollywood with daily guest stars. We were next door to the bungalow of Elizabeth Taylor and Eddie Fisher, her husband of the moment, who happened to be another Algonquin regular. Down the lane was Marilyn Monroe, whose personal assistant befriended our housekeeper. One day, our housekeeper took Douglas and me along when she visited her new friend in Marilyn's bungalow. I remember meeting Marilyn's poodle and glimpsing a bed upon which white minks were piled. That was exciting, but not nearly as exciting as what Grandma Mary once saw *underneath* one of those minks.

Another highlight, arranged by Grandpa Ben, was for the Colbys to attend the filming of an Orwellian episode of *The Twilight Zone,* "The Obsolete Man (1961)," starring Algonquin regular Burgess Meredith (now best known as The Penguin on TV's *Batman* (1966) and as the trainer in *Rocky* movies (1976; 1979; 1982). Still, this trip's biggest excitement was yet to come. Our neighbor, Elizabeth Taylor, was up for an Academy Award for *Butterfield 8* (1960), a middling movie (starring her and Eddie Fisher) that she reportedly loathed. She was also recovering from a tracheotomy after near fatal pneumonia contracted on the set of *Cleopatra*.[1] Probably because of her illness, her sons, Michael and Christopher, were isolated a few bungalows away from her. Since Douglas and I were similar ages and types to them, plus we were right next door, some people mistook us for Elizabeth Taylor's sons. This may have explained the huge smiles and exceptional service when our housekeeper took Douglas and me anywhere in the hotel.

April 27, 1961 was the apotheosis of our trip, as my parents and grandparents attended the Oscars. Since it was the West Coast, the Oscars were pretty early. I watched the ceremony on TV with Douglas and our housekeeper. There was lots of fanfare at the Beverly Hills Hotel. I was still up when reporters surrounded Bungalow 7 as Elizabeth Taylor returned to Bungalow 6 after winning the Oscar for *Butterfield 8*. "I lost to a tracheotomy," said her close competitor, Shirley MacLaine (nominated for *The Apartment* (1960), which swept other awards including "Best Picture"). [2] Whatever the case, that evening comprised a picture that will play in my mind forever.

The next week, when my family returned to Long Island, I doubted that anyone at school would believe much about my trip. The details might seem like a fanciful tall tale to classmates at Woodmere Academy. Nonetheless, my Algonquin experiences and theatre knowledge put me in good stead the next fall at school auditions for our December show, Gilbert & Sullivan's *The Mikado*. We of the 6th grade would play the leads, my best opportunity to do a musical since Camp Swago! If I remember correctly, *The Mikado* was called our "Christmas show." The description was odd since most of the students were Jewish and many additionally went to Hebrew School. This was especially evident one morning when attendance was taken in French class. While other kids announced "Ici!," a smart aleck yelled out "Hinani!" (Hebrew for "Here"). Everyone giggled except the teacher.

After having been leading man at Camp Swago, I couldn't wait to audition for *The Mikado*. What helped me snag the title role was how well I could affect a Savoyard British accent, especially for a Lawn Guylandah. I owed this to years of Algonquin exposure to British guests and musicals like *My Fair Lady*. Doing the show at my school, I for once felt like a big cheese there (living up to the Colby name), rather than an uncoordinated outsider. The entire cast was spot-on, and *The Mikado* was a gigantic hit for Woodmere Academy. The show marked two other enduring highlights for me: the Gilbert & Sullivan influence would be prevalent in my 1982 musical, *Charlotte Sweet*; and I established a close friendship with our drama teacher, Sheila Rubell. "Miss Rubell" was also the drama teacher at my Hebrew School at Temple Beth-El, Cedarhurst, Long Island. That's where she double-cast me and my brother Douglas as "Mordecai" in a Purim show reworking songs by Gilbert & Sullivan. Douglas and I alternated performances singing a variation of "A Wand'ring Minstrel" with lyrics "A

Wand'ring Jew am I," to which our leading lady sang "And I'm his Cousin Esther."

I rekindled the friendship with Sheila Rubell decades later after I saw her play the lead in an off-Broadway revival of Sylvia Regan's *An American Family* (2000), produced by the Folksbeine Yiddish Theater.[3] In time, Sheila even appeared in a musical for which I wrote lyrics, *Meester America* (2007; book by Jennifer Berman, music by Artie Bressler).

Sheila Rubell at Woodmere Academy; Gordon Stanley and Sheila Rubell in Meester Amerika *(Photo: Joanna Lesnick Rosen).*

1961 was in many ways a banner year for the Colbys. For the time being, the friction between my parents had been salved by the glamorous trip to California, as had my father's relationship with the Bodnes, who treated us so royally in Bungalow 7. There was also the good news that my mother was pregnant with her third child. To boot, I began enjoying writing, an alternate avocation to acting. In contrast to being treated as "the cute kid" at the Algonquin, at school I was a so-so student, lousy at gym, who was called out for his dirty hands and "digging for gold" (i.e. picking my nose). However, I was now being praised for a knack at penning lyrics and poetry, likely developed through years of listening to show albums. My confidence was particularly boosted when I wrote the largest number of poems selected for a Woodmere Academy collection of verse (I came up with the title too, "Chock Full o'Thoughts").

Back at the hotel, Dad balanced managerial duties with Uncle Andrew. His friends included such Algonquin regulars as Lilianne Montevecchi and Joel Grey (who honeymooned at the Algonquin with his wife, Jo

Richard Nixon and Dad.

Wilder, and returned for anniversaries thereafter). On a given day, Dad greeted such visitors as Richard Nixon—whose biographer, Earl Mazo, was Grandma Mary's cousin (and brother of Sholem Aleichem translator Frances Butwin). At home, Dad found weekend nirvana playing his collection of Jazz LPs, often featuring performers who'd become his pals via the Algonquin: Oscar Peterson, Gerry Mulligan, Carmen McRae, and Ella Fitzgerald. Ella, who made the Algonquin her New York home, was close to everyone in our family. Whenever Grandma Mary was in her audience, Ella improvised lyrics to acknowledge her, such as "Bewitched,

Mom and Dad with Ella Fitzgerald.

Bothered, Mrs. Bodne, am I" or "We'll have Manhattan, the Bronx, and Mrs. Bodne too." Ella was the sweetest, most unassuming celebrity, who adored such things as show music, baseball, and—later on—the soap opera *All My Children* (1970-2011) (she'd drop everything when it was on).

Ella was also close to employees of the Algonquin. Bell captain Mike Lyons, who worked at the hotel since he was eighteen, recalled how Ella brought back Chinese food for the staff after a gig, which they all shared after midnight. Mike continued, "Then on Sunday morning she'd call down and say, 'Mike, bring me up some ice cream.' We'd bring her nine scoops, because that's how many flavors we had then. She'd eat it while she watched TV."[4]

I remember, when I was older, having breakfast with Ella as she burst into song. She was euphoric, having heard songs from the "new musical *Chicago* (1975)," singing to me, "The name on ev'rybody's lips is gonna be …Roxie." It beat anything you'd hear on the radio that morning.

An additional highlight of 1961 that brought my grandparents special delight was a hit Broadway comedy written by Jean Kerr, who—with her husband, critic Walter Kerr—was a longtime friend of my grandparents. Grandma particularly liked the title of Jean's play, *Mary, Mary*. Grandpa liked the fact that star Barbara Bel Geddes, playing the recently divorced title lead, would nightly deliver the lines, "Oscar, if the phone rings, it may be for me. The Algonquin is supposed to call and confirm my room for tonight."[5]

Another memorable 1960s hotel presence, dating back to the late 1930s and the original Algonquin Round Table, was pianist/actor Oscar Levant. Levant was also a renowned composer ("Blame It On My Youth," 1934), who'd been a close friend and interpreter of George Gershwin. He coined such witticisms as "I can remember Doris Day before she was a virgin" and "Schizophrenia beats dining alone." Round-Tabler Alexander Woollcott famously said of him, "There's absolutely nothing wrong with Oscar Levant that a miracle can't fix."[6]

Two stories about Levant at the Algonquin were reported by columnist Leonard Lyons. One story took place in 1962, when Levant and his wife June dealt with the hotel's one and only full-time passenger elevator (the other elevator was mainly used by staff and room service). Waiting for the elevator, Mrs. Levant complained to a bellhop about the long delay. The bellhop retorted, "Charles Laughton stayed here for twenty-eight years. He spent twenty of them waiting for this elevator."[7]

Lyons' second item was about how Levant once told a hotel maid, "Please bring me more blankets. You see, I didn't get much affection when I was a child."[8] Between Levant's extra blankets and Noel Coward's requested extra pillows, the Housekeeping Department could have supplied the Salvation Army.

Another witty couple frequenting the hotel was Henry and Phoebe Ephron, especially during the run of their hit comedy *Take Her, She's Mine* (1961). Henry, who'd met Phoebe when they were camp counselors, decided, "I have ideas—you can type—let's write a play."[9] The couple went on to co-create several successful screenplays, and four successful daughters: writers Nora, Delia, Hallie, and Amy Ephron.

And now for a round of connect the dots. Among the stars for whom Henry and Phoebe wrote was my grandmother's flasher, Marilyn Monroe (*There's No Business Like Show Business*, 1954). After Oscar Levant and Phoebe Ephron died, their spouses—June Levant and Henry Ephron— married each other. Later, Henry Ephron worked with Mary Chase, Jack Urbont, and me on an early draft of the musical, *Mrs. McThing*; June played hostess at some of our meetings. Moreover, she was pivotal in singer Michael Feinstein's career, introducing him to—and helping him land a job assisting—Ira Gershwin (brother of George Gershwin, who dated my Aunt Cyd). Michael Feinstein's career was further catapulted when my Uncle Andrew Anspach presented him as a performer at the Algonquin's Oak Room. Michael also recorded one of the songs on a CD of my lyrics,

Quel Fromage (2001). These scattered associations, from Marilyn Monroe to Elizabeth Taylor and Ella Fitzgerald, made me feel like Zelig, Forrest Gump, or a minor-league Kevin Bacon, a few degrees apart. But, of course, my experiences paled in comparison with those of my grandparents at the Algonquin Hotel. They seemed to know everyone.

The Algonquin at night. Courtesy of the Algonquin Hotel.

Chapter 6: *Could Jed Clampett be Jewish?*

The Beverly Hillbillies—*Donna Douglas, Max Baer Jr., Irene Ryan, and Buddy Ebsen (photo courtesy of Photofest): and the Bodnes.*

In August of 1962, another Algonquin Kid was born, my brother David Bodne Colby. He was the unequivocal hit of the year at our house.

Colby Family: Sidney, Michael, Renee, David, and Douglas.

In September of 1962, a series was born that was the unequivocal hit of the television season. Created by longtime Algonquin guest, Paul Henning, the TV show was titled *The Beverly Hillbillies*. The show was about a folksy Southerner who strikes it rich in oil, then moves his family to an incongruously sophisticated setting. My Aunt Norma Mazo, Grandma Mary's sister, opined this TV family was—at least in part—based on my grandparents, the Bodnes.

It may have been pure coincidence, but there were undeniable similarities pointed out by Aunt Norma, aspects that may have influenced Paul Henning during his stays at the Algonquin. Of course, my family, though down-home types, were *not* hillbillies by any means. And it boggles the mind to imagine *The Beverly Hillbillies* as Jewish. On the other hand, there's the fact that Grandpa Ben Bodne was an oilman from Tennessee who never made it through school, parallel to the show's protagonist, Jed Clampett, (played by Buddy Ebsen). Secondly, the family names on the show were

Phil Silvers and Ben Bodne. Photo: Lucas Monroe-Lucas Pritchard courtesy of Museum of the City of New York.

Clampett as well as Bodine: like "Bodne" with an extra "i." Grandpa Ben's pet name for his wife was "Granny," the appellation given the show's female lead (Irene Ryan). The name of Jed's daughter, Elly Mae (Donna Douglas) was similar to Renee ("REE-knee") Mae, my mother; plus both Elly Mae and Renee Mae were lovely yet tomboyish. Another parallel was how the show's simple Southerners took up residence in the most soigné of neighborhoods, surrounded by celebrities. Possibly the pièce de résistance was the episode in which Phil Silvers, as con man Shifty Shafer, tried to sell Jed the Brooklyn Bridge and the Algonquin Hotel.

Paul Henning had previously written for radio (*The George Burns and Gracie Allen Show*, 1950) and for films (*Bedtime Story*, 1964) in addition to TV (*Bob Cummings Show*, 1955; *The Real McCoys*, 1957). Some of his shows had rural settings. Yet *The Beverly Hillbillies* had the unique premise of country folk suddenly becoming city nabobs. In an interview about the origins of his hit show, Henning declared, "I'd always had a great affection for hillbillies. I think that started when I was a boy scout. I went to camp in the Ozarks ... I loved their humor ... I thought if you could take someone from a real hillbilly family and somehow transplant them to a modern city. My first thought was New York. And then I thought this would mean expensive location trips. And why not transplant them to Beverly Hills where you have the same sophistication. And to make that possible they had to suddenly become affluent."[1]

Accordingly, Henning's influences predated the Bodnes. Still, it was understandable how Aunt Norma suspected the Algonquin and the Bodnes did provide some food for thought. What's more, there was Henning's follow-up show, *Petticoat Junction* (1963), about a country inn additionally beautified by the owner's daughters, Betty Jo, Bobbie Jo, and Billie Jo. Henning had actually almost used more than one daughter on *The Beverly Hillbillies* but waited for this sitcom to feature several.[2]

To be honest, there's less likelihood that *Petticoat Junction* had any relationship to the Algonquin. Henning knew of the pretty Bodne daughters, Renee Mae and Barbara Ann, but it's implausible that he was influenced by minutiae such as Barbara's sometimes being called Bobbie. Further, he acknowledged that *Petticoat Junction* was based on an inn run by the grandparents of his wife Ruth, "a little hotel beside the railroad track in a town called Eldon, Missouri, and how she and her cousins would go there in the summertime ... and how they were always warned by the grandparents not to have anything to do with the traveling salesmen."[3]

My mother and her sister never had to worry about traveling salesmen at the Algonquin. Nonetheless, there's no doubt that the Algonquin was

Aunt Bobbie, Dad, and Mom.

a favorite spot of Paul and Ruth Henning and alumni of Henning's shows. Among his stars who stayed there were Buddy Ebsen, Donna Douglas (who became a good family friend), Eva Gabor (of *Green Acres*, 1965); plus Linda Kaye Henning (daughter) and her husband Mike Minor (both actors on *Petticoat Junction*). All enjoyed a heaping helping of the Bodnes' Southern hospitality.

The Southern hospitality was equally popular with famous foreign families in the 1960s. It's where you'd find the Michael Redgrave family, including film director Tony Richardson (*Tom Jones*, 1963), then married to Vanessa Redgrave and father of

Mike Minor and Linda Kaye Henning at Algonquin. Source unknown.

Actors and actresses who come to New York know that the place to meet your friends is at the Algonquin Hotel. In their cocktail lounge-lobby, any time of day, you're bound to see one of your favorite stars. When Hayley Mills came to town, she met with Catharine Allegret, Simone Signoret's daughter, to discuss

Hayley Mills and Catherine Allegret at the Algonquin.

future actresses Natasha and Joely. The hotel was likewise where Italian film director Roberto Rosselini, divorced from his third wife Ingrid Bergman, was often visited by their children, Robertino and the twins, Isotta and Isabella Rosselini (future star of *Blue Velvet*, 1986). Furthermore, it was the favorite New York hotel for the family of Oscar winner John Mills. He stayed there with his writer wife, Mary Hayley Bell, son Jonathan, and daughter Hayley. Seen, too, was his other daughter Juliet (TV's *Nanny and the Professor*, 1970). In 1962, "in [their] suite at New York's Algonquin Hotel,"[4] Mr. and Mrs. Mills discussed their clan with interviewer Chrys Haranis for *Photoplay* magazine:

> "I wanted to find out how Mills felt about the career his two daughters had chosen. "Mary and I," Mills began . . . "have not tried to push the children into the business. But neither have we sought to discourage them." Mrs. Mills interrupted, "We have made it a strong point . . . to ease the way for our children if they wanted to go into show business. So we gave the children names that would look good on a marquee."[5]

Then there was Laurence Olivier. Olivier was perhaps the longest-running British idol at the Algonquin. In the early 1960s, while Olivier appeared on Broadway in *Beckett* (1960), he romanced and married his third wife, Joan Plowright, also at the hotel during her Tony-winning run in *A Taste of Honey* (1960). They later returned with their three children. According to Olivier's biographer Francis Beckett, since 1930 when Olivier first became a star visiting New York, "he started a regular love affair with the Algonquin Hotel, which persisted all his life."[6] His attachment to the Algonquin was so profound that his second wife, Vivien Leigh, made a special, sentimental trip there. Though divorced, she was still in love with him and asked to visit the room where he customarily stayed. Even without him present, it was compensation for this plaintive actress to retrace where he so often resided.

Through the years, Olivier became very fond of my grandparents and vice versa. When Olivier was sick with a bad cold, Grandma Mary cooked her Jewish penicillin, i.e. homemade chicken soup, for him. And who could blame him for being grateful? Grandma made the best Southern chicken soup (and matzo balls) I ever tasted.

Closest of all to my grandmother was Simone Signoret, who stayed at the Algonquin with her singer/actor husband, Yves Montand, and daughter Catherine Allegret. Signoret was one of France's all-time great actresses. Her French films included *La Ronde* (1950) and *Les Diaboliques* (1955); in Hollywood, she won the Best Actress Academy Award for *Room at the Top* (1959). As for Montand, he was among the most debonair entertainers ever seen at the Algonquin, even counting Tyrone Power, Charles Boyer, and Douglas Fairbanks Jr. Signoret and Montand discovered the Algonquin via their friend, Norman Granz, the legendary Jazz producer and Algonquin regular who launched *An Evening with Yves Montand*, Montand's smash 1959 Broadway (and American) debut. Like Laurence Olivier, Signoret and Montand fell in love with the hotel on first visit, staying there during the show's run. In Signoret's biography, *Nostalgia Isn't What It Used To Be* (1979), the actress wrote:

"A few snobbish Americans had laughed at us when we had announced ... we were going to stay at the Algonquin in New York. The Algonquin! That was the place to go twenty or thirty years ago, when Mr. So-and-so and Mrs. So-and-so and Miss So-and-so lived there, wrote their music, their plays, or their terrible reviews which demolished everyone else's plays. Since we'd never heard of any of those So-and-sos, we'd let them talk, and instead of going

Simone Signoret. Photo courtesy of Photofest.

to one of those big palaces they suggested, we followed the advice of Uncle Norman; out-of-date provincials that we were, we were going to stay at the Algonquin.

"The Algonquin is like La Colombe. It belongs to a family, the Bodnes. If we had lived at the Waldorf-Astoria, I doubt very much whether we would ever have met Mr. Waldorf or Miss Astoria. At the Algonquin, the Bodne family awaited us in the lobby.

"The lobby reminded me of the smoking room of the Savoy, with its mahogany and overstuffed armchairs; it reminded me of the lobby of the Alkron, with all its traffic; and it reminded me of a Viennese teahouse, with the quiet good manners of all that bustle.

"Mrs. Bodne said she was sure that Catherine [Simone's daughter from an earlier marriage] would join us very soon. That one sentence said it all. Welcome. I don't know you but I do. Your show is going to be a success, you'll see; I know you're only going to bring over your daughter if it works. This is my way of saying good luck."[7]

Through the years, my grandmother and Signoret grew even chummier. Grandma babysat when Simone's young daughter, Catherine Allegret visited her mother. She was Signoret's confidante during difficult periods, as when Montand engaged in a brief but highly publicized affair with Marilyn Monroe (during the making of the film *Let's Make Love*, 1960). In fact, Signoret once called Grandma one of her truest friends in the world. Many felt similar affection. Grandma was someone who made New York feel like home to notables from far and near.

My grandmother was anything but perfect. She could be meddling, illogical, and displayed habits like picking from tablemates' plates while they were eating. Yet, to those she loved, she was the most generous of souls. She was truly the matriarch of the Algonquin, with a hospitality that transcended just Southern comfort.

Chapter 7: *A Mazel Tov from Robert F. Kennedy*

Robert F. Kennedy photographed on February 19, 1968 by Jill Krementz.

People are surprised when I tell them my bar mitzvah celebration did *not* take place at the Algonquin. But let's be honest. The first words that jump to mind after you say "bar mitzvah" aren't "The Algonquin Hotel." So please accept the first of several apologies in this chapter when I admit I'll be focusing on other matters than the Algonquin as I describe the details of my bar mitzvah (albeit the hotel plays a major role).

The date of my bar mitzvah was October 24, 1964 at the Conservative Temple Beth El in Cedarhurst, Long Island. This was a great time for the event, a month after *Fiddler On the Roof* had opened on Broadway (September 22), when having your band playing "Sunrise Sunset" was still a fresh novelty.

Frankly, I feared that few of my friends, who were few to begin with, would attend. You see, I was not part of our class's in-crowd. I was part of a B-circle of less popular and prominent students. Even within that B-circle, I faced a major problem. A classmate with many of the same

The Algonquin Kid becomes a man.

friends as me, Robert Finkel, was having his bar mitzvah on the very day of mine. Moreover, Robert Finkel was comparatively cool and athletic, plus an expert on sports (he wanted to be a sports broadcaster). He bordered on the A-circle.

How could I compete with Robert in coaxing people to attend my event? I was the last kid chosen on a sports team (classmates would ask,

"Can't we just skip him?"). I was teased for being physically immature (my voice wouldn't change for a few years, and even then you'd hardly notice). I was a target of bullying on the lunch line (by no less than John Burstein, who grew up to be the jolly "Slim Goodbody" on the *Captain Kangaroo* TV show, in 1976).

Despite having attended Woodmere Academy since kindergarten, I had *never* been one of the in-crowd at the school. There weren't that many kids at Woodmere Academy who shared my main interests: Broadway musicals and DC Comics books. The comic book fixation may have made me seem extra geeky. By the age of twelve, I subscribed to *Variety* (the show biz trade paper) and various DC Comics books. My most prized bar mitzvah gift was a copy of the first issue of *Batman*, not exactly what you imagine in terms of Jewish studies, even if its creator, Bob Kane, was a member of the tribe.

Still, my love of comic books did result in an abiding friendship with my classmate, Peter Meyer. Peter often visited my house to peruse my voluminous comic collection. I visited his house, too, bringing along a batch of my latest editions. Peter's home was a comforting one, with exceptionally calm parents and a cheerleader sister, compared to my house, where my parents were fighting again. Unfortunately, I botched even that friendship the day Peter insisted on playing a game he had invented, a William Tell-style type of darts. Peter had us take turns throwing tiny metal darts at a target right *over* our heads. After he'd successfully missed my head, I begged Peter, "Please don't make me do it, don't make me do it, I'm a klutz!" He said, "Oh just try it once—you can do it from up close where the dart will have to miss me." Peter was wrong. I threw the dart smack into the middle of his forehead: a mishap for which no apologies would suffice. Fortunately, it was a superficial wound and Peter recovered to brave it to my bar mitzvah. Yet we weren't as likely to get together after that, especially with sharp objects around. Subsequently, I refused to try archery with anyone!

Flash forward decades later: Peter's cheerleader sister became recognized by her married name, Elizabeth Glaser. This heroic woman founded the Elizabeth Glaser Pediatric AIDS Foundation. This occurred after she and her daughter, Ariel, terminally contracted AIDS during a hospital transfusion when she was pregnant with Ariel. In her remaining time, Elizabeth achieved milestones promulgating AIDS awareness. Today, I feel deeply privileged to have known the family. Yet no one could have envisioned this bittersweet future when, as I child, I visited the Meyer home.

Back in 1964, one could only hope my bar mitzvah skills surpassed my expertise at darts. I had been slow in learning my particularly long haftarah

Elizabeth Meyer Glaser, courtesy of Elizabeth Glaser Pediatric AIDS Foundation.

(the portion of the Bible I was chanting). I didn't want to be an embarrassment to my family, who were inviting relatives from Charleston, friends from Beverly Hills, and many regulars from the Algonquin. The invitation list included Jazz greats Ella Fitzgerald and Oscar Peterson, as well as Charleston's former Governor Ernest (Fritz) Hollings. A Monsignor from Charleston, a friend of my grandparents, would be attending, the first bar mitzvah he'd witness in his many decades of religious ceremonies. Also on the list was Jane Wyman, the Oscar winner and ex-wife of Ronald Reagan, who was staying at the hotel at the time.

Rather than be intimidated, I utilized this motley list like a showman touting marquee names to entice people to my event. In retrospect, it was somewhat gauche to act like P.T. Barnum. I have to apologize to Robert Finkel for such a sneaky strategy. Yet ultimately, our turnouts were quite evenly divided from a class of approximately twenty-five students. The Lord had worked in beneficent ways.

My reception was not at the Algonquin, but at the Middle Bay Country Club—Oceanside, Long Island—where the Colbys were members. Still, the Algonquin Hotel teemed with visiting relatives and out-of-town guests. Grandma Mary, something of a one-woman ticket agency, had her hands full since out-of-towners wanted tickets to the current Broadway hits.

Bodnes at the bar mitzvah.

Shows included Barbra Streisand in *Funny Girl* (1964); Algonquin regular Carol Channing in *Hello, Dolly!* (1964) (whose scenic designer Oliver Smith had redecorated the Algonquin); *A Case of Libel* (1964) (based on *My Life In Court*, the 1961 best-seller by Louis Nizer); and especially the newly opened *Fiddler On the Roof.*

Algonquin party for opening night of A Case of Libel: Louis Nizer, star Van Heflin, Grandpa, Mom.

Most of our family history mirrored the Jews in *Fiddler on the Roof,* who'd fled Cossacks and European shtetls in the early twentieth century heading for America. Someone with an even closer association to that musical was a guest from Washington DC, Grandma's cousin Earl Mazo, brother of Frances Mazo Butwin, who'd written the English translations on which *Fiddler On the Roof* was based. Earl was well-known in his own right as a biographer of Richard Nixon and political correspondent for *The New York Herald Tribune* and *The New York Times*. He authored articles attempting to prove that Nixon had beaten John F. Kennedy in the 1960 presidential race, detailing how the election "was stolen [by Democrats] in Chicago and in Texas."[1] Nixon himself interceded, asking Mazo "to stop writing his series because the country couldn't afford a constitutional crisis at the height of the Cold War."[2] Mazo told *The Washington Post*, "I thought he was kidding, but he was serious . . . I looked at him and thought, *He's a goddamn fool.*[3] Earl was devastated years later, when it was Nixon who was exposed during Watergate as the less than honorable President. Nixon would be forced to flee his quarters faster than Tevye and his daughters.

In years ahead, I, like Earl Mazo, would have my own personal connections to *Fiddler On the Roof.* In 1979, Maria Karnilova—the Tony Award-winning original Golde of the show—was the leading lady in a reading of my musicalization of Jean Anouilh's *Time Remembered,* (a play I first read in my French class at Woodmere Academy). I likewise had the honor of writing speeches at two New York benefits spoken by Sheldon Harnick, lyricist of *Fiddler On the Roof.*

Still, let's return to this chapter's main subject, the day of the Bar Mitzvah. It finally arrived on a beautiful October morning in 1964. Anxious and early, with my parents and brothers beside me, I crept up the steps of Temple Beth El. There, a Southern relative or two greeted us with a "Shalom, y'all." Colbys, Bodnes, Mazos, Cohens, and even a Monsignor gathered at shul to watch me make the transition to Jewish adulthood, regardless of my baby face, braces, and unchanged voice. My rabbi was the distinguished Edward T. Sandrow, whose daughter, Nahma Sandrow, became a chronicler of Yiddish Theatre and who co-wrote the musicals *Vagabond Stars* (1982) and *Kuni-Leml* (1984). All I remember about Cantor Dubrow is that he would huff and puff and turn red as borsht trying to teach me my tropes. Of our invitees, Ella Fitzgerald and Jane Wyman canceled out at the last minute. Ella was ill (but sent me a deluxe paint kit), while Jane Wyman—according to Grandma—"wasn't in the habit of going to bar mitzvahs." Nonetheless, the shul was filled with the likes of Louis Nizer and former Governor Ernest Hollings.

Ernest Hollings had grown up in Charleston, socializing with all the Bodnes. A politically active Democrat from early on, he served as Senator from South Carolina from 1959-1963. The year of my Bar Mitzvah was a transitional one for Hollings. He'd lost a bid for a seat in the Senate, then eventually won in 1966, serving as U.S. Senator for thirty-six years through 2003. The Hollings and the Bodne families remained close, attending each other's major family events through the years. In a Congressional Record testimony to my grandfather, Hollings called him "White Knight of the Algonquin Round Table . . . As fine a man and gentleman as you will ever meet. A wonderful friend."[5] Further, Hollings arranged for a very special present at the end of my bar mitzvah day.

Somehow I made it through the service sounding like I knew what I was doing. Then everyone made the exodus from Beth El to the reception

(Top) M/M Ernest Hollings, M/M Earl Mazo. (Seated) Ruth Goodhill and
M/M Louis Nizer.

at Middle Bay Country Club. My parents decided my bar mitzvah theme would be "Around the World," with decorations from countries like England, France, and Italy. I have no idea why that theme was chosen. At the age of thirteen, I had never traveled outside of the U.S. and was deeply frightened of flying thanks to Grandma Mary's warnings about horrific plane crashes.

The reception was capped by the snazzy Jazz performance by The Oscar Peterson Trio. Classmates on the dais were given autograph books as gifts. Everyone was impressed by the entertainment, even observers who weren't invited. Hara Kestenbaum, my girlfriend at the time, pointed out someone peeking in, whom we both knew from summer camp. Even though he wasn't invited, that someone not only attended the same camp but was a member of Woodmere Academy (a grade ahead of me), Temple Beth El, and Middle Bay Country Club. His name was Jack Feldman, and he went on to write the song "Copacabana" (1978, with Barry Manilow) and the Tony-winning lyrics of Broadway's *Newsies* (2012).

The Oscar Peterson Trio and the Colbys.

Bar Mitzvah dais. On the right of Michael are Hara Kestenbaum and Peter Meyer.

After Middle Bay, people convened for a concluding night nosh at the Colby house back in Hewlett. That's when Mom, Dad, Douglas, and I pulled a Houdini finale. While guests were meeting and eating, the Colbys disappeared from our home to join Senator Hollings elsewhere. We didn't even have a chance to say anything to our guests. So, for anyone that night who might be reading this, my belated apologies! Still, our bar

Ernest Hollings and Grandpa. Photo courtesy of BB Ross Studios.

mitzbehaviour reaped as great a DC thrill as any comic book. It was time for Hollings' special bar mitzvah present. We joined Hollings in the campaign bus of a famous politician running for—and about to become—the latest Senator of New York. The location was right across from the firehouse in Woodmere, the town neighboring Hewlett. The streets were chockablock with this politician's followers, as the Colbys boarded the campaign bus of Robert F. (Bobby) Kennedy. Kennedy had been attorney general during the "Camelot" years of his late brother, President John F. Kennedy (the president who'd once said, "When I was growing up, I had three wishes: I wanted to be a Lindbergh-type hero, learn Chinese, and become a member of the Algonquin Round Table"[6]). Robert F. Kennedy was also a vital force against organized crime and major crusader for Civil Rights.

Michael and Douglas at end of reception.

The Colbys sat alongside Ernest Hollings in a row of foldout chairs right behind Robert F. Kennedy, as he gave an electrifying speech. From the bus, I saw two girls from my class in the crowd, one who'd been at Robert Finkel's bar mitzvah and one from mine. They eagerly waved to me, far more impressed that I was on that bus than by anything I could have done at my bar mitzvah. When Kennedy finished his enthusiastically received speech, he turned around to greet visitors on his bus. Ernest Hollings introduced me to him, mentioning it was my bar mitzvah day, to which Kennedy replied, "Mazel Tov." He then stated he would have liked to have attended but was preoccupied elsewhere. I didn't believe for a second that he would have attended, but those were exhilarating words to hear. I could just imagine the clamor of my classmates to offer their new autograph books for *his* signature.

My bar mitzvah may not have been at the Algonquin, but it was a doozy of a day!

Chapter 8: *As William Faulkner Wrote at the Algonquin...*

William Faulkner (photo courtesy of Photofest), James Thurber (photo courtesy of Photofest), Gore Vidal (photo © S. Bukely/Shutterstock.com).

"I feel that this award was not made to me as a man, but to my work—a life's work in the agony and sweat of the human spirit, not for glory and least of all for profit, but to create out of the materials of the human spirit something which did not exist before.

"...I believe that man ... is immortal, not because he alone among creatures has an inexhaustible voice, but because he has a soul, a spirit capable of compassion and sacrifice and endurance. The poet's, the writer's, duty is to write about these things. It is his privilege to help man endure by lifting his heart, by reminding him of the courage and honor and hope and pride and compassion and pity and sacrifice which have been the glory of his past."[1]

The above is an excerpt from the 1950 Nobel Prize acceptance speech of William Faulkner, which was written in his room at the Algonquin. I've often stood in awe of the writers who stayed at the Algonquin, trying to fathom what made them tick. Their creativity stemmed from such a spectrum of sources.

There was Gore Vidal, whom I saw at the hotel while he was working on the political play, *The Best Man* (1960). Vidal developed his interests at the side of his blind grandfather, Senator Thomas Gore of Oklahoma, for whom he "was required early on to read grown-up books . . . mostly constitutional law and, of course, the *Congressional Record.*"[2]

Eudora Welty and Reynolds Price photographed by Jill Krementz at the Algonquin Hotel on May 17, 1972. All rights reserved.

There was Eudora Welty, whom I'd befriend in years to come, when I assisted on a musical version of her novella, *The Robber Bridegroom* (1942). Inspired by her father, an amateur photographer,[3] she preceded her writer's career behind a camera, with a remarkable exhibition of photographs evoking Mississippi during the Great Depression.[4] Through her photographer's eyes, she likewise created literary depictions of lives and loss in small-town Mississippi, including the Pulitzer Prize-winning novel *The Optimist's Daughter* (1972).

I especially identified with Algonquin writers who built order out of the turmoil of their past. James Thurber, with one eye blinded by a childhood accident, couldn't participate in sports and other physical activities but compensated with an unusual wit and imagination.[5] Arthur Miller, whose affluent New York family lost almost everything in the 1929 Wall Street Crash,[6] infused his plays with ruminations on failure, loss, and depression. Whatever their muses or demons, these writers spun their experiences into art that, to borrow from Faulkner, "lifted" the hearts of people everywhere.

As for me, I was witnessing plenty of drama at home, where the conflicts between my Brooklyn-born Dad and my Southern Mom sometimes played out like scenes by both Arthur Miller and Tennessee Williams. Coupled with the ever-present friction at 1340 Paine Road, loud disputes often started and ended the day. On our Sunday ride to a restaurant lunch, my parents would squabble to the extent that my mother flung open the car door, threatening to jump out. Another incident occurred when I was in my game room playing pool with a friend. We suddenly saw my dad's arm crashing through the glass of a window-door: he had staggered backwards in the next room during a fight with Mom. The aftermath didn't add well either. My dad retreated to his well-stocked, glass-mirrored bar. My frustrated Mom beat her fist against things, even once injuring her hand. Thank goodness the Colbys had a protective housekeeper or two to clean up.

Nevertheless, I found comforting ways to write this all off. I escaped daily commotion through my DC/Superman magazines, where goodness always saved the day. I then created little comic-book stories about heroes conquering chaos, adventures I wrote and illustrated in small booklet form. When I visited the Algonquin, I showed them to Grandpa Ben, who stored them all in a drawer in his office. I haven't a clue what happened to them except, obviously, Grandpa never sent them to any of his publisher friends. He did, however, introduce me to Algonquin regular, Jack Liebowitz, who published DC Comics and took me on a personal tour of their offices, watching artists at work, which, for me, even beat a trip to Disneyland. I only wish I could have shown my cartoons to James Thurber, the writer/cartoonist who lived at the hotel until his death from pneumonia in 1961. My daydreams, populated by fantastic heroes, were not unlike those of Thurber's famous character, Walter Mitty.

As time passed, I did become a "published writer" of sorts. I penned postcard comments printed in the "letters to the editor" pages of almost every known comic book, both in DC publications and, ultimately, Marvel Comics. The contents of the postcards seem somewhat silly now, but they made me feel accomplished at the time. Across the Atlantic, a "fan" in Dublin tracked me down, sending me a gorgeous Shamrock calendar and asking to be my pen pal, discussing comic books. Unfortunately, he ceased writing when I sent the lad a card wishing him a "Happy Rosh Hashanah" (around then, I started to realize that Jews weren't the world majority, except perhaps in Hewlett and Woodmere).

To this day, the name "Michael E. Colby" can be Googled on the Internet to locate my old letters, including suggestions for new superheroes, e.g. "Sport Youth" ("he is a champion in every type of athletics."); and "Venus Vamp" ("she can make others handsome or ugly and can make people love anything."). Such brainstorming foreshadowed my creating a Circus of Voices in the show, *Charlotte Sweet*, where everyone has a special ability (high voice, low voice, fast voice, etc.), ultimately triumphing over adversity.

There was one memorable response to my letters that I especially wish I'd saved. A girl, who lived a few blocks from me in Hewlett Harbor, got

Dear Editor: Five letters of the alphabet can describe the latest issue of ACTION COMICS: G-R-E-A-T! The story, "The Great Superman Impersonation", was terrific and the artwork was superb. The Supergirl story in the same issue, involving the entire "Superman family", was even better. The plot certainly had me guessing. Only one thing bothers me. In the coming attractions you announced that this story wasn't a "Dream, Imaginary Story, Magic Spell, Red Kryptonite Illusion, or a Hoax. But in the end we found out it WAS a Hoax!"Error or not? —Michael E. Colby, Hewlett Bay Park, Long Island, N. Y.

(You're right. Webster defines "hoax" as: "A deception for mockery or mischief." Please forgive us for our deception; we guess our enthusiasm for this story ran away with us.—Ed.)

JIMMY OLSEN'S *Pen Pals*

Dear Editor: I think that those readers who are constantly protesting that Lucy Lane treats Jimmy Olsen in a humiliating fashion, as though he were dirt, owe you an apology. I suggest they refer to the story in your September issue, "The Nine Lives of Jimmy Olsen," in which she turns out to be genuinely concerned about his safety. I think she's become quite interested in Jimmy, and I'm looking forward to seeing her marry our cub reporter hero.

Michael E. Colby, Hewlett Bay Park, L.I., N.Y.

(Don't jump to conclusions about Jimmy and Lucy tying the marital knot until you read the story, "Jimmy's Inter-Dimensional Romance," in this issue.—Ed.)

Michael E. Colby, L.I.: "SPORT YOUTH – he is a champion in every type of athletics."

"I think Eclipso is great," says Michael E. Colby of Hewlett Bay Park, N. Y. "I hope you never stop publishing his stories!"

Dear Editor: I enjoyed the recent story, "The Immortal Lois Lane", in which Lois went back into the past and met the famous Leonardo Da Vinci . . . and also met the notorious poisoner, Lucretia Borgia. However, in this story, as in many other of your time stories, the female villainess always turns out to look just like Lana Lang. Couldn't you have a story where Lana Lang goes into the past and meets a villainess who looks like Lois Lane?

Michael E. Colby, Hewlett Bay Park, L. I., N. Y.

(That's a clever new switch you've suggested, and we'll get to work on it pronto. Thanks for the idea.—Ed.)

Michael E. Colby, Hewlett Bay Park, L.I., N.Y. - "Venus Vamp. She can make others handsome or ugly and can make people love anything."

Montage of letters—from Michael E. Colby—to DC Comics.

a hold of one of my unfavorable notes to Marvel Comics. Wasting no time, she wrote directly to my Hewlett address. That girl, Joan Lieber, was the daughter of the writer/president of Marvel Comics, Stan Lee. Coincidentally, she'd attended Woodmere Academy for a few years. Appalled that a boy from Hewlett could criticize *Spiderman*, she so fiercely defended the Marvel Universe, I never again dared to send disapproval to her father's offices.

"The Circus of Voices" in Charlotte Sweet: *(counterclockwise:) Polly Pen, Jeff Keller, Michael McCormick, Lynn Eldredge, Merle Louise, and Mara Beckerman. Photo by Elizabeth Wolynski.*

Of course, I never encountered anything like the universe-threatening events found in comic books. Yet, in the winter of 1965, the Colbys faced a real-life adversity that sent us flying, almost as fast as Superman, to the Algonquin for safety. The calamity happened during a cold, snowy evening after a brand-new cook, on the job her first day, had prepared a sumptuous dinner. The dinner was beautifully garnished and meticulously served, course after course. Everyone was highly impressed—for the moment, that is—until we all went to bed. Our new cook, before taking a shower, turned up the electric heater right near her bedroom curtains. Soon, it wasn't just dinner she had cooking. Between her hysterics ("Lord, what have I done!") and my mother's Southern screams ("Hay-elp!"), the scene felt like a surrealistic melodrama. My father sustained minor injuries trying to put out the flame, while I phoned the fire department. Then, our family and new cook fled to a neighbor's house, some of us tramping barefoot through the snow like *The Little Match Girl.*

Still, there was a silver lining to this storm. The damage would require us to live at the Algonquin while repairs took place at home. As tired and shaken as I was, my mind was secretly exclaiming *Hooray! Hooray! Algonquin, we're on our way!* By 6 p.m., the Colbys arrived at the hotel to live for the next month, minus our poor new cook, whose conflagration led to her professional firing.

My brother, Douglas, and I traveled each weekday between the Algonquin Hotel and Woodmere Academy, mostly via train. No matter how humdrum a day, I looked forward to returning to the glamorous hotel at night. By day, I was a student receiving an excellent education at Woodmere Academy. By night, I was the Algonquin Kid again.

Every evening, or so it seemed, my grandparents introduced me to some new notable. Producer and TV host David Susskind, a friend of my grandparents, frequented the hotel to tout his new musical, *Kelly* (1965). The man was a giant in the field of television, but not so much in theatre. He didn't visit as often once *Kelly* opened and closed in the same evening. The unanimous pans for this show about a man who jumps off the Brooklyn Bridge might have tempted its investors to do the same.

Notwithstanding, the Algonquin parade, unlike *Kelly*, never halted. While dining with my grandparents in the Rose Room, I sat near actors who one day would display both an Oscar and Tony Award on their mantels. Christopher Plummer was often around, as were Maureen Stapleton and Helen Hayes. Reputedly, the Algonquin was where Hayes first met her future husband, Charles McArthur, whose playwriting credits included *Twentieth Century* (1932) and *The Front Page*. Spotting her across the Blue Bar, he tentatively approached her, scooped up a bunch of peanuts, and declared, "I wish these were emeralds." Years later, on their 25th anniversary, he gifted her with a bunch of emeralds, declaring, "I wish these were peanuts."[7]

In addition, around the 1960s onward, the Rose Room was the setting where Sherlock Holmes enthusiasts—the Baker Street Irregulars—held regular gatherings known as "Mrs. Hudson's Breakfasts," which was named after the fictional detective's landlady. The events included evocations of scenes from the Arthur Conan Doyle series. Resident Algonquin actress Enid Markey even played Mrs. Hudson on occasion.[8] Deerstalking caps made it easy to detect who some members were.

Most distinctly, this was a period where a diverse wave of 1960s cultural figures made a splash at the hotel. Andy Warhol, the pop art icon, could often be spotted in the lobby or Rose Room. As a fourteen-year old, I didn't quite know who he was; he looked to me like an actor from *The Twilight Zone*.

Joan Baez, the activist and Folk music legend, was the Algonquin's visiting visionary. In her career, she marched alongside Martin Luther King Jr. in the civil rights movement, toured with Bob Dylan, inspired Vaclav Havel in his fight for a Czech Republic, and organized opposition to the war in Southeast Asia.[9] Yet she seemed the most laid-back of ladies when

The Algonquin Kid observes an array of guests in the lobby. (Top row) Joan Baez, Brendan Behan, Tennessee Williams, Peter Ustinov, Dick Van Dyke, Julie Andrews, and Helen Hayes. (Bottom row) Christopher Plummer, Groucho Marx, Carol Channing, Angela Lansbury, John Gielgud, and Rudi Gernreich. Illustration by Dennis Potter.

Grandma Mary introduced her, an impressive figure with her flowing sable hair and earth-mother outfits.

Another example of cultural cool was fashion designer Rudi Gernreich, one of several fashion trailblazers—such as Mary Quant and Donald Brooks—who visited the Algonquin. Gernreich treated my grandparents like family (or, as they say in Yiddish, *mishpocher*). As a Jewish teen in Austria, Gernreich fled with his mother to the United States when Hitler invaded his country. Every time I met him, he seemed the quintessence of the "mod 60s" look, a truly chic version whom Austin Powers would have traded his mojo to match. A crusader for gay rights, as well, his iconoclastic fashions were, in many ways, his retaliation to a Fuhrer who banned nudity in art and homosexuality in Germany.[10] Gernreich created unisex designs, see-through blouses, mini dresses, and the topless bathing suit.[11] Grandma Mary would sometimes buy fashions from designer guests for herself, her daughters, and her sisters. Yet with Rudy, she stopped at his handbags.

Meanwhile, back at Woodmere Academy, something unusual happened to me. I was *first* to be chosen on a team, not last. It wasn't in gym but in English class, where our project was to create an epic poem in iambic pentameter. We'd studied Coleridge's "The Rime of the Ancient Mariner" and now it was our turn to divide into teams of two, tapping into our inner Shakespeare. Regardless of weaknesses in other school activities, I'd always been facile at any project involving poetry and rhyme. Listening to all those show albums and Gilbert & Sullivan had paid off. Everyone wanted to be on my "iambic pentameter" team. I don't remember exactly whom I chose, but our resulting epic about the bravery of men in space during this 1960s space race was wonderfully received; it earned the highest grade in the class. I hardly achieved anything like the writers I'd met at the hotel. I was hardly any kind of superhero. But at least the Algonquin Kid was having an all around good time—for the moment.

Chapter 9: *The British Are Staying!*

British subjects: Sir Noel Coward; Lord Laurence Olivier and wife Dame Joan Plowright. Both photos courtesy of Photofest.

To this day, the Algonquin has been so closely associated with British artists that its marquee was part of the cover of *The British on Broadway*, a book by Elizabeth Sharland. Devoting a section of her 1999 chronicle to the hotel, Sharland wrote:

"The Algonquin Hotel . . . has been the home to most of the British contingent of actors for over 50 years. What hotel in the world could boast of a guest-list like the Algonquin? — Noel Coward, Gertrude Lawrence, John Gielgud, Laurence Olivier, Charles Laughton, Bea Lillie, Jonathan Miller, Ian McKellan, Peter Ustinov, David Hare, the Redgraves, Jeremy Irons, Anthony Hopkins, Trevor Nunn, Tom Stoppard, Peter Hall, Angela Lansbury and Diana Rigg."[1]

Reasons for this affinity are many. Firstly, situated on West 44th Street between 5th and 6th Avenues, the hotel is a short walking distance from most Broadway theatres. Equally appealing has been the hotel's intimate size, Edwardian décor, and hospitality. It wasn't just the menu of Dover sole, London Broil, and Yorkshire Pudding. Even when the hotel was in 1940s disrepair, British stars, such as Laurence Olivier, recommended the hotel to friends and colleagues. There's a droll story about British actor

Ralph Richardson, Olivier's good friend, who stayed there in 1946, just before my grandparents bought the place. Biographer Garry O'Connor wrote how Richardson used his room to practice an old hobby of his, oil painting. Richardson phoned his New York agent requesting him to "send someone round to the hotel to help me hear my lines . . . and would she mind posing in the nude."[2]

In the 1960s, you'd find that newcomer, Peter O'Toole, sitting in the lobby celebrating his big break as the title role in the film, *Laurence of Arabia* (1962). Alan Bates flirted with the hotel operator via the switchboard. You'd step into the small elevator face to face with Robert Shaw (*Jaws,* 1975), Donald Pleasance (*Halloween,* 1978), and Judi Dench. It was like watching BBC in person.

In 1962, cavorting about were the stars of the British import, *Beyond the Fringe*: Alan Bennett, Jonathan Miller, Peter Cook, and Dudley Moore. *Beyond the Fringe* was the smash revue starring and co-written by this quartet, catapulting the careers of all four. Alan Bennett became best-known as a writer, winning countless awards for such plays as *The History Boys* (2006); these honors included The New York Drama Critics Award, given at the Algonquin. Intellectual Jonathan Miller was a true Renaissance Man. Originally a practicing physician, he became an acclaimed British TV personality, stage director, and sculptor. Even among the intelligentsia of the Algonquin, the 6' 4" Miller towered.

Dudley Moore and Peter Cook branched off as a famous comedy team. They are best known to Americans together in such movies as *Bedazzled* (1967) and *The Wrong Box* (1966), as well as Moore's solo appearances in *10* (1979) and *Arthur* (1981). Both actors lived at the Algonquin during their glorious return to Broadway in the 1973 revue, *Good Evening.* That's when I was privileged to spend time with the genial, generous Moore. My brother, Douglas, and I met him one day to play songs we'd written for a proposed musical version of Moore's film *The Wrong Box.* Since Moore was an acclaimed musician, as well as a comedian, his chuckling over some of my lyrics was music to a teenager's ears. On other occasions, I remember noticing how, even though Cook was the tall, aristocratic looking one, it was usually Moore who was accompanied by beautiful women. This fact was acknowledged by Barbara Walters in a TV tribute. She declared "despite his height . . . he had always been a ladies' man. Some called him 'cuddly Duddly.'"[3]

Though many Oscar winners stayed at the hotel, there was a preponderance of Britishers who received the "Supporting Actor" award: including Donald Crisp (*How Green Was My Valley,* 1941), Hugh Griffith (*Ben Hur,*

1959), Peter Ustinov (*Spartacus,* 1960 and *Topkapi,* 1964), John Mills (*Ryan's Daughter,* 1970), and John Gielgud (*Arthur,* 1981). Ustinov multi-tasked on Broadway: a consummate actor, director, and/or a playwright—sometimes all three (*Photo Finish,* 1963). Among his famous quips were: "I'm convinced there's a small room in the attic of the Foreign Office where future diplomats are taught to stammer;" and "The only reason I made a commercial for American Express was to pay for my American Express bill."[4] Once, my grandmother greeted him at lunchtime in the Oak Room, saying "I'll be seeing you in the matinee today of *A Funny Thing Happened On the Way to the Forum* [a 1972 revival that actually starred Phil Silvers, not Ustinov]." Ustinov replied, "Oh, you'll love it! And make sure to visit me backstage afterwards." Ustinov's naughty side was again evident when, against the backdrop of the usually staid Algonquin, he discovered a favorite possession was missing from his room. Discreetly he promised a reward to the Algonquin staff for anyone who could locate that lost bag of weed. This is a story that was recently told to me by former bellman Will Sawyer. I doubt my grandparents ever knew of Ustinov's stash (the closest Grandma Mary ever came to mentioning weed was joking that she'd like her spaghetti with "marijuana sauce").

The more often I visited my grandparents, the more I became aware of this Who's Who of English channels. The British contingent bridged countless categories. Novelists such as Anthony Burgess (*A Clockwork Orange,* 1971) and Laurence Durell (*Justine,* 1969). Movie greats, such as Julie Christie (Oscar'd for *Darling,* 1965) and Peter Finch (Oscar'd for *Network,* 1976). Stage directors like Peter Brook (Tony'd for *Marat-Sade,* 1964) and Peter Hall (Tony'd for *The Homecoming,* 1967). For decades, writer Alec Waugh (*Island In the Sun,* 1957) lived part of every year at the Algonquin.[5] Making at least one annual trip, too, was Ray Cooney, Britain's premiere writer of Feydeau-like sex farces, whose *Run for Your Wife* (1983) ran nine years in London's West End. Playwright John Osborne returned year after year with another imported smash: viz *The Entertainer* (1958), *Luther* (1963), and *Inadmissible Evidence* (1965). Especially impressive, according to Bellman Tony Cichielo, was Osborne's giving Cichielo the biggest tip he ever got, a $100 bill (back when orchestra tickets sold for $9).[6]

In addition, during the late 1960s and early 1970s, the Algonquin played host to countless new English playwrights working on Tony Award-winning shows. These included: Christopher Hampton's *The Philanthropist* (1971), which received four nominations; Simon Grey's *Butley* (1973, won Best Actor for Alan Bates); and David Storey's *The Changing Room* (1973, won Best Supporting Actor for John Lithgow). Tom Stoppard topped

Sir Peter Ustinov. Photo courtesy of Photofest.

them all with four Best Play wins for *Rosencrantz and Guildenstern Are Dead* (1967*)*, *Travesties* (1975), *The Real Thing* (1985), and *The Coast of Utopia* (2006).

At the height of the theatre season, you'd likewise spot British theatre producers, either importing their shows to New York or keeping up with

British producer Harold Fielding.

the latest Broadway offerings. Two producers were especially close to my grandparents, serving as reciprocal hosts any time the Bodnes visited London. One was Peter Bridge, an intense producer largely responsible for advancing the career of the prolific playwright Alan Ayckbourn (often called England's equivalent to Neil Simon). Bridge produced Ayckbourn's first Broadway show, the British farce *How the Other Half Loves* (1971), making some difficult choices. One good choice was having Ayckbourn stay at the Algonquin, where he'd later launch many a Broadway triumph (including *Absurd Person Singular,* 1974; and *The Norman Conquests,* 1975). A questionable choice was taking a delectably British farce and having Ackybourn rewrite it as an American comedy to star Phil Silvers and Sandy Dennis (albeit their presence helped raise the capitalization).[7] The gambit didn't quite work. The show was like a close-to-ingenious Rube Goldberg construct with one essential part, the distinct British humor, missing.

When *How the Other Half Loves* opened to mixed reviews and a disappointing run, Peter Bridge took it badly, becoming another example used by Grandma Mary to dissuade me from going into the theatre. Bridge's mood swings were severe: going from Nirvana to near nervous breakdown. Nevertheless, he was a kindly man—passionate about family and theatre—whose young son stayed in his Algonquin suite during New York visits, including for Bridge's Broadway hit, *The Man in the Glass Booth* (1968). That son was Andrew Bridge, who grew up to be a three-time Tony Award winner, notably as lighting designer for *The Phantom of the Opera* (1988). As for Alan Aykbourn, his future New York hits all retained their original English settings.

My grandparents' best producer friend was the legendary Harold Fielding. This always jolly and elfin impresario produced new London musicals, as well as United Kingdom premieres of Broadway classics. He made a stage star out of Tommy Steele, one of Britain's first big Rock and Roll idols.[8] It was for Steele that Fielding commissioned the creation of *Half a Sixpence* (1963, London; 1965, Broadway), the hit musical which Steele toplined in London, on Broadway, and on film. Among Fielding's stellar imports to London were *The Music Man* (1961, with Van Johnson), *Show Boat* (1971, with Cleo Laine), and *Mame* (1969, with Ginger Rogers),. As reporter Dennis Barker wrote, "His ambition was to make the West End a rival to Broadway as a venue for musicals . . . with such shows as *Charlie Girl*, which he launched in 1965 and which ran for 2,202 consecutive performances."[9]

When I took my first trips to London, in the company of Grandma Mary and my brother Douglas, it was Fielding who regaled us with dinners and backstage visits to his musicals, *Show Boat* and later *Gone With the Wind* (1972). The musical version of *Gone With The Wind* was a typically lavish Harold Fielding production, complete with muslin wisteria trees, the wounded soldiers/railroad scene, plus antebellum costumes to suit any cotillion. Happily, Harold Fielding allowed Douglas and me an insider's perspective. I'll never forget the staged burning of Atlanta, which Douglas and I watched from the theatre wings. Scarlett (June Ritchie) struggled on-stage with a real horse tied to a wagon, within which—unseen by the audience—the "pregnant" Melanie (Patricia Michael) was applying make-up to look sickly. I never found out if that was the same wayward horse who, on opening night, received much attention by taking the greeting "Merde" too literally. I might have seen the standby (or should I say the "gallop-by").

Unfortunately, some of the critics also dumped on *Gone With The Wind*. Though it ran through the year, it was not a success. Still, Fielding was accustomed to the occasional flop, the most costly being a musical about the showman Fielding emulated, *Ziegfeld* (1988), which lost a then-staggering £1.3 million. Yet Fielding had developed a thick skin through far worse experiences. He once flew on a Constellation plane, whose roof was crashed into by a smaller plane, whereby the dead pilot fell into Fielding's lap. Despite the other plane's wreckage, the Constellation plane made a perfect landing. Having survived such circumstances, Fielding buoyantly believed "flying was the safest form of travel."[10] I'm particularly grateful Fielding didn't mention this incident to my grandmother before she booked our flight to London.

Beyond theatre folk, British fashion icon Mary Quant was another fixture at the hotel. Trailblazing the way for designers like Rudy Gernreich, it was Quant who originated the miniskirt, hot pants, and waterproof mascara.[11] She epitomized "Swinging England" as much as Twiggy and The

1960s ad featuring Mary Quant. Source unknown.

Beatles. Following up, she popularized the micro mini, "paint box" makeup, lace-up boots, and the plastic raincoats that became the rage in the U.S. and England during the 1960s.[12]   Though never sported by the Bodnes or Colbys, these styles did materialize on some of my more daring female classmates.

Most importantly, Quant showed savvy by making her designs affordable to the average working girl. If that weren't insightful enough, when asked what she liked best about the United States, she replied "The Algonquin Hotel, corn beef on rye, and your telephone system." I would guess the sight of Quant's modish models in the lobby—incongruously flanking such early American movie types as Lillian Gish and Edward Everett Horton—was my nearest experience to a psychedelic acid trip.

American actor Edward Everett Horton surrounded by British guests including Mary Quant, Diana Rigg, Quant models, Julie Christie, and Peter O'Toole. Illustration: Hannah Chusid.

The Irish side of the United Kingdom was well-represented, too, at the Algonquin. Frequent guests included the great Irish playwright Brian Friel (*Dancing at Lugnasa*, 1991), "doyenne" of Irish literature Edna O'Brien (*Saints and Sinners*, 2011),[13] and actor Jack MacGowran. A member of Dublin's Abbey Players and renowned interpreter of Samuel Beckett plays, MacGowran died at the Algonquin in 1973, right after completing his scenes for the film *The Exorcist* (1973).

Still, it was the British contingent that most influenced me. To this day, when I've worked as a substitute teacher in New Jersey, some students will inquire, "Are you from England?"

I reply, "Only by osmosis." No doubt, the British connection was accentuated by my days at the Algonquin.

Chapter 10: *Musicals "R" Us*

Bodnes and Charles Abramson dining in the Rose Room at the Algonquin.

1966 was a very good year to have a grandmother who liked taking her grandkids to Broadway musicals. In January, we saw the incomparable Gwen Verdon in the first musical of the year, *Sweet Charity* (1966). Grandma had one of her "Oops, maybe I shouldn't have brought the kids" moments watching a show about undulating, hustling, dance hall hostesses. But we adored it anyway, and Grandma explained, "Those girls just shake like that to stay in shape." We'd had a similar experience a few months earlier when Grandma took us to *Man of La Mancha* (1965), whose heroine was Aldonza, a "kitchen slut reeking with sweat."[1] At least Aldonza reformed by the end of the show. I'm not sure how Grandma would have explained some of the musicals today. She even had a hard time saying the title of *The Best Little Whorehouse in Texas* (1978), which she called "The Best Little House on the Prairie."

In March, Grandma treated Douglas and me to opening night tickets for *It's A Bird...It's A Plane...It's Superman* (1966): theatre heaven for this fan of both DC comics and Broadway musicals. Grandma herself found special delight taking us to *Mame*, wherein Angela Lansbury nightly announced, "See you Tuesday at the Algonquin." As if things couldn't get better, during the Summer, we saw three glorious revivals, the first two with their original stars: Ethel Merman as Annie Oakley in *Annie Get Your Gun* (Lincoln Center), Vivian Blaine as Miss Adelaide in *Guys and Dolls* (City Center), and *Show Boat* featuring Barbara Cook, David Wayne, and one of Grandpa Ben's favorite songs, "Make Believe" (Grandpa's other favorite was "Gentle On My Mind," which he sometimes called "Gentile on My Mind").

Still, it was in the fall when we saw a musical that would be a watershed event for me. The capper was the original production of *Cabaret* (1966). This breathtaking show, demonstrating how musicals could be both entertaining and illuminating, made writing musicals my ongoing goal. As a Jewish teen, I could, for the first time, comprehend how something as evil as Nazism took root. At the start of the show, the audience saw a glamorous, sensual Berlin beckoning like a siren song, led by the epicene emcee, the unsurpassed Joel Grey. Soon the setting became a bustling cabaret/nightspot where wine, women, and *whatever* were available. It was not a blatantly decadent setting—no grotesques with track-marks like in recent

Charles Abramson, producer of All the King's Horses.

revivals—but a naughty, seductive mirror of an era still daring, and only later deathly. At its pulse was the baby-faced kewpie doll, Sally Bowles (Jill Haworth), and the American writer, Cliff Townsend (Bert Convy), being drawn into the hypnotic undertow, as the audience followed their example. Like a nightmare overtaking us, Hitler's chorus dulcetly sang "Tomorrow Belongs to Me," and the musical grew darker and darker. Every song dazzled us, while the show insinuated its message: don't turn a blind eye to what's really happening in the world or you may succumb to the consequences. By the conclusion, I was overwhelmed by the possibilities of what a musical could achieve.

After an exhilarating weekend of theatre-going, I returned to our Long Island house, freshly restored after our big fire. There, life was anything but entertaining. I faced escalating arguments between by parents that spurred my insomnia on some nights, followed by dreams so ferocious I often woke screaming.

Fortunately, I knew weekends at the Algonquin meant visits to musicals where, as often as not, "people sing when sad, lights are pink and gold, villains booed when bad, happy endings told."[2] I also had the chance to meet creators of musicals and better understand the magic they made.

One of my guides to bygone musicals was the theatrical agent and former producer, Charles Abramson. He was a walking encyclopedia on theatre history who loved sharing his knowledge with me. His career harked back to the 1930s, when he presented two musicals, *All the King's Horses* (1934) and *Orchids Preferred* (1937). A close friend of my grandparents, the debonair, mustachioed "Mr. Abramson," as I called him, reminded me of an avuncular version of actor Don Ameche. He would evoke the glories of a time in which Broadway was the center of the entertainment world and he'd pay nightly visits to new musicals by Rodgers and Hart, Jerome Kern, Cole Porter, and George Gershwin. His own circle of associates had included Preston Sturges, Philip Burton (Richard Burton's adoptive father), and the agent/producer Charles Feldman, for whom Mr. Abramson negotiated films ranging from *The Glass Menagerie* (1945)[3] to *What's New Pussycat?* (1965)—the sublime to the ridiculous.

Mr. Abramson reveled in verbally reliving the past. Sometimes he told stories so lengthy that he didn't realize I'd fallen asleep. Yet, divorced and having no children of his own, he devoted time to members of my family as if they were his own. Moreover, he encouraged my writing and helped me in any way he could. It was he who introduced me to a couple, staying at the Algonquin, who would be pivotal in my pursuits: actor Teddy Hart and his wife, Dorothy. Teddy was the brother of one of my favorite lyricists,

Two sides of actor Teddy Hart. Photos courtesy of Larry Hart II.

Lorenz Hart, who'd been another regular at the Algonquin before he died in 1943. Teddy was gifted, as well, the originator of roles in two classic musicals, *One Touch of Venus* (1943) and *The Boys From Syracuse* (1938), the latter co-written for him by his brother. Dorothy was dedicated to both men. She was instrumental in preserving the legacy of Lorenz Hart after he died, plugging his shows and writing his biography. She was also delightfully eccentric, with a sensitivity to the cold air that led her to wearing oversize furs in summer and coming down with pneumonia after a drink with too many ice cubes.

During the 1940s, Lorenz Hart had bolstered the confidence of another Algonquin guest I grew to know. The two men met after Alan Jay Lerner returned from serving in World War II, facing a shaky marriage and concerned that his poor vision (blind in one eye from a boxing incident) might impede his future. According to Lerner's biographer, Gene Lees, Larry Hart became a mentor and "the man who did most to make him [Lerner] believe that he had talent to make a life as a lyricist."[4] As lyricists, Hart's and Lerner's work habits could not have been more diverse. Dorothy Hart told me that Larry could lock himself in a room and ten minutes later deliver the words to "Ten Cents a Dance (1930)," featuring ingenious rhymes like "Sometimes I think I've found my hero,/ but it's a queer ro-/mance."[5] Alan Jay Lerner took long spans writing his lyrics, struggling nine days on *Gigi*

(1958) to come up with "She's so oo-la-la-la-la, / So untrue-la-la-la-la,/ She is not thinking of me."[6]

Both men wrote songs my father blissfully played on his stereo as sung by the likes of Ella Fitzgerald and Frank Sinatra. Additional songs by Hart, written with composer Richard Rodgers, included "Where or When (1937)," "Thou Swell (1927)," and "There's a Small Hotel (1936)" (the last one my parents' wedding theme). Lerner's included "I've Grown Accustomed to Her Face (1956)," "Get Me to the Church On Time (1956)," and "Almost Like Being in Love (1947)" (which title *should* have been my parent's wedding theme). Hart and Lerner were also alike in substance dependency. Hart was an alcoholic, Lerner a smoker, amphetamine-taker, and uncontrollable nail-biter. He chewed his nails so badly that he wore white gloves to discourage himself. My grandmother cited Lerner as another example of what show business does to people, saying, "He doesn't have fingers, he has knobs."

Lerner and his most frequent collaborator, Frederick (Fritz) Loewe, both stayed at the Algonquin on and off throughout their careers. Some might say writing musicals was their first love beyond any wives. Maurice Abravanel, the famed conductor who directed the music for Lerner and Loewe's *The Day Before Spring* (1946), reportedly stated:

> "I liked Fritz and Alan both as human beings. But they were strange human beings. Alan's first wife, Ruth, was a lovely . . . girl. I sat with her after the premiere of *The Day Before Spring*, because Alan didn't pay any attention to her. She told me she was alone. Alan didn't live with her. Alan would call her maybe once every two or three weeks. He and Fritz totally neglected their wives. They both lived at the Algonquin. I couldn't help feeling sorry for the two women . . . ."[7]

Nevertheless, staying alive became more important to Frederick Loewe than composing. This was especially true when, working on *Camelot* at the Algonquin, he suffered a massive coronary. Lerner did briefly coax him out of retirement, and back to the hotel, to collaborate on two projects: a stage version of their Oscar-winning movie *Gigi*; and a new movie musical based on *The Little Prince* (1974)—which, incidentally, was co-produced by Grandma Mary's second cousin, Joseph Tandet. Yet neither project succeeded.

Lerner ultimately clocked in eight wives and thirteen Broadway musicals, among them, the Lerner and Loewe hits, *Brigadoon, Paint Your Wagon* (1951), *My Fair Lady,* and *Camelot.* My grandparents saw most of the musicals and wives, albeit Lerner's shows sometimes ran longer than his marriages. I sat and talked to Lerner when he had high hopes for his last musical, *Dance a Little Closer* (1983). Collaborating with composer Charles Strouse (*Bye Bye Birdie*), he multitasked as lyricist, librettist, and director of this musical based on *Idiot's Delight*, a play written in 1936 by Algonquin Round-Tabler Robert E. Sherwood. As we sat, Lerner radiated confidence. He asserted how well the musical's early performances were going, particularly proud because it starred his eighth wife, British actress Liz Robertson. Sadly, he was as oblivious to reality as Sally Bowles was in *Cabaret*. *Dance a Little Closer* was roundly panned, lasted one performance, and received the nickname "Close a Little Sooner." However, Lerner did something very right on the show. This time, while the show was being developed, he lived at the Algonquin *with* his wife. It was probably his happiest marriage: he and Liz Robertson stayed together until his death did them part.

Another veteran lyricist I knew through the Algonquin was Irving Caesar, my grandparent's friend and the nicest Tin Pan Alley mensch you'd ever want to meet. He led a fantastic, long life. He grew up knowing the Marx Brothers. He was lyricist for George Gershwin's first hit tune, "Swanee (1919)," which, as recorded by Al Jolson, outsold all Gershwin's other songs. His other songs included "Animal Crackers in My Soup" (1935; composers: Ray Henderson and Ted Koehler), "Just a Gigolo" (1929; music: Leonello Casucci), and—from the Broadway musical *No, No, Nanette* (1925)—"I Want to Be Happy" and "Tea For Two" (music: Vincent Youmans).[8] In 1971, Caesar was in major demand because of the smash Broadway revival of *No, No, Nanette*, as directed by another Algonquin regular, Burt Shevelove (the great co-librettist—with Larry Gelbart—of *A Funny Thing Happened on the Way to the Forum*, 1962).

I recall visiting Irving Caesar's office around that time, a place which writer Mark Steyn described as:

> "[A] step back in time . . . The sheet music covers are quaintly dated, the faded photographs show singers and writers long dead, and each chair has its own spittoon. Littering the floor, stacked up against desk legs, are dozens of awards . . . most for 'Tea For Two' as 'Most Performed Song of the Decade'—not in the twenties, when it was written, but in 1984, 1985, 1986, 1987 . . . 'They give it to me every year,' sighs Caesar heading for his hundredth birthday. 'I don't know what to do with 'em any more.'" [9]

During my visit, Caesar recounted how he originally improvised the words to "Tea For Two" as a dummy lyric that people told him to keep.

Lyricist Irving Caesar. Photo courtesy of ASCAP.

He relished telling this story; I'd heard it at least two times before when he made guest appearances at events. But, as a bonus just for me, he sang the "Stonewall Moskowitz March," whose lyrics he'd co-written with Larry Hart for the Ziegfeld musical *Betsy* (1926). Sample lyric:

> "My name is Stonewall Moskowitz.
> I'm no Doctor of Philoskowitz.
> I've got money in the bankowitz.
> I'm as good as any mankowitz."[10]

After hearing the song, it was clear to me why it never reached the popularity of "Swanee."

Most treasured of all such Algonquin introductions was my meeting E. Y. ("Yip") Harburg, one of my two lyricist idols, alongside Lorenz Hart. Harburg's contributions to shows such as *Finian's Rainbow* (1947) were lyrical equivalents, years ahead, to the accomplishment of *Cabaret*: they entertained while edifying. Though not as dead serious as the message of *Cabaret*, Harburg's lyrics were memorable social commentaries cushioned in whimsy with catchy tunes by such composers as Jay Gorney, Burton Lane, and Harold Arlen. Such Harburg songs were "Brother, Can You Spare a Dime? (1930)," "When the Idle Poor Become the Idle Rich (1947)," and "It's Only a Paper Moon (1933)."

Lyricist E.Y. Harburg and Michael.

Harburg, who was blacklisted during the 1950s for his views, also wrote wildly witty political verse, such as in his book of poetry *Rhymes for the Irreverent*:

> "We've licked pneumonia and T.B.
> And plagues that used to mock us,
> We've got the virus on the run
> The small pox cannot pock us.
> We've found the antibodies for
> The staphylo-strepto-coccus.
> But oh, the universal curse
> From Cuba to Korea,
> The bug of bugs that bugs us still
> And begs for panacea!
> Oh, who will find the antidote
> For Pentagonorrhea?"[11]

It's amazing that this cynical verse came from the same man who wrote the wistfully child-like lyric to "Over the Rainbow" (music: Harold Arlen).

During our conversation, I was touched when Harburg acknowledged that his all-sung and rhymed "Munchkinland" sequence in *The Wizard of Oz* (1939) was inspired by similar scenes written by my other idol, Larry

Hart, for movies like *Love Me Tonight* (1932). I myself would one day write several musicals that were all-rhymed and all-sung.

I might have never been introduced to these marvelous musicals and veteran writers, if not for my grandparents, the Bodnes, especially Grandma Mary. She had no idea what an outlet they'd become for me, shining light on darker aspects of my own life. *Cabaret* would remain my favorite musical, closely followed by Rodgers and Hammerstein's *Carousel* (1945), where people in a tumultuous marriage are unable to express their love, coming to blows instead. *Carousel* struck a chord with me in a home where my parents were fighting so constantly that expensive steps were taken to conciliate their marriage. Urged by my father, the Bodnes arranged for them to receive family counseling with a therapist at Johns Hopkins University. My parents, Douglas, and I traveled to Baltimore so our testimonies would give the therapist the fullest picture of our family dynamic. Unfortunately, Grandma Mary decided to influence the results. After going to all this trouble and expense, Grandma coached Douglas and me on what we should say. We were to claim my mother's intense agitation, later diagnosed as OCD, were mostly the fault of my father and his drinking. Grandma Mary thought that information would help the therapist fix things at home without causing stigma to her daughter. I realize Grandma thought she was handling the situation correctly, protecting her daughter. She was part of a generation of immigrants that wanted the best for their children but acted from the heart rather than psychological acumen. Needless to say, when the Colbys returned from Baltimore, the fighting just got worse. Like in *Cabaret*, a blind eye had been turned on the truth and, eventually, our family would encounter consequences.

Chapter 11: *Learning the Ropes*

Gathered in the Rose Room: Louis Nizer, humorist Harry Hershfield, writer Konrad Bercovici, Joe DiMaggio, Ben B. Bodne, and Variety *editor Abel Green.*

Despite my theatre aspirations, my family repeatedly reminded me, "There's more security in the hotel business!" For several summers, my brother Douglas and I gave it a try. Starting when I was about fifteen, Douglas and I would either be driven to the hotel by my father, on his way to work there, or just stay over at my grandparents' 10th floor suite at the Algonquin. Then, we spent weekdays learning the ropes in various jobs.

Sorting files and bills in the reservations office might have seemed routine under ordinary circumstances, but not when you're helping to make arrangements for Jason Robards and Colleen Dewhurst, or Jeanne Moreau and François Truffaut. I learned more about French films through my summer job than by going to the movies. A special list of incoming VIPs could be found on a pad kept by hotel's head secretary, Irene McCarthy. Even when I wasn't working thereabouts, I often climbed the stairs to sneak a peek at the list.

Douglas and I also did stints as switchboard operators, alongside the hotel's professional operators. Connecting a forest of wires in and out of jacks, we plugged through the week as if in a scene from *Bells Are Ringing*

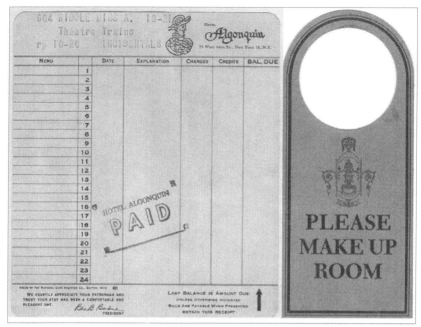

Algonquin souvenirs: bill and room service sign.

(1959). Alas, those switchboards have now gone the way of the spinning wheel, the butter churn, and the carrier pigeon.

The most enjoyable job was working as a clerk behind the front desk. Grandma Mary took me to Brooks Brothers to find just the right navy blue suit to wear. In what must have seemed like a Little Rascals remake of *Grand Hotel,* I stationed myself behind the check-in desk and assisted the head clerk. Thus, guests would be greeted by a baby-faced fifteen-year-old prompted by a dapper desk clerk, the two of us resembling a ventriloquist and his puppet. I remember that Grandma often sat nearby, while I worked at the front desk, I guess sometimes to warn guests, sometimes to kvell about her well-groomed prodigy. Regular guests mostly smiled, knowing who I was, and others took it in stride. I myself keenly benefited from this learning experience—and a small weekly stipend. Plus, I got better acquainted with some of the hotel's remarkable guests.

Even after James Thurber passed away, the Algonquin continued to be "A Thurber Carnival" (to borrow the title of the 1960 Broadway revue in which Thurber played himself and for which he won a special Tony Award). Thurber's framed cartoons could be seen in the hallways from floor to floor; and his widow Helen still lived at the hotel. Daily, I handed out her mail, which she received with what seemed like the same cordiality she would show an adult. Everyone at the Algonquin adored her. She had been nicknamed "Mr. Thurber's Seeing-Eye Wife" since, after he lost his sight, she oversaw his writings and drawings.[1] Later I read how she also reversed her husband's shrewish image of women, as patterned on Thurber's abrasive first wife, Althea. Ironically, reporter Dannye Romine described how Helen's sunniness spurred some heat from the editor at *The New Yorker*:

> "Thurber's plans to marry Helen a month after his divorce from Althea made editor [Harold] Ross edgy. He feared Thurber's nagging-wife characters . . . would disappear if Thurber happily remarried. The thrice-married Ross dispatched humorist Robert Benchley to try unsuccessfully to dissuade Thurber.
>
> "Thurber's shrews did, in fact, dwindle over the years. The couples in his later stories evidence . . . a more equal balance."[2]

Behind the desk, I likewise encountered a longtime friend of Thurber's, author E. B. White. The two men even wrote an unlikely book together, *Is Sex Necessary?* (1929) (When Helen Thurber first met James, this book had just been published, and Helen grabbed his attention with her introductory comment, "Well, Mr. Thurber, *is* sex necessary?"[3]).

As for E. B. White, he was an extremely shy man, who disliked public-ity and feared public appearances.[4] He was most-famous for his bestiary children's books, *Stuart Little* (1945) and *Charlotte's Web* (1952), neither obviously inspired by his stays at the Algonquin. One could argue that when construction was underway in the neighborhood, White may have spotted a mouse or two, resembling Stuart Little. Still, White found most of his inspiration from the animals at his permanent home, a farm in Maine. He cited, "I had been watching a big grey spider at her work and was impressed by how clever she was at weaving. Gradually I worked the spider into the story that you know [*Charlotte's Web*]."[4]

E. B. White was especially fond of the mattresses at the Algonquin, calling them the most comfortable and sleep-inducing he'd ever experi-enced. My uncle, Andrew Anspach (the hotel's co-manager), sent a hotel mattress directly to White's farm, for which White couldn't have been more grateful. With his shyness and pleasure in sleep-inducing mattresses, it's no wonder that White co-wrote *Is Sex Necessary?*

During the time I distributed guest mail into slots at the front desk, it was easy to become confused when the name "Wilder" appeared: film director Billy Wilder, playwright Thornton Wilder, and composer Alec Wilder all stayed there. Alec Wilder *lived* at the hotel for forty years until his death in 1980. As a child, he visited there with his mother.[5] As soon as

Alec Wilder.

he was old enough, he moved in, between trips around the world. Wilder treated my family like, well, family—always happy to talk. A tall, slim figure, he had a professorial air with his grizzled hair and slightly rumpled tie and jacket. He was a mostly self-taught composer. His music ranged from classical to jazz. His songs, including the standards "While We're Young" (1944, lyric: William Engvick) and "I'll Be Around" (1942, lyric: Wilder), were recorded by such artists as Frank Sinatra and Tony Bennett.[7] Back in 1949 and 1950, he also hosted a weekly Sunday event at the Algonquin's Stratford Suite, the elegant meeting room on the 3rd floor, where singers performed to orchestral tracks of his music. Wilder reported:

> "Before we knew it, these Sunday evenings had become a fashionable event to attend. All manner of prominent theatrical and

literary people came. I recall that one Sunday evening Leonard Bernstein and Marc Blitzstein volunteered to help us get the right balance between the orchestra recording and the 'live' voice of the leading singer. I don't think Nancy Walker missed one of those Sunday evenings . . . One evening I happened to look up from my hot seat at the piano to see William Faulkner . . . sitting in the first row of chairs."[6]

I often saw Alec Wilder in the lobby, doing such fascinating things as writing out music charts for Frank Sinatra. He wrote a definitive book on music, *American Popular Song: The Great Innovators, 1900-1950* (1972), the basis for an acclaimed National Public Radio series he hosted during the 1970s. He was a paradox of erudite sophistication and impish humor who loved conversing with children, eased through *The London Times* crossword puzzle in ink, and was known to blow bubbles even at formal dinners.[7] Singer Marian McPartland cited how he never held back his opinions. According to McPartland, he so disliked Peggy Lee's recording of "While We're Young," he told Lee, "The next time you come to the bridge [of the song], jump off!"[8]

Also visiting the hotel was a veteran movie star who arrived with a surplus of suitcases. Dana Andrews, who gave unforgettable performances in movies, such as *Laura* (1944) and *The Best Years of Our Lives* (1946), was very close to my family, as was his wife, Mary (Grandma Mary seemed to love guests who shared her name). Bellman Tony Cichielo declared, "If the man had fifteen pieces [of luggage], it was nothing."[9]

Dana Andrews may have had an excess of luggage, but he had a minimal ego. He attributed his first big break to luck:

"I had just made my first movie . . . They put up a huge sign. 'The Westerner,' it said, 'Starring Gary Cooper and Dana Andrews.' I had exactly four lines in the picture. Nobody had ever heard of me. But the publicity department had done that for all the billboards. They thought Dana was a girl's name, and I was the girl in the picture, and that it looked more exciting to have Cooper and a girl. If I'd used my first name, 'Carver,' [he was born Carver Dana Andrews] maybe I'd never have made it."[10]

On several occasions, Dana Andrews spiced up lunches with my family, sharing stories of old Hollywood, with little asides about everything from director Otto Preminger's voice of terror to actress Joan Bennett's battle of the bulge. Little did I know that, decades later, I personally would

Dana and Mary Andrews.

be responsible for the actor's starring at the Berkshire Theater Festival in Stockbridge, Maryland. As a consultant there in 1977, I arranged for his being cast in William Inge's *Come Back, Little Sheba*. Dana was simply magnificent. Being a reformed alcoholic, who'd become a vital spokesman for AA, Dana gave poignant resonance to the role of Doc Delaney, a character whose drinking problem devastates his marriage.

In addition to my other jobs at the Algonquin, I spent a few days helping out in the housekeeping department, which took up the entire

13th floor. Set apart from the rest of the hotel, the department could only be reached by a single stairway or service elevator. The floor was full of washing machines and linen presses, as the chief housekeeper coordinated maid service via walkie-talkies. Every now and then, something unexpected would be reported. For example, there was one ordeal faced by a maid that was right out of a creature feature. Entering a room to make up the bed, she found a large box from which issued horrible hissing sounds. Like Pandora about to release the evils of the world, the maid daringly pulled open the lid of the box. Out crawled an invasion of slimy, slithering snakes making the maid back away screaming. Turned out the guest was a collector of reptiles, who smuggled more than a few of his friends into his room. Stumbling backward, the maid tipped over another box from which rose leaping lizards. Running to take refuge in the bathroom, she received the biggest shock of all: within the tub gazed an open-mouthed alligator. Fortunately, she escaped becoming room service lunch, as other employees rushed to her rescue. Still, the guest was sent packing. Except

Thelonious Monk. Photo courtesy of Photofest.

for the Algonquin Cat, the Algonquin had a fairly strict "no pets" policy, certainly no zookeepers and company.

The 13th floor also held a short stairway leading up to the hotel roof. It was on the roof that a Jazz legend almost hit his final note. From the late 1950s on, Thelonious Monk was hailed as one of the most innovative Jazz pianists. A popularizer of Bebop, he is the second most recorded Jazz composer after Duke Ellington.[11] However, he had a history of difficulties and erratic behavior. He was largely subsidized through the patronage of an Algonquin habitué, and Rothschild descendant, Baroness Pannonica de Koenigswarter. He spent many hours in her Algonquin suite, rehearsing, composing, and hanging out with such other Jazz greats as saxophonists, Sonny Rollins and John Coltrane.[12] Monk apparently wandered around the hotel, as well. Somehow, one day, he found his way to the roof. Fortunately, he was closely followed by Bell Captain Tony Cichielo. According to Cichelo, he stopped Monk from leaping off the roof. "Monk had one foot off the top. I grabbed him by the shoulder. I said, 'Where are you going, Mr. Monk?'"[13] Monk couldn't improvise an answer.

It remains a mystery why the unpredictable Monk was up on the roof. But, it's fortunate Cichelo checked in on him or Monk might have joined Preston Sturges, James Thurber and a few others who checked out, permanently, at the Algonquin.

My Algonquin apprenticeship concluded with several weeks of working in the food steward's department. This department was located in a part of the Algonquin that few saw, the hotel's "underworld": the basement and subbasement. To do this, the good news was that I absolutely had to stay in my grandparent's apartment, so I could rise at 5:30 a.m. each weekday. The bad news was that I had to rise at 5:30 a.m. By 6:00, I ventured down to the steward's basement office. It was stocked with shelves of foods, alongside small freezers and a big closet-size one. Through the day, I helped the steward unload supplies, phone around for the best food prices, and prepare fruit baskets for guests—skills for which Woodmere Academy never prepared me. Often, when I stepped into the big freezer, I thought of the movie *Hell's Kitchen* (1939), in which Dead End Kid Bobby Jordan was trapped in one such ice box and froze to death. Luckily, Grandma Mary regularly phoned in, so I knew the steward would never let anything like that happen to me.

Down the foyer were other freezers and meat lockers full of every kind of edible. One flight below was the liquor and wine sub-cellar. This wasn't typical Algonquin glamour. Instead of Mary Quant models and famous songbirds, I was looking at hanging beef and barrels of fish. Still, I was rolling up my sleeves and working hard.

It was my father's idea to put me in the steward's office. He rightly posited that, if I were to go into the hotel business, I should learn all departments from top (housekeeping) to bottom (wine cellar). Nonetheless, my grandparents—especially Grandma Mary—disliked the idea of my being out-of-sight at menial labor like lifting heavy boxes. I didn't mind at all. In my pampered Algonquin mode, it was the only solid exercise I could get. Still, that led to more clashes between my father and my grandparents. Those clashes reverberated throughout the family. After all the effort to indoctrinate me, my summer ended with reasons *not* to want to go into the hotel business.

Young Douglas and Michael at a piano at home; David, Michael, and Douglas Colby in the lobby.

Chapter 12: *This Doesn't Happen at the Holiday Inn*

Melina Mercouri, Orson Bean, and the cast of Illya, Darling *(1967). Photo courtesy of Photofest.*

Not every hotel could claim live bouzouki music resonating through the halls. In 1967, the musical version of the Greek movie, *Never On a Sunday* (1960), was rehearsing for Broadway, and many of its creators were staying at the Algonquin Hotel. Grandpa Ben, who'd complained about the music in *My Fair Lady* and walked out of a backer's audition for *Kiss Me Kate*, finally agreed with Grandma Mary that this show was a surefire hit. The musical, titled *Illya, Darling*, had the biggest advance sale of the season thanks to its credentials. Melina Mercouri would be recreating her celebrated role of Illya, the independent darling of a brothel in Piraeus, Greece. In her seductively husky voice, she'd be singing a score by the quintessential Greek composer, Manos Hadjidakis. The songs included his Oscar-winning title tune from *Never On a Sunday*, the film on which the show was based.

Mercouri's husband, American film director Jules Dassin, arranged for Mercouri and Hadjidakis to join him at the Algonquin. Dassin had been one of the many artists blacklisted during the McCarthy era who'd found the hotel to be an apolitical haven. Before the blacklist, he'd directed such American film classics as *The Naked City* (1948) and *Night and the City* (1950). Afterwards, he fled to Europe, helming *Rififi* (1955) and *Topkapi* (1964). Dassin actually began his career as an actor in New York Yiddish Theatre[1] and

Composer Manos Hadjidakis (Photo courtesy of ASCAP). Grandma dancing with me on another occasion.

was the leading man in the movie *Never On a Sunday*, which he also wrote and directed. He couldn't sing, so actor Orson Bean would be playing his role in the musical.

Illya, Darling was Dassin's return to the Broadway stage, where he'd previously directed *Two's Company* (1952)—believe it or not—a musical revue starring Bette Davis. Davis wasn't exactly the go-to person for musicals or altruism, but she personally got Dassin hired for this show during the blacklist.

In any case, my family couldn't have been more excited, as the Dassins and Hadjidakis spent afternoons rehearsing new material at the hotel, with a full contingent of musicians on hand. Live bouzouki performances were certainly classier hotel accompaniment than elevator music. Grandma took me on a personal tour of their floor when I visited, sometimes dancing in the halls to the music. She even knocked on the Dassins' door to say hello to those rehearsing.

The show also involved veterans from three of the most successful musicals ever, producer Kermit Bloomgarden (*The Music Man*), lyricist Joe Darion (*Man of La Mancha*), and choreographer Oona White (*Mame*). How could it miss being a winner? Well, they said that about Thomas E. Dewey, too. As Mercouri stated: "*Never on Sunday* changed my life twice.

With the film, I became known. And with the play ... I lost everything I owned."[2]

Still, despite bad reviews and being financial quicksand, the musical ran nine months on the strength of Melina's Tony Award-nominated (and previously Oscar-nominated) performances. The Bodne family was rooting for it, right from its ill-fated tryout. Grandpa Ben and Grandma Mary took my brother Douglas and me on the train to Philadelphia for our first out-of-town theatre event. Everyone loved the experience, if not necessarily the show. We went backstage and Grandma tactfully spoke for all of us, expressing her genuine enthusiasm. It was certainly thrilling to get a backstage look at designer Oliver Smith's vivid Piraeus set, then greet Melina and Jules Dassin alongside our favorite Algonquin bouzouki players (who toured with the show since the musicians union didn't have many *American* bouzouki players).

Moreover, *Illya, Darling* wasn't the only show we saw in its Philadelphia tryout that weekend. We attended the even more ill-fated *Love in E-flat*

Credits for Norman Krasna's Love in E-flat.

(1967), a new comedy by the heretofore successful playwright Norman Krasna. Krasna had written a string of Broadway hits that were turned into even more profitable movies, including the comedies, *John Loves Mary* (1948) and *Sunday in New York* (1961)—whose film versions respectively starred Ronald Reagan and Jane Fonda. His screenplays included *Princess O'Rourke* (1943, Oscared for Best Original Screenplay) and *White Christmas* (1954, with Fred Astaire and Danny Kaye). His love of theatre had begun decades earlier, when he saw *The Front Page*, the celebrated play by two Algonquinites, Ben Hecht and Charles MacArthur. As a crash course in playwriting, Krasna retyped that play's script more than twenty times in order to assimilate its style and structure.[3]

Grandma Mary introduced me to Krasna while he was staying at the hotel in pre-production for *Love in E-flat*. Impressed by my knowledge of theatre, Krasna, father of six, took an immediate paternal liking to the sixteen-year-old Algonquin Kid. He even asked me for advice on actresses when the show's star needed to be replaced (he'd moved to Switzerland and wasn't familiar with the names agents were offering). The actress who'd been let go was Susan Oliver, whom I recalled from a terrifying episode of *The Alfred Hitchcock Hour*. Her replacement was Kathy Nolan, Kate of TV's *The Real McCoys* (1957-1963), who'd also been in that terrifying "Hitchcock" episode. Krasna was bowled over I knew valuable information like that.

Not only did I get to attend the out-of-town tryout of *Love in E-flat*, I attended the Broadway opening as Norman Krasna's guest! In fact, while he watched from the back of the theatre, he let me sit with his lovely wife, Erle, who was also the widow of Al Jolson. I was deeply honored by that gesture, and then devastated when the show received tepid reviews. Nonetheless, I made it my mission to try and save the show. Back home in Hewlett, I became a one-boy publicist, phoning people randomly and pretending to be a recorded message proclaiming, "See Broadway's notable new hit, *Love in E-flat*! Hurry now to the Brooks Atkinson Theatre while tickets are available." My calls didn't work; the show lasted a mere twenty-four performances.

Another "Algonquin playwright" I had the honor of knowing was Thornton Wilder. The winner of two Best Play Pulitzer Prizes—for *Our Town* (1938) and *The Skin of Our Teeth* (1942) (and a third Pulitzer for his novel, *The Bridge Over San Luis Rey*, 1927)—he was surprisingly humble. Kindhearted as Kris Kringle, he took the time to send my parents a personal note of encouragement about my writing skills. Then again, Wilder seemed to take delight in everything that was happening, whether it was something as simple as hearing I received an "A" on a school essay or the phenomenal success of *Hello Dolly!*, the musical version of his play *The Matchmaker* (1955).

However, Wilder did have a conspicuous shortcoming: forgetfulness. A doorman at the hotel was quoted as saying:

> "One day he [Wilder] came out of the hotel door, and I said, 'Taxi, Mr. Wilder?' He nodded vaguely. I hailed a cab, and he got in the door, got out the opposite door, walked across the street and drove off in a parked car. I only hope it was his car—he's so absent-minded!"[4]

I myself spent an evening with Wilder I'll never forget. I'd been invited by Charles Abramson (my "Uncle Charlie") to join him for a cocktail hour chat with Wilder and the legendary Jed Harris, also staying at the hotel. That night, I felt like a page at Camelot observing royalty. Moreover, I witnessed the great divide among artistic temperaments. On one side of the lobby table was Wilder, whose knowledge of history, language, and literature colored his conversation with inspiring insights. On the other side was Jed Harris, who talked all evening about Jed Harris. He was the producer, director, or both of such classics as *The Front Page*, *The Crucible* (1953), and

The Algonquin Kid is reminded of Santa, Don Ameche, and the Big Bad Wolf sitting with Thornton Wilder, Charles Abramson, and Jed Harris in the lobby. Illustration: Hannah Chusid.

Wilder's *Our Town*. Yet, largely due to his unpleasantness and duplicity, he had fallen on hard times, about to be kicked out of the Algonquin for not paying his bills. According to Harris' biographer Martin Gottfried, Harris had worked with all the greats and made enemies of most of them.[5] Laurence Olivier based his interpretation of the venomous Richard III on Harris.[6] Walt Disney is said to have used Harris' features as the basis of the Big Bad Wolf in the cartoon, *The Three Little Pigs* (1933). George S. Kaufman reportedly asked that his ashes to be thrown in Harris' face.[7]

As the evening progressed, I could see why. Harris was not good company. He rolled his eyes when Wilder extolled the current crop of Broadway playwrights. He interrupted Wilder repeatedly to give his less flattering opinions, nettling Wilder by calling him "Thorny." He barely let speak the customarily loquacious Mr. Abramson. Then, Harris' vainness reached a Himalayan peak when he cited how he'd turned down directing Wilder's *The Skin of Our Teeth*, as if he'd escaped a burning building. It came as no surprise that, when the bill arrived, Harris ducked out and Thornton Wilder paid for the get-together. To this day, I can brag, the playwright of *Our Town* treated me to two Coca Colas.

The contrast between Wilder and Harris was an object lesson on what constitutes a life well spent, or squandered, in theatre. As Grandma Mary told me, toward the end of his life, Jed Harris's genius had turned into dodging his creditors, rather than creating stage magic.

Regardless of Jed Harris, I observed lots of glamorous and inspirational guests at the Algonquin who *did* pay their bills during the late 1960s. I was in Grandma Mary's apartment when she was visited by Jacqueline Kennedy Onassis with another frequent Algonquin guest, Greek actress Irene Papas. I saw Princess Grace Kelly dining in the Rose Room. Coretta King passed me in the lobby.

Heading of "The Lyons Den," syndicated and carried in The New York Post.

Of course, spending my weekdays at high school on Long Island, I missed many Algonquin doings I could only wish I'd seen. Perusing old Leonard Lyons column in the *NY Post*, I'm in awe of what my grandparents hosted every day:

"All seven judges of the Court of Appeals lunched at the Algonquin yesterday—the first time in court history that they've all convened in New York."—*The Lyons Den*, 2/2/1968

"CANDIDACY: At the Algonquin yesterday, Arthur Schlesinger Jr. [U.S. historian/Special Assistant to JFK], told of his meeting Sen. Vance Hartke (D-Ind.) ... Hartke stated that LBJ would not run for reelection."—*The Lyons Den*, 4/2/1968

"Sen. [Eugene] McCarthy left Esquire's Algonquin party to fly to France. An aide explained: 'Gene wants to get away from those who ask when he's coming out for Humphrey.'"— *The Lyons Den*, 11/13/1968

"Stalin's daughter Svetlana Alliluyeva, dined with the literary set at the Algonquin."— *The Lyons Den*, 4/4/1969

There was even an item about me in a Leonard Lyons column:

"Mrs. Ben Bodne, whose husband owns the Algonquin, sent her grandson a daily allotment of caviar while he was away this summer. Mrs. Bodne dotes on the boy, who dotes on caviar."—*The Lyons Den*, 8/27/1968 [8]

This item was placed while I was taking a two-week summer course at Syracuse University in Journalism. Grandma had recently introduced me to caviar during lunch at the Algonquin. Since I didn't smoke, drink, or take drugs, she decided I deserved at least this one indulgence while studying hard.

No matter her faults—and how she'd spoil me at times—Grandma remained my strongest support system through the years. She never missed a chance to get Douglas and me involved in something she knew we'd enjoy. She even arranged for us to be present when movies were made at the Algonquin. One weekend, Douglas and I sat on the sidelines while the multi-million dollar movie, *Star!*, was being filmed in the Algonquin Rose Room. As with *Illya Darling*, there were high expectations for this 1968 movie, combining many elements that had in 1965 made *The Sound of Music* one of the most successful movies of its time. The same director (Richard Wise) and producer (Saul Chaplin) oversaw this next screen musical for superstar Julie Andrews, who'd again be playing a biographical character, this time the British actress Gertrude Lawrence rather than Maria Von Trapp.

LOBBY (with buffet in distance) is sketched at top left. Julie Andrews (above), in scene from the forthcoming film "Star," shot at the Algonquin, reads opening-night reviews.

Irene Papas and Jacqueline Kennedy Onassis. The making of Star! with Julie Andrews (from clipping, source unknown).

The scene filmed at the Algonquin portrayed an opening night party for Gertrude Lawrence. In the movie, the characters would be rejoicing at their opening night raves. In reality, nobody rejoiced over the lukewarm reviews received by *Star!* The film did, however, receive seven Oscar nominations; it won zippo.

By coincidence, another movie filmed at the Algonquin was up for an Academy Award that year for Documentary Feature. The movie was *The Young Americans* (1967), a tribute to the All-American singing group by that name who toured the U.S. Written and directed by Alexander Grassoff, a friend of the Bodnes, the movie included the unlikely plot development that a company of thirty-six smiley teens would be staying—and rehearsing—at the compact Algonquin. Grandma Ben gave Grassoff a special deal, especially since Grandpa was always generous to friends and the hotel would be spotlighted. Grandma even talked Grassoff into using Douglas and me as extras. The scene featuring the Colby Brothers took place in the Rose Room, during a breakfast conference between one of the Young Americans and his adult supervisor. I was at a table directly in back of that charismatic Young American. I would be seen prominently jabbering to Douglas. Months later, when my family attended a preview of the movie at a Long Island cinema, we were disappointed to discover that only part of the Colby Brothers were on-screen. I was seen, but only Douglas' hand was visible in the corner frame. Nonetheless, Douglas's hand was quite lively, gesticulating and pouring milk into a bowl of cereal. He could have gotten a Jergen's Hand Lotion commercial out of this showcase.

The biggest surprise of all was that *The Young Americans*—a movie hardly anyone saw (except my family)—*won* the Academy Award for Best Documentary that year, at least, temporarily!   For a brief while, I could brag that I'd made my movie debut in the "Best Documentary of the Year." Unfortunately, I soon learned that the film's too early release date should have disqualified it. *The Young Americans* was retroactively declared ineligible, one of the few movies ever to have an Oscar revoked.

The Rose Room in the 1980s: Broadway designer Oliver Smith's sketch and postcard photo of the room as he designed it.

I must admit some of the experiences weren't the sort to make anyone eager to pursue show business. Yet I was one lucky kid to live them. Let's just say my family never had experiences like these when we vacationed at the Holiday Inn. Every visit to the Algonquin would be like a special holiday, sometimes like Thanksgiving, sometimes April Fools Day, yet always a day to remember.

Chapter 13: *Who Knew?*

The years 1968-1970 were not the most invigorating at the Colby home. My father had reached a point where he could no longer endure the tension of working under Grandpa Ben at the Algonquin. He and Mom were going through something of a separation, while Dad took a job as manager to a hotel in Washington DC to prove he could, literally, manage on his own. Mom, in turn, was extremely upset and sometimes vented her feelings on those still at home. Consequently, I had trouble focusing on schoolwork and was faltering academically.

On the other hand, there was the Algonquin, where I could always experience dazzling events and characters and, beyond any MacDonald's, happy meals. Fortunately, during my father's absence, my grandparents encouraged my visiting them as much as ever, to make things easier for my mother. In fact, my grandparents sometimes let me get away with all

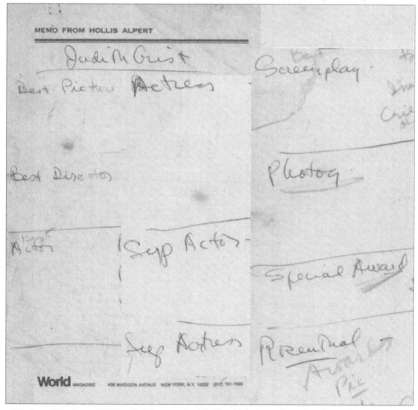

National Society of Film Critics patched ballot (deleting choices). Critic Hollis Alpert was the group's founder.

manner of mischief. The Stratford Suite on the third floor was the scene of a typical antic. The Suite was where various critics' organizations would vote for the "bests" of the year, and I would sneak in afterwards, gathering and perusing the ballots. During my Christmas vacation at the hotel, I gathered the ballots from the National Society of Film Critics. Come June, I leafed through the votes of the New York Film Critics Circle. I knew the winners of these awards hours before official announcements were circulated. How many teenagers could make that claim?

Skipping ahead a few years, there was an especially hush-hush upshot. Actually, at this particular time, I was away at college, and Douglas inspected the ballots early one evening, making a shocking discovery. He told me he'd gone to the Stratford Suite to practice on the piano there. He found the ballots, and, after a perusal, realized something was amiss. He took them up to another guest at the hotel—our friend Dorothy Hart (sister-in-law of Lorenz Hart)—and she corroborated the something amiss was a mess! He phoned me at college, asking, "What should I do? What should I do?" He'd uncovered a major miscount by the New York Drama Critics on the winner for Best Play of the 1972-73 Season. David Rabe's *Sticks and Bones* (1971) had been circled as the winner with 36 voting points, while Jason Miller's *That Championship Season* (1972) was cited as runner-up with 27 points. Yet the latter play had actually received more votes (37 points). The critic who tallied the votes apparently wasn't good at math. Meanwhile, preliminary announcements had already gone out that *Sticks and Bones* was the winner (as would be reported in that evening's edition of *The New York Times*).

Douglas wanted my advice on whether he should reveal his finding, worrying which would be a worse embarrassment: exposing the Critic Circle's big mistake *or* the fact a Bodne grandson had been peeking at the ballots. I replied that truth must prevail, at least in terms of which play was the rightful winner. We couldn't just stand by and let this egregious error remain. The next morning, he presented the ballots to our Uncle Andrew Anspach, who—as the Algonquin's manager—reported the discovery to Henry Hewes, critic for *The Saturday Review* and president of the New York Drama Critics. By the next day a formal media announcement was made:

> *"Drama critics goof.* Henry Hewes ... said the ballots which were counted by him and Clive Barnes, critic for *The New York Times* and vice president of the group, had been inaccurately tallied at the Monday meeting. 'We somehow overlooked 10 points for 'Championship Season' that were caught when we recounted after

the meeting. The group is trying to figure out what to do, because newspaper ads have already run proclaiming the victory of 'Sticks and Bones.' One ray of hope for an understanding among everyone involved in the blooper was that both plays were produced by the New York Shakespeare Festival headed by Joseph Papp."[1]

Overnight, the New York Critics Circle saved face by giving awards to both shows, with *Sticks and Bones* receiving a special "Runner-up" citation. Still, it was generally believed that Henry Hewes saved the day. Until now,

That Championship Season. *Artwork: Raymond Kursar.*

it was never revealed how the error was really caught. My brother Douglas was the true Sherlock who unearthed the truth.

Not that there wasn't a certain amount of impropriety involved. But teens will be teens, though not many can alter award outcomes. Then, soon after, my brother and I were pushing the limits again when we took a trip with Grandma Mary and Grandpa Ben back to the Beverly Hills Hotel. There, Douglas and I called the hotel operator to page nutty fictitious names at the celebrity-filled poolside. Some of these concocted names were "Ginger Hollywood," "Burt Toast," and "Liza Allyatellmy." Once, in succession, I even paged the "four questions" from the Passover Seder: "Manny Shtanah," "Lilah Hah*zeh*," "Michael Halay*lawf*" and so forth. Who knew?

Overall, though, Douglas and I were little gentlemen; otherwise, Grandma Mary would never have introduced us to the latest Algonquin guests of note with whom she schmoozed. For instance, there was playwright Mart Crowley, living at the Algonquin during the run of his off-Broadway smash, *The Boys In the Band* (1970), a breakthrough in the gay rights movement. There was Jack Valenti, a close confidant of President Lyndon Johnson, who (from 1966-2004) served as a president himself—of the Motion Picture Association of America. Valenti implemented the MPAA Rating System for films that "gave new meaning to letters like G, R, and X"[2] while replacing the obsolete Hays Production Code that had banned on-screen nudity, profanity, and other controversial elements.[3] Of course, those are items we can now see every day on TV. Still, Valenti shared many an Algonquin lunch with high and mighty members of the entertainment world, forging the industry's future.[4]

Another steady face at the hotel was Mario Puzo, whose new book, *The Godfather,* would be released in 1969, and who lunched with his editor, William Targ. Targ, an Algonquin regular and editor-in-chief at G.P. Putnam's Sons, had bought Puzo's novel—the eventual source of two Oscar-winning Best Pictures—for a $5,000 advance after two other publishers rejected it. Published the following year, *The Godfather* became the most profitable novel ever for Putnam, selling about 21 million copies internationally.[5] It was said that, "Any book that passed through his [Targ's] hands became as good as it could be." Mario Puzo called Targ "the Godfather of editors."[6] Targ was also blessed to be married to the glamorous literary agent, Roslyn Targ, whose luminaries included Samuel Beckett, Henry Miller, and Saul Bellow.[7] Knowing people like the Targs, I always felt I was shaking the hands that guided literary greatness.

Shaking hands with another Algonquin married pair, Audrey Wood and William Liebling, I always felt I was shaking the hands that guided

William and Roslyn Targ. Photo courtesy of Roslyn Targ.

theatre greatness. This pair ran the Liebling-Wood Agency, with William Liebling representing actors, and his wife in charge of playwrights. Liebling promoted the careers of such stars as Marlon Brando, Audrey Hepburn, and Elizabeth Taylor.[8] Audrey Wood, perhaps her era's most revered agent of playwrights, discovered and/or nurtured Tennessee Williams, William Inge (*Picnic; Come Back, Little Sheba*), Carson McCullers (*The Member of the Wedding*, 1950), and Robert Anderson (*Tea and Sympathy*, 1953). Fortuitously, she arranged for many of them to stay at the Algonquin. In fact, it was at the Algonquin (or the "Algon-queen" as he called it[9]) that Tennessee Williams first became famous, many years before. This milestone, upon the Broadway opening of *The Glass Menagerie*, was recounted by reporter Dan Sullivan for the *Los Angeles Times*:

> "It [recognition] had come to him at age 34, after a 15 years of bumming the country and literary odd-jobbing. To suddenly wake up in the Algonquin Hotel in New York City and find yourself the most famous young playwright in America was not, somehow, reassuring. Williams remembered later that he had ordered a big meal from room service and by mistake poured chocolate sauce on the steak, spoiling both . . . I feel like I've been giving interviews

all my life," he said a reported thirty years later in the dining room of that same hotel." [10]

Audrey Wood, Tennessee Williams, and Carson McCullers. Photo via University of Texas.

Sad to say, Tennessee Williams and Audrey Wood dissolved their association in 1971, in part because of his drug use, in part when she became a scapegoat for his late-career flops. It was an especially rough period for Audrey Wood. She was still recovering from the loss of her husband, Bill, in 1969. Around this period, I saw this tiny woman, who'd helped so many artists, sitting silently by herself in the Algonquin lobby. Resembling an antique porcelain doll, she had a marked fragility for such a powerful woman. I myself was one of those fortunate to have been helped by her: she was always encouraging and wrote my college recommendation.

Another figure sitting in the lobby around 1968—even more imposing, at least bulk-wise—was character actor Victor Buono. The mammoth Buono was best known as Bette Davis' unctuous suitor in *Whatever Happened to Baby Jane?* (1962); his portrayal of King Tut on a two-part episode of *Batman* (1967); and his boundless appetite. The later made him a perfect fit as Alexander Woollcott (the Algonquin Round-Tabler) on a 1971 TV episode of *It Was a Very Good Year*. Where he was *not* a perfect fit were the chairs at the Algonquin. One day, Buono perched his 6'3" 310 pound frame[11] into one of the lobby's plush armchairs, miscalculating the mass distribution. Suddenly, the lobby was in an uproar as Buono learned he couldn't extricate himself from the chair and bellmen scurried to find a solution. The hotel engineer had to be called to dismantle the chair, piece

Actor Victor Buono didn't take an Algonquin armchair lightly. Photo courtesy of Photofest.

by piece, thereby excavating King Tut. The saving grace for Buono was that this incident didn't occur via a bathtub or toilet.

Around this time, a very different sort of icon and Algonquin regular burst on the scene: Canadian singer-poet-songwriter Leonard Cohen. Cohen was a discovery of John H. Hammond, the record producer who was likewise instrumental in the careers of Billie Holiday, Bob Dylan, and Bruce Springsteen, to name but a few.[12]

Cohen's style is one that might have been embraced by such Algonquin cynics as Dorothy Parker and George S. Kaufman: he has been called the "poet laureate of pessimism," "the grocer of despair," and "the prince of bummers."[13] His song hits, including "Suzanne" (1966) and "Hallelujah" (1984), were popularized by such Folk artists as Joni Mitchell, James Taylor, and Judy Collins. In person, Cohen proved a paradox of creative cynicism and personal virtue. For example, as described in Ira B. Nadel's biography, Cohen was known to be a devoted father and a pious Jew:

"A December 11 [1982] entry in a journal describes him in Room 700 of the Algonquin Hotel in New York with a Chassidic prayer book, his father's *tefillin* and woolen *tallit* [prayer shawl], a box of Barton's Hanukkah candy, and a set of Hanukkah candles, all in preparation for celebrating the festival with his children."[14]

Leonard Cohen. Photo courtesy of Photofest.

As further proof of the complexity of this man, in 1996 he became an ordained Rinzai Zen Buddhist monk. What I can say with certainty is that he was extremely kind to me and a champion of my work on the musical *Charlotte Sweet*. By pure coincidence, the album of *Charlotte Sweet* was the only musical theatre recording ever produced by the aforementioned John H. Hammond, Leonard Cohen's early advocate.

Another champion of my theatre pursuits was the unforgettable Taubie Kushlick, whom I met in my early teens and called my "Auntie Mame." This producer/director/actress was a prime mover of desegregation, promoting both integrated audiences and employment in Johannesburg, South Africa. She and husband Dr. Philip Kushlick made annual visits to the Algonquin every theatre season. We bonded there over our love for the musical, *Cabaret*. If ever there was a synthesis of Harold Prince, Hermoine Gingold, and a locomotive, it was she. In fact, she produced and directed many of Prince's shows in Johannesburg, including *Fiddler on the Roof*, *Cabaret*, and *A Little Night Music*, in which she played the same role as Gingold. In a survey book, listing her as one of the 100 "Most Influential South Africans of the Twentieth Century," it's stated:

> "Her personality was so forceful, her entrepreneurship so adventurous, her successes (and her failures) so epic, that given the demographic changes that have shaped our culture since her day we are not likely to see her likes again."[15]

I and my "Auntie Mame" shared long-distance phone conversations when I apprised her of the latest shows in New York. In 1982, I flew to Johannesburg, spending a glorious week as the Kushlicks' guest at their casa. Taubie gave me a grande-dame tour of the country, with visits to local theatres, the animal reserves, and the area of Soweto. Visiting Soweto was particularly eye-opening, as I witnessed the primitive living conditions Black citizens were finally surmounting. It was comparable to the Reconstructionist South I'd heard about from my family and history books, as South Africa evolved into a land of greater justice and freedom.

Every day with Taubie was a lark. She set up local interviews that we gave together, declaring: "[re when I was a kid:] He once warned me not to attempt *A Little Night Music* [one of her flops]. At that age, he showed foresight."[16] Through the week, she fascinated me with tales of how—as a woman, a Jew, and a human rights advocate—she had overcome countless hurdles in her career. This visit was a turning point for me. When I returned to the United States, I was inspired to myself co-produce the

Michael with the Kushlicks in the Algonquin lobby; Taubie in newspaper clipping.

original showcase production of *Charlotte Sweet*, and not be weighed down by rejections or setbacks.

The Kushlicks even flew around the world to attend my wedding in 1986. Once asked if she'd ever retire, Taubie answered that she'd given up even pretending that was possible, "How do you write your own death sentence?"[17] To the end, she was busy with theatrical endeavors, planning a recording of her extremely popular production of *Jacques Brel is Alive and Well and Living in Paris* (her 1970s production was the longest-running show in the country's history).[18]

When I was a kid and first met Taubie, I never anticipated this lasting friendship or where it would lead me. Nor did I always realize the import of some guests I saw. Discoveries awaited me on every visit to the Algonquin. Much of it would impact my future. But, at the moment, who knew how?

Chapter 14: *Moving Days*

High school graduation picture. Photo: Kamen Images.

It was June, 1969: a time for me to say goodbye to Woodmere Academy and hello to my college years, outside of New York. You'd think that would mean I'd see less of the Algonquin, but just the opposite would prove true.

I hadn't been the best student but was accepted at a few colleges, deciding to attend American University (AU) in Washington DC. Grandma Mary was particularly pleased because AU was close enough for me to take the Amtrak rather than fly, yet far enough away so that I wouldn't drive (early on, my driving had even prompted my Driver's Ed instructor to grab the keys and walk away from the school car in frustration). No matter what form of transportation I took, I had to report to both my mom and grandmother when I arrived safely. My family kept close tabs on all my travels: I had to *secretly* take my first New York subway ride, at the age of sixteen with my experienced classmate, Sam Hagan, telling Grandma Mary it was a taxi ride.

Another bonus of attending school in Washington DC was that I could spend time with my father, Sidney, who was doing everything he could to manage a troubled local hotel. Months earlier, my mother, brother Douglas, and I visited him there. The highlight of that trip was attending the tryout of a new musical everyone loved: *1776* (1969). Of course, I had no idea that my first professional theatre experience, five years later, would be working for its producer, Stuart Ostrow (*Pippin*, 1972; *The Apple Tree*, 1966). That fall, I spent a good deal of prized time visiting my father at the hotel he managed. This particular hotel seemed a bit rundown, and the food tasted like an unthawed TV dinner. Still, I kept that to myself and stuck to salads (sometimes literally) when my father said I could order all I wanted. During our conversations, I was reminded of the happier times we'd spent together. How, when I was ten, he recorded me singing along to tracks of Frank Sinatra and Doris Day on his extensive reel-to-reel taping equipment. The laughs we had when he took Douglas and me every summer to Rockaway Playland, with its Fun House, Hall of Mirrors, and Penny Arcade. The drives to New York City, when he'd always listen to William B. Williams playing Ella Fitzgerald, Tony Bennett, and other favorites on WNEW radio. Going with him at an early age to hear the likes of Peggy Lee and The Supremes—live. He'd been so handsome and vital once, it was heartbreaking to see him looking a bit bloated, his hands shaking when he held a coffee cup. Still, at least around me, he wasn't drinking.

Back at American University, for the first substantial time, I started excelling as a student. AU wasn't as competitive as Woodmere Academy; and I wasn't distracted by fights at home anymore. Furthermore, there was abundant excitement on-campus. I saw compelling on-stage drama like the production of a great playwright who was new to me: Lanford Wilson. His future play, *Talley's Folly* (1979), would receive the New York Drama Critics Award at the Algonquin. AU adventurously presented Wilson's *The*

Memories of Dad: at my first birthday; with Douglas and me in Florida; with his recording equipment as I recorded.

Madness of Lady Bright (1964), whose transvestite title role was played by student Ernest Thompson, himself the future playwright of the stage and film hits, *On Golden Pond* (1979, play; 1981, film). Likewise, there were real-life dramas on-campus and throughout Washington DC, especially political protests during this school year that was overcast by the Vietnam War.

The academic stimulation at AU was a turning point for me. I was taught by my all-time favorite English teacher, Mrs. Patton, who believed in me more than any previous teacher. Wearing 1960s horn-rimmed glasses, Mrs. Patton looked like a cross between TV's Eve Arden on *Our Miss Brooks* (1952) and Jane Wyatt on *Father Knows Best* (1954). Even when I thought I'd bungled her test, she pointed out how well I'd done, quoting my answers to our class. My scholastic insecurities took a hike. I may not have used drugs or alcohol in college, but I became intoxicated with English poetry. Mrs. Patton turned me on to Romantic and Victorian poetry. Soon, I understood why Robert Browning was reportedly Cole Porter's favorite poet, as Browning became mine, too. Browning's work burst with intricate rhyme and psychological depth comparable to what I later admired in the lyrics of Lorenz Hart and Stephen Sondheim. Browning packed his poems with such rhyming invention long before Hart juxtaposed "Dietrich" and "sweet trick"[1] or Sondheim paired "It's so/Schizo."[2] In Browning's "The Glove (1945)" alone there was "foremost" and "adore most," "well swear"/"elsewhere" and "fresh hold"/"threshold".[3] In addition, one century before Cole Porter's *Kiss Me Kate*, Browning was writing sophisticated character studies in the poem "Rabbi Ben Ezra (1860)" ("Grow old with me/The best is yet to be"[4]) and the soliloquy "Porphyria's Lover (1834)," whose ending of a deranged lover strangling his sweetheart is as complex and chilling as lyrics from *Sweeney Todd* (1979):

> "That moment she was mine, mine, fair,
> Perfectly pure and good. I found
> A thing to do, and all her hair
> In one long yellow string I wound
> Three times her little throat around."[5]

Years later, my reverence for Robert Browning was an immediate source of bonding between me and actress/composer Polly Pen, who graced my show, *Charlotte Sweet*, and is a descendant of the poet's wife, Elizabeth Barrett Browning. Other major poems I first read in Mrs. Patton's class included: Tennyson's "The Lady of Shalott" (1842), whose isolated tapestry-maker would inspire the song "A-Weaving" in *Charlotte Sweet*; and Christina Rossetti's "Goblin Market" (1859), which Polly Pen would one day adapt into an acclaimed off-Broadway musical.

After my exhilarating fall semester at AU, my morale took an unfortunate southward slip when I returned home to Paine Road, Hewlett, on my December break. Feeling left behind by my father, my mother was in an especially sullen mood. When I arrived home late and tired, we got into an argument escalating into a screaming match. After the quiet semester at college, I realized screaming was not a requisite of everyday life. I became so upset I took the ten-minute walk to our Hewlett station, caught the 1:00 a.m. train to New York, and ambled through the darkness to the Algonquin. There, a groggy Grandma Mary said I could stay for the night, and even longer if I wished. That's all I needed to hear. On that night, I actually *moved* from Long Island to one of the guest rooms at the Algonquin, making the hotel my permanent residence for the next seventeen years. Sometimes family fights can have their compensations.

I saw a lot of my grandparents anyway. Months earlier, the Bodnes had taken me, along with my brother Douglas, on a four-city summer tour as my high school graduation present. Our first stop was New Orleans, where my grandparents' best friends, attorney-author Louis Nizer and his wife, Mildred, joined us. I remember how we all sat around the TV in a hotel suite watching history in the making—the original moon landing—with Grandma Mary expressing (perhaps in jest) that the event might mess up the universe. The visit to New Orleans was capped by a series of sumptuous meals, especially at Galatoire's, the restaurant mentioned in *A Streetcar Named Desire* (1947). There, either Grandpa or Mr. Nizer arranged for a

Louis Nizer tablecloth sketches of Mary Bodne, Ben Bodne, Mildred Nizer, and Renee Colby.

private room and a southern dinner that would have put Paula Dean to shame. Mr. Nizer arranged quite a few memorable experiences in my life, such as the time he invited my grandparents, along with Douglas and me, to observe him at the Supreme Court. There, he defended the 1971 movie, *Carnal Knowledge*, against obscenity charges. As usual, he won the case.

Another observation made by intimates of Mr. Nizer was that no table-cloth or linen was safe in his presence. Seated at a table, he would take out a Magic Marker and sketch anyone in view, ruining countless cloth napkins at the Algonquin and elsewhere. My family had a whole collection of Nizer portraits they thought might be valuable one day, varying in quality and often with food stains (more like shrouds of tureen than the Shroud of Turin).

After bidding farewell to the Nizers and N'Orleans, our four-city tour continued in Dallas, Las Vegas—where we saw the razzle-dazzle Vegas shows of Petula Clark and Barbra Streisand—and finally Beverly Hills. The Bodnes and Colby boys were back at the Beverly Hills Hotel, now sharing a suite and poolside cabana. We had a special deal there since Grandpa was friends with its owner, another Jewish hotelier named Ben: Ben Silverstein. This hotel boasted even more celebrities than you'd see at the Algonquin. At the pool, our cabana neighbors were producer/publicist Irving Mansfield and his wife, novelist Jacqueline Susann. Susann was at the pinnacle of best-selling popularity with her sex and drug-filled page-turners, *Valley of the Dolls* (1966) and *The Love Machine* (1969). Deeply tanned, with a full raven coif, and statuesquely parading a tiger-skinned bathing suit, she looked to me like she was just about to make a jungle movie. I remember her raving about the hotel's foot-long frankfurters, which she called "the wild thing." I also recall her profound sadness the day the news arrived that Sharon Tate, who'd starred in the film *Valley of the Dolls* (1967), had been killed by the Manson gang (August 8, 1969).

During our week in Beverly Hills, the poolside was also where Douglas and I would hang out with a sixteen-year-old New York girl, Leslie Sank, who idolized actress Barbara Stanwyck. Leslie had memorized full scenes from Stanwyck movies and soon had me reciting dialogue from *Sorry, Wrong Number* (1948), which is still embedded in my memory today: "They said you were a criminal, Henry. A desperate man. And said you wanted me to . . . to DIE."[6]

The Stanwyck veneration led unexpectedly to an evening wherein I was able to acquire a Stanwyck memento for Leslie at the Hollywood restaurant, Chasen's. My grandparents had taken Douglas and me to Chasen's on one of the many nights when Barbara Stanwyck dined there.

Barbara Stanwyck. Photo courtesy of Photofest.

She was accompanied by Detroit gossip columnist, Shirley Eder, whom my grandparents knew and greeted. As if out of a movie, Shirley and Barbara Stanwyck joined us at our table for dessert. Stanwyck talked about how radically Hollywood had changed, about how much she missed her ex-husband Robert Taylor (who had recently died), and about the Jewish foster parents she'd had as a child. When coffee was served, she reached for a cigarette, whereupon I grabbed a match at our table and lit it (in those days, there were matches at all the tables). After the euphoria of lighting Stanwyck's cigarette, I put the match away in my pocket and gave it to

Leslie the next day. I knew Leslie would want the match that had served Stanwyck so well; and I was right—Leslie held onto it like a lucky charm. Years later, when a thief stole her wallet, Leslie was especially upset that the match was inside, lost forever.

It turned out that Chasen's was the restaurant we visited most frequently during our trip. That was fine with me: I could live on their super-creamy banana cake and Caesar Salads—the best ever—cholesterol shock and all. The owner, former vaudevillian Dave Chasen (born in Odessa, Ukraine, like Grandma Mary) was another good friend of my grandparents. He and his elegant wife, Maude, always stayed at the Algonquin. He was so fond of the hotel that he kept a framed photo of it on display at his restaurant, right near a picture of W.C. Fields dressed as Queen Victoria. Chasen began his restaurant after receiving a loan of $3,500 from *The New Yorker* editor, Harold Ross, based on the delectable chili and ribs Chasen would cook up for Algonquin Round-Tablers like Dorothy Parker and Robert Benchley.[7] It was at Chasen's Restaurant where Dave Chasen invented the "Shirley Temple" cocktail as a special treat for the child star. It was there that Ronald Reagan proposed to Nancy Davis. Stars such as Frank Sinatra and Groucho Marx had their own booths there.[8] Moreover, Chasen's chili was so craved, Elizabeth Taylor ordered buckets of it over in Europe when she filmed *Cleopatra* (1963).[9]

On a second evening at Chasen's, Mr. Chasen took us back to his office just as Jackie Gleason phoned him to announce Gleason's engagement to second wife Beverly McKittrick. Another night, Mr. Chasen, out of his love for my family, circulated around the restaurant asking guests to sign autograph books for Douglas and me. The signees, all eating there on a single night, ranged from Art Carney to Boris Karloff. Regrettably, after Dave and Maude Chasen passed away, this legendary restaurant closed its doors in 1995. Tinseltown will never see its likes again.

Meanwhile, there was more unhappy news in my family. While I was flourishing academically and taking grand trips, my father Sidney was struggling; the job in Washington DC had not worked out. He was back in New York, unemployed and exuding defeat, returning to my mother and Paine Road. My grandparents, who'd been antagonistic toward Dad, did an about-face and welcomed him back as an Algonquin manager. Grandma felt particularly bad for him. In turn, my father did everything he could to reconcile and make up for lost time with the family. Yet nothing could reverse what was happening. Above all, he was in terrible shape. His emotional vulnerability was compounded by the long-term effects of alcohol and smoking. At home he would sleep through weekends and experienced

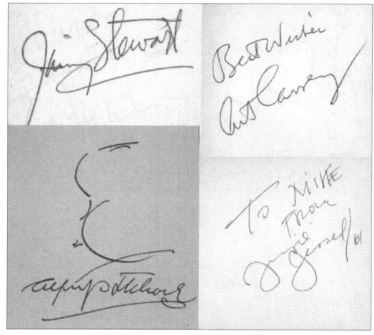

Autographs from Chasen's: (clockwise) Art Carney, George Jessel, Alfred Hitchcock, and James Stewart.

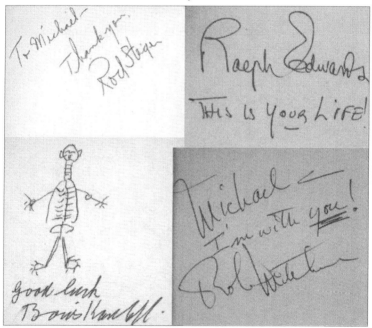

More autographs from Chasen's. (clockwise) Ralph Edwards, Robert Mitchum, Boris Karloff, and Rod Steiger.

delirium tremens. His hallucinations included his imagining a lamp was a huge snake, whereupon he momentarily went after it with a baseball bat.

Then came the worst night the Colby family had ever gone through. I was in my Algonquin Room in New York, when I received the phone call from Douglas. Our parents had been arguing at home. I don't know if Dad had been drinking or was just in poor shape to begin with, but Douglas reported the awful news: Dad had taken a bad fall down the second-floor stairs at home. At the bottom, he lay unconscious on the white linoleum floor, a puddle of blood surrounding his head. An ambulance arrived and rushed him from Long Island to New York University Hospital where my father received brain surgery to relieve a subdural hematoma.

Sidney Colby in his Algonquin office.

Upon Douglas' call, I hurried to the hospital and joined the family to wait through the surgery, which ended very late. My mother was hysterical in disbelief. Grandpa Ben and Grandma Mary were notified on vacation in Italy; they booked the next flight to New York. Around midnight, I was ushered into see my father, his head shaved after surgery. It was the last time I saw him—he passed away that night, August 31, 1970. He was forty-three years old.

I've often wondered how much longer my father might have lived if not for the repercussions of his marriage and working at the Algonquin. The fantasy Algonquin life had a very dark underside for him, a tragic fact I can never forget. Notwithstanding, I'll always be grateful for being in Washington DC that last year and the deeply moving days I had with him in DC and through the years. When I visit the Algonquin nowadays, I still imagine him in the lobby—his youthful self—looking like he could be one of the stars staying there. Of all the ghosts I've envisioned at the hotel, I never dreamed my young father would be one. Life at the Algonquin, though it went on, would never really be the same.

Chapter 15: *Excelsior*

The storybook aura of the Algonquin had been shattered by my father's death. Our family questioned whether the fantasies he'd fulfilled there had turned into something of a devil's pact. Still, there was nothing we could do to change the course of events but honor his memory, be there for each other, and do our best to go on with our lives. In the Jewish tradition, that is the purpose of shiva, our mourning period. With my grandparents making most of the arrangements, mourning went hand in hand with eating—to ease the pain.

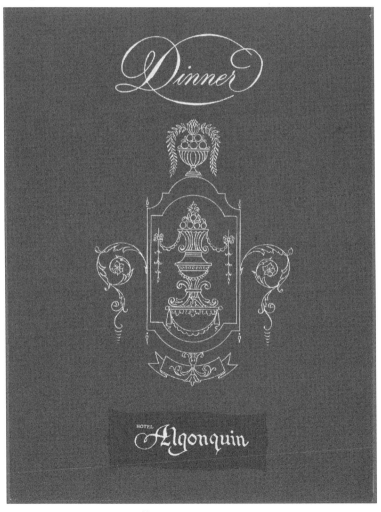

Algonquin menu cover.

Food, be it Jewish or Southern, was always treated as an all-purpose support system in my family. It may not have reversed a situation but it sure made the present a lot more bearable. Growing up in Long Island, no matter how tough or miserable a week, I looked forward to the kitchen wizardry whipped up by Louise, our housekeeper from Charleston. Best of all were feasts she prepared on Fridays: fried chicken, ice tea, Grandma Mary's recipe for matzo ball soup, and chocolate pie made with that Jewish-home staple, My*T*Fine pudding.

Once I moved into the Algonquin, the accent on food, if anything, intensified. Grandma Mary's theme song might have been "As Long as She Feeds Me." She seemed at her happiest when she could provide my favorite dishes (often taking a bite herself) as if that were the ultimate demonstration of affection. She had regal repasts served to me via Algonquin restaurants and/or room service. It didn't matter that I was a light and picky eater. She'd make sure I was sated during my college breaks and later during my fulltime occupancy at the Algonquin. Minute steaks, squab stuffed with wild rice, Caesar salads, and the pick of the day's lobsters: these were reserved for me and other family members (albeit, the lobsters weren't the best training for my future with Andrea, my Kosher-keeping wife). Then there were the after-theatre buffets with hot corned beef and pastrami sandwiches, apricot torte, and the Algonquin's own variation of Chasen's chili (I never liked chili, but all my increasing number of friends did; ditto in regard to the hotel's popovers, roast beef au jus, and Yorkshire pudding).

Algonquin menu.

Even if New York food critics didn't always rave about the Algonquin menu, I thrived on it. A bonus was visiting Grandma's home kitchen on the 10th floor. There, you might smell the beckoning aroma of her soups. Grandpa Ben could be found at the dining room table, savoring Grandma's lima bean or cabbage soup, in which he dipped a heel of pumpernickel. Another favorite was her schav, made with eggs, sorrel, and sour cream. A grateful Bellman, Will Sawyer, recounted how she would cook a specialty he'd take home to his very Irish Catholic family at Thanksgiving: "This strange delicious Jewish dish called kugel [noodle pudding]."

Of course, food could not eliminate the deep shadow that hung over us right after my father's death. Still, there were other occurrences that helped distract. Foremost, not long after the loss, I left my residence at the Algonquin for Evanston, Illinois, to start my sophomore semester at a new college, Northwestern University (NU). American University had given me the confidence and grades to transfer to my first choice college, NU, with its exceptional Drama and Journalism departments. I was particularly enthused at the prospect of submitting lyrics to the Waa-Mu show, NU's celebrated annual revue. During the next couple of months, I must have submitted dozens of lyrics for consideration, mostly rejected (naughtily, I also submitted some esoteric lyrics by Cole Porter and Lorenz Hart which were rejected, as well). Fatefully, "The Telepathic Twosome"—my one lyric that got into that year's show, *Thanks a Lot* (1981)—was co-sung by student

Program cover from Waa-Mu show, Thanks a Lot *(1971); "The Telepathic Twosome" sung by Charlotte Luporini and Michael McCormick. Pictures courtesy of Brian Nelson, Northwestern University.*

Michael McCormick. Years later, McCormick would appear in *Charlotte Sweet* and topline the Broadway revival of *1776* (1997).

Theatrical ambitions were everywhere at NU. Waa-Mu alumni had included Warren Beatty, Cloris Leachman, Sheldon Harnick, Walter Kerr, and Ann-Margret. Though I knew there were far more skilled performers at NU, I mustered the courage to audition for the Waa-Mu cast, stumbled through the dance combination, and even received a callback. I'll never forget waiting backstage with other auditioners, including some hyper-histrionic students who were junior versions of types I saw at the Algonquin. One was hitting unearthly notes, one discussing her Broadway credits, and another somersaulting—seemingly to intimidate the competition. To calm my jangled nerves, I chatted with one pretty girl, Laura Weil, who ended up in the show. Years later, I saw Laura during intermission at *Charlotte Sweet*. She had no memory of me but was cordial. She proudly stated she now worked at a theatre agency and was visiting to scout leading lady, Mara Beckerman. Then she asked what I was doing at the show, to which I answered "I wrote it for Mara." I felt, after what I saw at the Waa-Mu audition, I was entitled to a little hubris.

Another benefit at Northwestern was its trimester set-up, which allowed me month-long trips back to the Algonquin during the December and March height of the Broadway season. Within those months, it was easier than ever for me to catch up on shows now that I lived at the hotel, so nearby the theatre district. One show I saw three times was *Applause* (1970), the backstage musical based on my favorite movie, *All About Eve* (1950). It was the perfect lesson in how a musical can evolve from trifle to triumph. Its tryout in Baltimore occurred while I was still at American University, so I took a train from Washington DC and joined Grandma Mary, attending the out-of-town premiere. The premiere was a mishmash of tentative performances, rambling scenes, and hit/miss numbers. Lauren Bacall, playing the acerbic Broadway actress Margo Channing, was ideal in the role originated in the film by Bette Davis, even if her singing was in its own orbit. But Diane McAfee, a talented young actress, didn't quite have the command or menace to play Margo's scheming protégée, Eve Harrington. Perhaps to compensate, her big solo, "Halloween," about her role's ruthlessness, included an overhead movie of the topless, writhing McAfee that literally exposed the naked truth about Eve. Concurrently, my grandmother was also writhing, seated next to her "innocent" grandson, with an audience expression reminiscent of "Springtime For Hitler."

Months later, during my spring vacation, I saw a vastly improved show at its Broadway opening. The book was tighter and funnier, songs had been reworked or replaced, and I witnessed how one actor can transform a show. Penny Fuller had taken over the role of Eve Harrington in a performance as dynamic as Bacall's. At last, the musical had an Eve comparable to Anne Baxter in the movie: a dragon lady in the guise of a sweet ingénue. The nude movie projections were gone; there was no need to distract from the brilliance of Fuller's "bitch showing her claws" rendition of "Halloween" (and I don't think this decision was just based on someone seeing Grandma Mary's expression in Baltimore).

Still, for me, *Applause* was at its pinnacle when I saw it for the third time, in January 1971. That's when Anne Baxter—the original Eve (whom I'd recently met via my friend Dorothy Hart)—succeeded Lauren Bacall as Margo Channing. You see, a major reason Anne Baxter was originally cast in *All About Eve* was her resemblance to the first actress signed to play Margo Channing, Claudette Colbert, who dropped out because of a ruptured disc. The intention was to create the illusion that Eve and Margo were younger and older variations of the same persona. With the magnificent Anne Baxter and look-alike Penny Fuller playing opposite each other, that original goal was finally achieved (rapture for a longtime fan of *All About Eve*).

Around this time, there was another show that excited me even more: the breakthrough musical, *Company* (1970). It was enhanced by a scintillating score by Stephen Sondheim and book by Northwestern/Waa-Mu alumni George Furth (Northwestern was even mentioned in the show). *Company* was the most innovative musical since my all-time favorite *Cabaret*, likewise produced and directed by Harold Prince. More a "concept musical" than a conventional plot-driven show, *Company* was about a New York bachelor living vicariously through his friends as they celebrate his 35th birthday. I saw it many times, in an era when tickets were still between $2 and $12. During one of those visits, I invited my brother, Douglas, who was staying at the hotel on vacation, to join me. At the eleventh hour, he phoned my room saying he had to cancel because he "had to operate." I took this to mean he was filling in for the Algonquin telephone operator, which he did from time to time when on vacation. I replied, "Can't the hotel find someone else? I don't think I can get anyone new to use the matinee ticket this late." He responded, "You don't understand—I'm in the hospital about to have an emergency appendectomy—I *have* to operate!" It was one of the rare times Douglas turned down theatre tickets.

Company would ultimately have a profound effect on my personal life, as well. Years later, when I was thirty-four (and still living at the Algonquin), I had an epiphany. I envisioned my own 35th birthday in a dark space occupied solely by cake candles, an orchestra, and voices singing of my solitary status. I decided there and then I wanted a more conclusive wind-up than *Company*. Within the year, I achieved my candle wish of a permanent leading lady. Through resolve, focus, and tremendously good fortune, I met and soon married my wonderful wife, Andrea.

Another highlight of New York back in 1971 was an off-Broadway play to which Grandma Mary took me since it was co-produced by Warren Lyons, the son of the Bodnes' good friends, columnist Leonard Lyons and his convivial wife, Sylvia. Their close acquaintances were a Who's Who of cultural greats, including Moss Hart, Ernest Hemingway, Charlie Chaplin, and Dorothy Parker.

John Guare. Photograph: Paul Kolnick.

The up-and-coming playwright whose work Warren Lyons produced would soon have his own award-winning position in American culture: his name, John Guare; his play, *The House of Blue Leaves* (1966). Among the first of numerous awards the play received was the New York Drama Critics citation as "Best American Play," presented at the Algonquin. John Guare became a stalwart visiting the Algonquin, always kind and enthusiastic to members of my family. He would win two other New York Drama Critics Awards: for *Two Gentlemen of Verona* (1971; which also won the Tony as Best Musical) and for *Six Degrees of Separation* (1990; Best Play). In 1974, he wrote a play of special interest to my family, *Rich and Famous*, which Grandma Mary and I attended as Guare's guests at the New York Public Theater. We eagerly awaited the show, directed by Mel Shapiro (who'd helped make *House of Blue Leaves* a classic) and featuring the virtuoso cast, William Atherton (also from *House of Blue Leaves*), Ron Leibman, and Anita Gillette (my favorite Sally Bowles in *Cabaret*). The show was a droll comedy about the tribulations of a New York playwright. However, within fifteen minutes of the play's start, I witnessed a theatre no-no. Conspicuously, Grandma Mary was snoozing. Now, this was not unusual for Grandma. She visited the Land of Nod at movies, matinees, opening nights, you name it. But, after all, we were John Guare's guests, it was a small theatre, and— for all I knew—Guare might be around to spot us. So, I sat there, trying to focus on the show and praying for the best. Then the reason we'd been invited to the show in the first place became obvious. William Atherton, as playwright Bing Ringling, picked up a phone and delivered the line "Hello??? Algonquin Hotel?? I'd like to leave a message . . . ."[2]

All it took was that word "Algonquin" to bring Grandma to her senses. Out of a sound—accent on "sound"—sleep, Grandma sprang upright, exclaiming for all to hear, "Who said 'Algonquin'?! Who said 'Algonquin'?!" I had to subdue her, as the play shifted to a scene set "outside to the left of the fabled Algonquin Hotel."[3] John Guare's scene not only featured the hotel but mentioned its name several more times. Now Grandma was at full attention. She watched and beamed through the scene. Then, upon its completion, she returned to the Land of Nod, while I just enjoyed the show.

Coincidentally, *Rich and Famous* was also the name of a 1981 George Cukor film that featured scenes at the Algonquin Hotel (it's where Jacqueline Bisset, as a famous writer, conducts an affair with a *Rolling Stone* reporter [Hart Bochner]). Other movies in which the hotel is spotlighted include such now forgotten titles as *Wives and Lovers* (the 1963 Van Johnson film that at least produced a famous Burt Bacharach title song), *Fitzwilly* (1967,

Movies associated with the Algonquin Hotel.

with Dick Van Dyke), and *They All Laughed* (1981, a Peter Bogdanovich film with Audrey Hepburn and John Ritter).

My grandparents themselves cast an aura of "rich and famous" with their chauffeur-driven, sable-brown Rolls-Royce—a Phantom V. Algonquin visitors often saw the car parked right outside, emblazoned with a license plate featuring my grandfather's "BBB" initials. The Phantom V, specially designed in 1964 for my grandparents, had an even more impressive history after my grandparents eventually sold it. In early 1980, Yoko Ono reportedly bought it as an anniversary gift to John Lennon (tragically, this was also the year of Lennon's assassination). In 1984, she auctioned it at New York's Sotheby's to raise funds for children's charities. Now I can't hear The Beatle's "Ticket to Ride (1965)" without thinking of that car.

Surrounded by the "Rich and Famous" at the Algonquin, I naturally daydreamed of a time I might be "rich and famous" on my own. Back at NU, I was surrounded by students with even stronger ambitions than mine, particularly in the drama department. Nonetheless, I persisted. Even if most of my lyric submissions at Waa-Mu were rejected, there was always another project to which my hopes were pinned. It was the musical I was writing, with my brother Douglas as composer, based on the movie, *The Wrong Box* (1966). I held fast to those hopes, even though, at ages nineteen and sixteen, we weren't exactly Broadway veterans.

Meanwhile, in 1971, there was a truly rich and famous Algonquin guest whose credentials *assured* his getting produced, though his one musical was received in a way for which no writer would bargain. Leon Uris was one of the most successful American novelists of his time, with a series of best-sellers including *Battle Cry* (1953), *Mila 18* (1961), *Topaz* (1967), and *QB VII* (1970). His most famous book was *Exodus* (1958), the epic about the birth of Israel that was translated into more than fifty languages and became the largest seller since *Gone With the Wind* (1936). Uris was a self-educated author who never graduated high school, yet parlayed his experiences in the Marines and such countries as Palestine into a multi-million dollar fortune.[4] He was so fond of the Algonquin, it was where he held his third wedding, to photographer Jill Peabody, in a lavish Jewish ceremony. I got to watch their Rose Room reception from the sidelines.

Shortly after the marriage, Uris was approached about turning *Exodus* into a musical with the hope it would be the greatest Jewish-style hit since *Fiddler On the Roof*. Certainly, "This Land Is Mine (1960)"—the theme from the film *Exodus* by Pat Boone and Ernst Gold—had been a smash. The musical would be titled *Ari* (1971), taken from the name of the book's protagonist, Ari Ben Canaan, a leader in the movement to establish Israel. According to Uris' biographer, Ira B. Nadel:

> "Uris had always loved the theatre, hoping, from his youth, to be a dramatist. His productions in the marines had furthered that desire. Although his career as a novelist and screenwriter flour-ished, he still wished for a Broadway success."[5]

In fact, back at the age of six, Uris wrote an operetta inspired by the death of his dog.[6] However, he lacked the requisite experience to write the book and, especially, lyrics for this new musical. The problem was compounded by his choice of composer, Walt Smith, "a musician and res-taurateur," whom Uris knew from Aspen. Uris had chosen Smith after admiring the special wedding march Smith wrote for the Uris' marriage ceremony—sweet, but not model credentials for Broadway.

After panned tryouts in Philadelphia and Washington DC, *Ari* hob-bled into New York, with Uris covering additional costs. This was one show even Grandma Mary couldn't recommend. At the preview I attended, the audience did an "Exodus" number during intermission. The nadir was a scene with a boatload of refugees, in which one dancing character—sup-posedly near starvation from a hunger strike—collapsed during the middle of a hora. I had to wonder what in heck motivated a starving refugee to dance a hora except, perhaps, an over eager choreographer. After nineteen performances, the result was hari kari for *Ari*.

In the aftermath, I suspect Grandma Mary tried her usual means of cheering people up: she sent Leon Uris trays of Algonquin comfort food, except turkey (which would have been too symbolic). The experience was yet another Algonquin illustration of the vagaries of theatre that would sharpen my perspective on events to come.

Leon Uris (photo courtesy of Photofest) and logo from Ari.

Chapter 16: *Coming Attractions*

Douglas and Dorothy Hart in the Rose Room.

Let's put on a show! That was the mantra during my time off from college—Douglas and I were auditioning our musical, *Where There's a Will* (a.k.a. *Fortune Tolled*). It was based on a favorite movie of ours, *The Wrong Box*, whose screenplay (adapted from a novella co-written by Robert Lewis Stevenson) was penned by the impeccable Larry Gelbart and Burt Shevelove, librettists of *A Funny Thing Happened On the Way to the Forum*. Douglas wrote beautiful and sprightly melodies, and it was my first attempt at writing a libretto for a musical set in Victorian England, an approach I refined on *Charlotte Sweet*. Blame it on our youth, but we hoped we'd soon be on Broadway with a musical having more than seventeen characters, elaborate production requirements, and no clearance on rights. We were determined to audition the score and, thanks to various connections, we did so for a formidable array of Broadway pros.

Among the first show folk for whom we auditioned were Teddy and Dorothy Hart. This took place during the summer of 1971 in a room with a piano at the Beverly Hills Hotel. Among my top fantasies fulfilled at that hotel was when the Harts responded enthusiastically. Teddy—brother of lyricist Larry Hart—was a veteran actor I admired in films, such as *Three Men On a Horse* (1936) and *Mickey One* (1965). Dorothy became a champion of my lyrics and, a few years later, engaged me as researcher for her biography of Larry Hart. Sadly, Teddy Hart passed away several months later, not long after my father died, but the affinity between families was fortified that evening.

Meanwhile, the auditions continued. Grandma, who'd often warned Douglas and me about the heartbreak of show business, did an about-face and morphed, essentially, into our unpaid agent. She somehow arranged for us to present our songs—sometimes performed by us, sometimes by real singers—for the likes of Shirley Bernstein, sister of Leonard Bernstein as well as manager of Stephen Schwartz (*Godspell*, 1971; *Pippin*; *Wicked*, 2003). That audition went okay; Shirley Bernstein even said she'd review our demo and script afterwards. I thought it was a promising sign when she phoned me back within days.

"Is this Mr. Colby?" she said respectfully.

"Yes, yes!" I answered.

She added, with what sounded like receptivity, "Well, I must tell you, I cahn't find enough enthusiasm to represent your work."

I was thrilled, interpreting what she said as boundless enthusiasm, and replied à la Sally Field, "Oh, Miss Bernstein. So you really, really like it!"

She rejoined, "Mr. Colby, you don't quite understand. I *cahn't* find enough enthusiasm! I *cahn't!*"

In addition, Grandma arranged for us to see a Broadway composer who was one of the smallest in height but a giant in talent: Jule Styne, composer of *Gypsy*, *Funny Girl*, *Bells Are Ringing*, and countless standards ("Three Coins in the Fountain," 1954; "Let It Snow," 1945; "Diamonds Are a Girl's

Jule Styne (photo courtesy of Jule Styne, Inc.); Linda Purl (photo courtesy of Linda Purl).

Best Friend," 1949). Styne was likewise a Broadway producer, responsible for the smash revival of *Pal Joey* (1952) with its score by Richard Rodgers and Larry Hart. He'd even once proposed a D'Oyly Carte-style repertory of Rodgers and Hart shows.

Regardless of how things turned out, Douglas and I felt honored to just be visiting his office, above the Mark Hellinger Theatre. Filling the walls and shelves were awards, posters, and pictures of this musical genius who'd been instrumental in the careers of Carol Channing, Ethel Merman, Barbra Streisand, Frank Sinatra, and many others. Styne went out of his way to be supportive to two hopeful teenagers; he leveled only minor criticism about anachronistic words. He was someone who could even make criticism seem like the highest of compliments.

I can't claim the same for some for whom we auditioned, like the producer who said our show "hadn't a Chinaman's chance" or the one who reacted to songs like he was smelling a loaded diaper. Then there was the morning we auditioned for another theatre idol, producer/director Harold Prince. Oscar Hammerstein II's words popped into my head because we were all "as jumpy as a puppet on a string."[1] The performance too was shaky, and Harold Prince—whose shows, *Cabaret* and *Company,* had been my touchstones—was blunt. He singled out my lyrics, saying I "needed to do more homework." For a week after that, I felt as low as a centipede's toe. But he was right: my writing skills needed considerable more honing. Years later, I felt redeemed when Prince wrote me an enthusiastic letter about *Charlotte Sweet.*

As much as I appreciated these opportunities, my insecurities worsened; I knew we were mainly being seen because of who our grandparents were. I reassured myself that family connections have helped open doors for many worthies. Yet, the fear would always be there that I couldn't make good on my own. Moreover, my father's experience cast a shadow. As he found, when he went to work at another hotel, it could be overwhelming for family members trying to live up to the stature of my grandparents and the Algonquin. Still, it was because of the heady fruits we'd tasted that the hunger would persist. And so did the auditions.

Perhaps the best audition Douglas and I gave was for producer Stuart Ostrow, whose *1776* remains one of my favorite musicals. I myself sang opposite a pretty student from Finch College, whom Leslie Sank—my friend who attended Finch—recommended. The singer's name was Sasha Purl. Years later, she became better known as TV actress and cabaret singer "Linda" Purl. She was charm personified and could have performed a musical version of *Jaws* (1975) and made it delightful. Accordingly, even though

Artist Al Hirschfeld at his drawing board. Photograph: Louise Kerz. By permission from the Al Hirschfeld Foundation.

Ostrow passed on the show, he was very encouraging. Indeed, a few years later, I would be working for him.

Leslie Sank recommended an equally impressive leading lady from Finch College to sing with me at another audition. Her name was Nina Hirschfeld. I only vaguely remember the audition (it was for my grandparents' friends in the Bodne 10th floor living room). Yet I'll never forget rehearsing at Nina's home, a townhouse on the upper East Side. You see, Nina hailed from an eminent show business family. Her mother was Dolly Haas, a German actress, who'd been in Hitchcock's film *I Confess* (1953) and who'd succeeded Mary Martin in the Broadway musical *Lute Song* (1946). Nina strongly resembled her mother, who had red hair and features like a Renoir painting. Her father was the definitive caricaturist of Broadway, Al Hirschfeld. I followed his work religiously and, on several occasions, saw him from afar at the Algonquin. He was an extremely distinguished looking gentleman with a long white beard; he resembled a cross between Prospero in *The Tempest* and my image of what God must look like.

Nina was also well known because her father customarily concealed her name, usually several times, in each of his drawings. The one exception was a caricature of Nina (titled "Nina's Revenge"), which he drew around the time she appeared in a 1966 City Center revival of *Where's Charley?*; in this portrait, he hid the name of her mother, Dolly.

For a theatre fan, entering the Hirschfeld townhouse was like awaking in Wonderland. His caricatures, both life-size and in miniatures, were everywhere. Each tile around the fireplace featured a cameo appearance: Ethel Merman, Mary Martin, Carol Channing, and The Marx Brothers. The wallpaper against the ascending staircase portrayed celebrities as if they were partying right in front of you: Tallulah Bankhead, Charlie Chaplin, Albert Einstein, George Bernard Shaw, Pablo Picasso, Eleanor Roosevelt, Ed Sullivan, and Marilyn Monroe. It was breathtaking.

As I left the townhouse, I had no idea of the circumstances under which I would return there a decade later. My second visit was in 1983, right when the *Charlotte Sweet* cast recording was being assembled. Al Hirschfeld had already done one caricature of the show, a profile of actress Polly Pen, after attending the same performance as critic Edith Oliver of *The New Yorker*, who wrote one of the show's most negative reviews. As an object lesson in how differently two people can react to the same performance, Hirschfeld had loved the show and was recommending it to his friends. Using Nina's home number, I dialed to see if he'd be interested in doing a caricature of the full cast for the album. His wife, Dolly answered the phone. I announced, "Hello, this is Michael Colby. I used to audition with your daughter Nina."

She replied, "Ya."

I added, "And you know my grandparents, the Bodnes of the Algonquin." She replied, "Ya."

I added, "And I wrote *Charlotte Sweet*."

She responded, "You wrote *Charlotte Sweet*! You wrote *Charlotte Sweet*! Al, get on the phone!"

The next week, I visited the Hirschfeld townhouse and picked up his illustration of the entire cast, which he joyfully handed over to me. It was one of the greatest thrills of my life, having my characters come to life on his easel and beholding admiration from a prodigy such as Hirschfeld.

There was another theatre figure who gave me tremendous early encouragement. His name was Ben Bagley, and he was quite a personality. A gaunt, chain-smoking rascal—devoted to his cats (at various times, Butch, Fogarty, and Emily)[2]—he had a slightly vampiric look as if he'd stepped out of an Edward Gorey sketch. He was esteemed for producing hit off-Broadway revues and unmatched recordings of lesser-known gems by master songwriters, from Rodgers and Hart to Leonard Bernstein. Through three small original revues he produced, he helped launch the careers of such Broadway mainstays as Charles Strouse, Lee Adams, and Michael Stewart (who together wrote *Bye Bye Birdie*), Tom Jones and Harvey Schmidt (*The Fantasticks*, 1960), and Sheldon Harnick. Among his future star discoveries were Beatrice Arthur, Joel Grey, Charlotte Rae, and Chita Rivera. Long before *Ain't Misbehavin'* (1978), he likewise popularized retrospective revues with the show *The Decline and Fall of the Entire World as Seen Through the Eyes of Cole Porter* (1965).[3]

Ben Bagley. Photo courtesy of Original Cast Records.

I met Ben Bagley through Dorothy Hart, when he joined her for dinner at the Algonquin. Always in need of money and generally hungry, he relished visiting the Algonquin's restaurants. Dorothy suggested I give him a demo recording of *Where There's a Will* (1970). He immediately responded to the Colby Brothers' songs, not just to return for meals, but because of Douglas's lovely melodies and my humor (one song he particularly liked was "The Cemetery Social Set," about Victorian society figures who hobnob from funeral to funeral: "All the upper crust of England can be found h'ya,/ Whether tête-à-tête or strictly in the ground h'ya."[4]).

His own recordings featured the cream of the crop: from consummate entertainers such as Dorothy Loudon, Barbara Cook, and Bobby Short, to stars not known for singing (with good reason), such as Katharine Hepburn, Joanne Woodward, and Joan Rivers. His liner notes were notoriously irreverent. Here's a relatively subdued example, describing a song from the Fred Astaire film, *Royal Wedding* (1951), on "Ben Bagley's Alan Jay Lerner Revisited" (1964):

> "The movie is chiefly memorable in that it introduced Winston Churchill's elfin daughter, Sarah, to millions of moviegoers. Perfectly cast in a musical, Miss Churchill sang almost as well as Margaret Truman, and danced even better."[5]

Other typical notes were from "Ben Bagley's Ira Gershwin Revisited" (1971):

> "This is the second recording [of this] song. The first was by that sweet little Irish colleen Ella Fitzgerald.

> "While hospitalized recently for hepatitis, I worked on a list of all the people I'd had carnal knowledge of during the past year in an attempt to trace the person who infected me ... If anyone reading this knows the whereabouts of Joan and Larry Rivers, tell them to get globulin shots. To requote that oft-quoted line of Erich Segal's, 'Sex is not a sin if you're sorry.'"[6]

Though he rubbed many people the wrong way, he couldn't have been nicer to me. I proved helpful to him, too. As researcher for Dorothy Hart, I tracked down some lost Rodgers and Hart songs, which he included on two of his albums. Still, what most endeared him to me was that anytime I was in the doldrums, especially after my work had been rejected, he somehow knew to phone me. Though it's not my manner to use profanity, it could be cathartic hearing Ben using his typical expression to describe anyone who was unnecessarily unkind: "that c***s*****!" (and the "c.s." didn't stand for Charlotte Sweet).

Another supporter of my work was right in my family, Aunt Cyd Mazo. For a while, Aunt Cyd lived at the Colby home in Hewlett, to help out when my father left for Washington DC. It was easy to see how Aunt Cyd had captivated George Gershwin during her younger days in Charleston. Then considered a great beauty, she was ingenuously attracted to him for himself not his fame. She regretted that she hadn't pursued him to New York and was distraught when he died. Since then, her life had been tough: she'd been twice divorced from the same difficult husband and had suffered a miscarriage during the marriage. Though she was exceptionally loving to all her nephews and nieces, Douglas and I became like surrogate sons to her (we alone were at her hospital bedside when she, a heavy smoker, passed away of emphysema).

Uncle Sammy Mazo (Grandma's brother) and Aunt Cyd.

During the period Aunt Cyd was at our house, she alleviated the screaming with jokes and laughter, whether pulling off one of her wigs or making cracks about our neighbors. She became one of the stars, along with my brothers, of the creative home movies I made—comic skits in the style of *Laugh-In* (1967). Grandma Mary sent her to chaperone Douglas and me on one of the trips to the Beverly Hills Hotel; she was present there at the audition for Dorothy and Teddy Hart, cheering on her nephews. It was also during that trip she crashed Sammy Cahn's wedding in the hotel's Polo Lounge (Cahn was the lyricist of songs including 1955's "Love and Marriage" and 1957's "Come Fly With Me"). Claiming to be "Peter O'Toole's girlfriend, Sue Mazo," she infiltrated the wedding reception as Douglas and I watched through a glass partition. We saw Aunt Cyd dancing along as the band, commemorating Cahn's second marriage, played the

Cahn-Jimmy Van Heusen standard "[Love is lovelier] The Second Time Around (1960)".

Aunt Cyd attended all my musicals that she could. She'd assert, "One day, when people know your name and sing your songs, please mention that I predicted it." I can't say Aunt Cyd's prediction was fully achieved, but I can acknowledge how much I appreciated and loved her.

Alas, no one ever produced *Where There's a Will*. Where there's a WON'T was the response to the idea of giving a million-dollar production to two youngsters who didn't even have rights permission. Still, I learned a lot from the experience. Uppermost, the experience made me more likely to create completely original, smaller-scale musicals, where I didn't have to worry about licensing rights or size. In time, I *was* able to get a Victorian musical produced, my own brainchild, the relatively modest *Charlotte Sweet*.

The auditions for *Where There's a Will* weren't the only coming attractions of future shows in my family during this period. Our uncle Andrew Anspach was pursuing ideas for a cabaret series at the Algonquin, although plans wouldn't be official until 1980. It was Uncle Andrew's goal to restore the hotel's policy of supper-club shows, dormant since around 1939 when Austrian singer Greta Keller briefly headlined there. Grandpa Ben resisted this idea, thinking that the supper club hadn't really caught on in the past, so why take the risk. Nevertheless, Uncle Andrew and his friend, publicist Donald Smith, explored ways to make this dream happen.

From childhood, Uncle Andrew held an ardent interest in the Arts, admitting, "Although I lacked the talent to make a life in the Arts, I have [shaped] a very happy life with the Arts."

As a pre-teen, he spent summers tap-dancing in top hat and tails at local theatres in Augusta, New Jersey and nearby communities. He learned piano, clarinet, and tenor saxophone well enough to play in assorted orchestras, and earned his first money at age seventeen ($25!) playing in the Jazz band at a graduation ball. After graduating Cum Laude from Newark Academy, he attended Yale, soon participating in both the Glee Club and the Dramat (their drama program). He earned the distinction of becoming the only Glee Club Manager in the history of Yale with a voice so off-key that he couldn't sing with the group he managed. It was years later, when he crossed paths with Donald Smith, that his aspirations would truly flourish. Their original plan was to make the Algonquin the permanent home of cabaret legend Mabel Mercer, for whom the devoted Smith worked many years as an unpaid promoter.[7] It was my good fortune that Uncle Andrew would sometimes bring me along, when he and Smith scouted cabaret personalities around town or attended Mabel Mercer's shows at the St.

Regis Hotel. Mabel Mercer was mesmerizing, less a full-out vocalist than a talk-singing interpreter mining the sorcery of a song lyric (typically by Hart, Porter, Hammerstein, and Coward)—the kind of performer a lyricist would adore. I was watching the embodiment of cabaret history while the future of cabaret was being formulated. I remember how, one night after seeing Mabel Mercer, Donald Smith invited Uncle Andrew and me to visit his East Side apartment decorated with pictures and other souvenirs of his inspirations, such as Fred Astaire, Ethel Merman, and Cole Porter. Smith was a large man with a Cheshire Cat face capped by wavy whitening hair. His conversation was colored by his strong Massachusetts accent and declaratives like "Did you see that knock-'em-dead gown Julie Wilson

*Donald Smith and Family Mercer (photo courtesy of The Mabel Mercer Foundation);
Uncle Andrew with daughters Roxanna and Elizabeth.*

waw!" and "That man should be tahhed and feathahhed faw what he did to that song!"

That evening, he and Uncle Andrew discussed how it was their duty to resurrect the elegance and high standards of past eras, as exemplified by Mabel Mercer. Those words proved prophetic not only at the inception of the new Algonquin cabaret series but in how Smith himself would in 1985 found the Mabel Mercer Foundation (dedicated to the perpetuation of the art of cabaret) and the New York Cabaret Convention.

Fortune smiled again and again as Uncle Andrew took Douglas and me to hear nightclub singers. Among father figures, Grandpa Ben was more interested in taking us to ball games, the Great American Pastime. Conversely, like my father Sidney, Uncle Andrew saw the Colby boys were more interested in the Great American Songbook. Thanks to Uncle Andrew, we experienced the best of the best in cabaret, veteran and newbie, venue to venue: e.g. Bobby Short (Café Carlisle), George Shearing (the Stanhope), and Steve Ross (Backstage)—who in place of Mabel Mercer was the triumphant opening attraction when the Algonquin's cabaret was re-launched in the Oak Room.

We even saw the venerable Bricktop: a once world-famous singer whose protégée had been Mabel Mercer at the popular Paris nightspot, Chez Bricktop. Bricktop's real name was Ada Beatrice Queen Victoria Louise Virginia Smith, a little long for a marquee.[8] Born to a poor African-American family in Virginia, she sang her way into high society, moving to Paris, where Gertrude Stein, Ernest Hemingway, and the F. Scott Fitzgeralds frequented her nightspot.[9] Cole Porter had written the song "Miss Otis Regrets (1934)" for her. Seeing her live, one felt in awe of what she'd accomplished and whom she'd known. There was also some sadness about the evanescence of her fame. So, I wouldn't dare correct her after she introduced a song with complete misinformation. The song was "Where Or When" written by Rodgers and Hart for *Babes in Arms* (1937). "And now," she announced, "I am going to sing 'Where Or When,' a song Noel Coward wrote just for me." What made the announcement extra ironic was the underlying lyric: "It seems we've stood and talked like this before ... But who knows where or when."[11]

Perhaps Bricktop's statement was in itself a coming attraction of how reality and imagination can blur in time, how what's transformative can be transitory, as well. Yet, pursuing theatre, I would learn it's essential to hold onto your illusions when the actuality is less consoling. As actress Ruth Gordon, an Algonquin regular, used to proclaim, "The only way to have a life in the Arts is never face the facts."

Thus, after all the effort and auditions, someone in the Arts *can* finally get a break (as occurred for me with *Charlotte Sweet* despite its short run). Sometimes dreams *do* come true, as with the resurrection of the Algonquin cabaret, even if success is relative (the cabaret closed in 2012 after thirty-two years). The bottom line is that even if the moment of achievement doesn't last, as it occurs, it is one of life's most precious rewards.

Chapter 17: *You Mean, That Arnold Schwarzenegger?*

Algonquin Christmas card by Barbara Westman.

Returning home for the holidays was a special treat now that home happened to be the Algonquin. I flew in after a morning of finals at Northwestern University and arrived at a lobby filled with glittery wreathes, mistletoe, and a glamorous golden Christmas tree. The Algonquin had several holiday traditions. For one, on Christmas Eve, all Algonquin guests received red-mesh stockings hung on their doors, filled with tangerines, candy canes, chestnuts, and other goodies. Then, there was the hotel's festive New Year's Eve. Celebrants would pack the Rose Room and lobby for dinner, furnished with every sort of noisemaker and flamboyant hat. As midnight sounded on the lobby's stately grandfather clock, the spotlight turned to Charley, the Chinese busboy, who'd worked at the hotel for decades. Looking like a skinny Father Time, he strutted up and down the aisles draped in a tablecloth, beating pots and pans like a gong, and becoming the shining Algonquin star of the moment.

Amid all the Yuletide cheer, my grandparents were Jews who would, to some extent, celebrate both Chanukah and Christmas. Actually, celebrating Christmas was quite common for Southern Jews of a certain generation. This is a phenomenon I discussed in detail when I once worked with Alfred Uhry, the Jewish writer from Georgia, whose plays, *Driving Miss Daisy* (1989) and *Last Night of Ballyhoo* (1996), portray such Jewish Christmasmania. Growing up in the Five Towns, I had both a traditional menorah and a not-so-traditional tree. The tree was justified and kosherized, with hanging Jewish stars, a plastic bulb I created depicting "Santa Claus' bar mitzvah" (his red hat served as a yarmulke), and more bulbs containing "Broadway" figurines designed by me: Joel Grey, Angela Lansbury, and—out of *Zorbá!* (1968)—Maria Karnilova. My father, who'd never celebrated Christmas, wasn't thrilled about this. Nevertheless, my brothers and I were elated to get gifts on both holidays. Plus, I always enjoyed being creative with that tree. At night, when everyone else was asleep, I would lie under the colorfully lit tree and observe the rainbow of reflections on our ceiling in the quiet of the night. Then on Christmas Eve, with holiday movies on TV and no one in the house fighting, I truly felt the peace on earth.

My knowledge of Christmas would come in handy in 1979. The occasion was right after an off-off Broadway group, the Lyric Theater of New York, presented a reading of *Another Time*, my first collaboration with composer Gerald Jay Markoe. The well-received show was a musical version of Jean Anouilh's *Time Remembered* (1957 Broadway premiere; a.k.a. *Léocadia*, Paris, 1940) featuring Maria Karnilova and Carolyn Mignini (*Tintypes*, 1980). Happy with our work, the company's artistic director,

Original cast of Ludlow Ladd *(1979): Jerry Crow, Beverly Robinson, Charles Michael Wright, Mara Beckerman, Spring Fairbank, John Schmedes, and Margaret Benczak. Photo: Elizabeth Wolinski.*

Neal Newman, asked if Gerry and I had a show they could do as a staged reading at Christmas time. We didn't. But that didn't stop me from saying, "You got it!" Then, this nice Jewish boy spent the perfect amount of time—twelve days—writing the first draft of a Christmas musical mixing every holiday cliché I could imagine. The result was *Ludlow Ladd*, an all-sung, all-rhymed operetta about an orphan boy, born on Christmas Eve, searching for a loving home. It was staged as one ongoing Christmas carol, where the performers could hold onto their scripts like carolers. They thereby didn't need to memorize. *Ludlow Ladd* was well-liked and received several subsequent productions. We were very lucky with this show, especially when we cast a soprano with an incredibly high voice, Mara Beckerman. Mara would become a continuing inspiration to me (incidentally, the same role was later played by another ingénue with an incredibly high voice, Kristin Chenoweth).

I look back now and realize that *Ludlow Ladd* was a subconscious reflection of my childhood. It featured squabbling parents and a chaotic holiday night assuaged by a beautiful Christmas tree, one that metamorphoses into a magical guardian named "Missus Pinecones" who sets things right. *Ludlow Ladd* was so much fun for everyone that Gerry and I wrote a sequel, expressly for Mara's high voice. The sequel, *Charlotte Sweet*, was pretty lucky, too. It received Drama Desk Award nominations for Gerry, Mara, and me. Once more, holidays were central to the plot. In it, "Ludlow

Christmas tree "comes to life" in Ludlow Ladd: *Spring Fairbanks, Charles Michael Wright. Photo: E. Wolinski.*

Ladd," the character born on Christmas Eve, is betrothed to "Charlotte," a high soprano born on St. Valentine's Day, culminating in a joyful New Year's scene. Even though many of my future musicals would contain Jewish themes, non-Jewish holidays and settings have figured prominently in others. Then again, I'm just following a long tradition when you consider the Jewish songwriters of such standards as "White Christmas" (1940, Irving Berlin), "We Need a Little Christmas" (1966, Jerry Herman), "Santa Baby" (1953, Joan Javits and Phil Springer), and "Rudolph, the Red-Nosed Reindeer" (1949, Johnny Marks).

Even after the holiday season, the Algonquin was a festive place to be as my winter break continued. Stepping into the elevator, I was elbow to elbow with such current stars as Burt Reynolds, Jean Stapleton, and Ellen Burstyn. In addition, there would be impressive celebrities whose faces weren't so recognizable, such as Oscar-winning filmmaker Costa-Gavras (*Z,* 1969), writer Studs Terkel, photographer Ansel Adams, and cartoonist Charles Addams (who was surprisingly straight-laced and personable in person, nothing like you'd expect of the creator, in 1938, of *The Addams Family*). In 1973, however, the hotel housed a bunch of especially atypical guests. Charles Gaines wrote about these visitors in *Men's Journal*. One was Arnold Schwarzenneger, an Austrian and four-time winner of the Mr. Olympia bodybuilding competition, who would go on to become a famed actor and governor of California:

"We had arranged for Arnold and a group of other bodybuilders to stay while they were in New York at that bastion of the delicately sensible life, the Algonquin Hotel, in whose small, exquisite lobby they were studied like metaphors in some obscure language. On this September morning a literary agent and I turned the corner onto West 44th Street off Sixth Avenue, and there was Arnold, walking like a wave breaking toward the hotel from the other end of the block, followed by a retinue of bodybuilders and their vivid girlfriends. He was wearing emerald green shorts. His centaur legs were a bright copper color from a new coat of Tan-in-a-Minute. A car full of his buddies turned onto 44th and slowed beside him, and suddenly the whole street was alive with bodybuilders, driving up in cars, coming out of the hotel. The doorman and the taxi drivers gaped: These huge, outrageous people seemed conjured from the sparkling air. There was laughter from one of the cars and a shout as it pulled off. Out in the street Arnold whooped mightily and kicked at the departing fender. There were maybe two dozen pairs of eyes in front of the Algonquin, and all of them watched his ornately carved leg wink outward in a high, floating punt that seemed to catch the New York morning smack in the bustle."[1]

It was the same writer, Charles Gaines, who launched Schwarzenegger's acting career. Gaines fought strong opposition to cast Schwarzenegger as a lead in the movie version of Gaines' novel about bodybuilders, *Stay Hungry* (1972). Yet, even without any acting experience, Schwarzenegger was a natural as muscleman Joe Santos. He won a 1976 Golden Globe as Best New Actor and became a movie icon.[2] Still, there's no denying, without this stroke of good fortune, Schwarzenegger probably would have lacked the muscle to make it in movies or politics.

I only wish, being away at college, I hadn't missed the spectacle of Arnold Schwarzenegger at the Algonquin. However, Schwarzenegger wasn't as incongruous with the hotel as one might think at first. After all, its then owner, Ben B. Bodne, had a background in competitive athletics. Remember, back in 1946, my grandfather purchased the hotel as a fallback position when he lost out in the bidding for the Pittsburgh Pirates. Yet Grandpa never gave up on sports. For a while, he juggled his Algonquin responsibilities with being co-founder (in 1948) of the Tournament of Champions, a public relations outfit that promoted boxing figures, such as Marcel Cerdan, Jack Dempsey, and Rocky Graziano.[3] The outfit was eventually sold to the Madison Square Garden group.

Arnold Schwarzenneger and other bodybuilders checking into the Algonquin.
Illustration: Dennis Porter.

Throughout his life, Grandpa's avocation was sports, both as an aficionado of all athletic events and as an avid golfer. He used to say he'd bring along two pairs of trousers when he played golf, "In case I get a hole in one." But baseball was his favorite. My cousin Roxanna Anspach Devlin recalls the fantastic times she experienced accompanying him when he had season tickets to the New York Yankees. His seats were right behind the dugout. He'd schmooze with the players on their breaks. If that weren't exciting enough for his pre-teen granddaughter, Grandpa introduced Roxanna to Reggie Jackson, pitcher Ron Guidry, catcher Thurman Munson, and center fielder Mickey Rivers. One day, when young Roxanna misheard Grandpa, thinking she was going to meet the cartoon character Yogi Bear, Grandpa instead presented her to Yogi Berra. He also taught her everything one needs to know about baseball to love it, and she did.

Grandpa took me to some exciting Yankee games, too, but it was evident I knew more about the musicals, *Damn Yankees* (1955) and *I Had a Ball* (1964), than I did baseball. Still, I could instruct Grandpa on who the guests were at the Algonquin, when he didn't know. He probably had no idea who George Spelvin was, even though the Algonquin was the monthly setting for "Friends of George Spelvin" lunches for *Playbill Magazine*. Theatre buffs know that George Spelvin is the name customarily given as a red herring for a role that either doesn't really appear or is covered by an

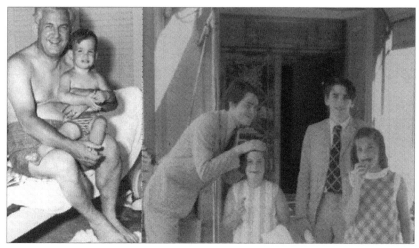

*More family photos: Grandpa Ben and young Michael in Florida; Michael and Douglas
with young Roxanna and Elizabeth Anspach.*

actor in a unrecognizable disguise.[4] The "Spelvin" lunches were held in the
Stratford Suite, hosted by Leo Lerman, the influential editor of *Conde Nast*
Magazine. These gala lunches began in November, 1970 and continued
for the next twenty years. At these luncheons, Lerman invited casts and
creators of current shows to mingle with *Playbill* advertisers.[5] Among the
shows feted were *A Little Night Music* (1974); *Pippin*; *Follies* (1972); *The*
Sunshine Boys (1974); and *Equus*. That meant, around lunchtime during
my vacations, I could literally take bets on "how many Tony nominees you
could squeeze" into the tiny Algonquin elevator.

Still, the theatricality didn't stop there. Besides the regular guests, there
were staff members who had high cultural aspirations, as described in a
New York Magazine article:

> "Many front-desk clerks worked in the arts—one showed his pho-
> tographs at O.K. Harris gallery, another wrote plays (featuring
> the guests), a third was an actor who had a walk-on part in the
> movie *Reversal of Fortune* and roles in several plays. The bartend-
> ers included a painter, a poet affiliated with the St. Mark's Poetry
> Project, and a few writers."[6]

Gordon Edelstein, who was once a waiter at the hotel (and who hails
from the Five Towns), is now the artistic director of the Long Wharf
Theatre and an acclaimed Broadway director. Tony Speciale, who clerked
behind the front desk, was artistic director of the Classic Stage Company
and directed Barry Manilow's musical, *Harmony* (2013). The place has

always been a magnet for artistic types; you should never take for granted the person serving you there.

In 1973, I *was* able to observe the return to the hotel of Alan Jay Lerner and Frederick Loewe. This time, they were working on their stage version of the movie classic, *Gigi*. The stage version had its problems. Yet, even with comparisons to the movie, the Broadway cast was topnotch. It included Alfred Drake, Agnes Moorehead, and my personal favorite, Maria Karnilova. Still, there was a hole in the center: a so-so "Gigi" where an enchanting ingénue was required. The actress originally cast during the tryout had been replaced by the understudy, but not sufficiently. The show could have used the magic I witnessed when the recasting of a vital role in *Applause* helped transform that musical into a hit. Moreover, I happened to know that, during its tryout, *Gigi* had a different understudy for the title role, a terrific one. Her name was Udana Power and she was a protégée of Alan Jay Lerner. I met her when she stayed at the Algonquin on another project. Winsome and adorable, she would have made an ideal "Gigi." Yet, during the tryout of *Gigi*, Udana dropped out as understudy when cast as Melanie Wilkes (the Olivia de Havilland role) in a musical version of *Gone With The Wind* (1973). I later had the occasion to see Udana as Melanie, and she was captivating, receiving excellent reviews—even though the show was panned. Ultimately, *Gone With The Wind* deflated, never making it to New York. But there might have been a happier ending for *Gigi*, had Udana stayed with the Lerner and Loewe show.

Udana Power in Gone With the Wind *(photo: Robert Armin); Maria Karnilova and Alfred Drake in* Gigi *(photo courtesy of Photofest).*

The situation reminded me of how success in the Arts is often predicated on a series of flukes. There are countless musicals that might have turned out very differently with actors who were seriously considered for leads but, for a variety of reasons, not cast. Imagine a parallel universe with the first-approached Mary Martin (not Julie Andrews) in *My Fair Lady;* Eydie Gormé as Polish Rose in *Bye Bye Birdie* (rather than Chita Rivera as Spanish Rose); Anne Bancroft (not Barbra Streisand) in *Funny Girl;* Nell Carter (not Jennifer Holliday) in *Dreamgirls* (1981); and Danny Kaye in *Fiddler On the Roof* (not Zero Mostel).

As far back as I can remember, I've been astonished by the vagaries of this profession. There have been so many actors I thought should be stars who never got that break. There have been shows that opened to just the right critic in *The New York Times*, when other critics disliked the show (the inverse are shows that were audience hits until some critics, perhaps cranky, got to them). Good or bad luck can be crucial in show business. Just look at how Arnold Schwarzenegger got started. Look at how fortunate I was that my grandfather bought the Algonquin instead of the Pittsburgh Pirates. Later in my life, serendipity was a major contributor to my own musicals: like the Christmas tree central to *Ludlow Ladd*; or the random audition of a high-voiced soprano that inspired *Charlotte Sweet*. Even my collaboration with the composer of *Charlotte Sweet* was based on a fluke: being introduced because Gerry Markoe, searching for a lyricist, phoned the first agent listed in the phone book, Charles Abramson.

In my future, there would be a multitude of flukes and what-if's. Fortunately, I'd be grateful for how it all averaged out.

Mara Beckerman in Ludlow Ladd. *Photo: E. Wolynski.*

Chapter 18: *Fast Forward*

My remaining years at Northwestern University zipped by, as I commuted between Evanston, Illinois and the Algonquin. While at NU, I could take the 45-minute train ride to Chicago to see theatre there. By sheer luck, one of Chicago's foremost stage companies, the Goodman Theatre, produced two Rodgers and Hart shows back-to-back during my NU years. Accordingly, I was able to catch up with Dorothy Hart as her guest for the Goodman openings of *The Boys From Syracuse* and *Pal Joey*. I also began a lifelong friendship with her son, Larry Hart II, a political consultant, who was born shortly after his namesake passed away.

Even though it was springtime at these opening nights, the cold-sensitive Dorothy would arrive in heavy winter coats, which she wore through the entire performances. An observer might paraphrase the Larry Hart lyric, "Spring is here, why doesn't the heat defrost her?" Still, it didn't matter; no one could be warmer than she to her friends.

Michael and Larry Hart II.

As a night owl living in Palm Springs, she was the one person I could phone in the middle of the night for advice and consolation. Then, on September 30, 1973, I was Dorothy's guest for a once-in-a-lifetime event: a University of Southern California tribute to Lorenz Hart, *Hart of the Matter*, featuring many of his original stars. I sat at a table with Mrs. Hart, her son, and several of Lorenz Hart's lifetime friends. The presentation itself was electrifying. Among original stars, Gene Kelly performed from *Pal Joey* (1940), Benay Venuta from *By Jupiter* (1942), and three-time Rodgers and Hart leading lady, Helen Ford from *Dearest Enemy* (1925). When Helen Ford spoke, she mentioned meeting Richard Rodgers at the Algonquin, and everyone at our table turned and smiled at me. Others appearing included Nanette Fabray (from *By Jupiter*, 1942), Shirley Jones and Jack Cassidy, Donald O'Connor, and Henry Fonda. In the audience were even more stars, such as Mae West (facing our table in a big white outfit) and Irene Dunne (who'd been the ingénue in Rodgers and Hart's *She's My Baby*, 1928). I thought that event couldn't be topped.

Yet it was. Fast-forward to June 1987, when Dorothy invited my wife, Andrea, and me to be her guests at a spectacular Centennial occasion. It was a weekend marking the 100th birthday of the still very lively director/playwright/producer, George Abbott, at the Great Lakes Festival in Cleveland, Ohio. Jumping in a cab on a busy Friday afternoon in Manhattan,

Joy and George Abbott. (photo courtesy of Joy Abbott).

Andrea and I barely arrived in time for our flight and then to the theatre for the opening event of the Centennial, a performance of the Abbott/Philip Dunning play, *Broadway*. Andrea and I didn't want to disappoint Mrs. Hart, who was there representing two Abbott alumni: her brother-in-law Lorenz Hart (who'd written lyrics on such Abbott shows as *Pal Joey*) and her late husband, Teddy, who'd acted in Abbott's shows, *Three Men On a Horse* (1937), *Room Service* (1938), and *The Boys From Syracuse*. With five minutes before the 8 p.m. curtain, Andrea and I rushed to our ringside seats, glimpsing rows of famous faces associated with Abbott. It was like a surreal dream to edge our way through rows where side by side sat Harold Prince, Nancy Walker, Betty Comden and Adolph Green, Eddie Albert, Maria Karnilova, Sheldon Harnick, Marian Seldes, and Joe Bova (whose kiddie TV show was one both Andrea and I grew up watching). Capping things, Andrea and I sat right nearby George Abbott and his wife, Joy, who also happened to be frequent occupants at the Algonquin. Only the week before, *People Magazine* interviewed him at the hotel, where he'd stated, "My legs may be gone, but my brain isn't. I've still got some more ideas, more plays I want to do."[1]

Throughout the birthday weekend, Andrea and I felt like Broadway history was flashing before our eyes. All these stage legends participated in symposiums describing their experiences on some of Abbott's 128 Broadway shows. I'd been to all-star events before, but not in a hundred years do I expect to encounter another Centennial like this one. It was a learning experience the equal of any course at NU.

During my years at NU, Grandma Mary was someone else who frequently met me in Chicago. Usually we'd spend the weekend together at the chic Drake Hotel. She knew I loved the food there, especially the Caesar salads and rice pudding, and, as a matter of fact, so did she. She also sometimes needed a break from New York City. Even though she herself could provoke Grandpa Ben, he was quite irascible to begin with, worsened by a hearing loss and periodic ear buzz that doctors couldn't much help. Even more upsetting to Grandma were regular phone calls—at all hours—from my mother, tirades blaming Grandma for perceived wrongs. Grandma would just sit there, quietly turning pale during my mother's rants, as if allowing her to vent would exorcise the situation. Grandma's fervent wish was for Mom to get over her anger and feel at peace. Ironically, it was Grandma's indulgence that undermined Mom's getting the kind of help she needed (e.g. how Grandma coached Douglas and me to side with Mom when my parents went for counseling years earlier). Fast forward: today my mother is in a far better state of mind, thanks largely to the medical and psychiatric care my brothers and I at last arranged for her—after my grandparents passed away. The saddest aspect is that this didn't happen earlier. It would have been a blessing for my grandmother and would have made a huge difference in both my parents' lives.

When I was a Senior at college, Grandma made one trip to Chicago where she and I grated on each other's nerves like nail files. Grandma didn't seem to understand that I had an upcoming college exam to focus upon. She had her heart set on a recommended restaurant in Chicago whereas I asked to just eat downstairs at the Drake Hotel. Tempers flared before we

Birthday party for Grandma Mary with Grandpa Ben..

went to her preferred restaurant. Inevitably, the evening wasn't pleasant; I made several comments about manipulation that she didn't like. The next morning, she decided it was important to clear the air, sitting me down for a talk on what she called my "belligerence."

"Michael, you said some awful things to me last night," she asserted.

"Grandma, I'm sorry, it's just that . . . ."

She continued with the demeanor of a wise philosopher. "Listen, I understand. I really do. I've lived a long time, and experience teaches you things. I've been through world wars, had to flee Russia, seen the world change. I've lost precious family members and witnessed many tragedies. I understand people, I've watched what goes on in our family, and I know just why you're acting this way."

"You do?" I replied, tears welling up in my eyes.

"Yes, Michael." She paused for a moment, and then with a profound sigh, shared her wisdom. "Michael, you were born with a mean streak . . . and you can't help yourself!"

Despite the distractions of the weekend, I did well enough on my exam. In fact, I got through NU with a higher grade average than I'd had at Woodmere Academy. During a single semester, I even got an A in two courses I was taking simultaneously: one on the poet William Blake, the other a comparative course on Gothic Literature and Horror Movies. The latter course was a snap for me. Alongside musicals and comic books, monster movies were my third major outlet growing up. I didn't need sports—they were too realistic.

After graduating from NU with a B.A. in English Literature, my major declaration was "New York City, here I come!" I enrolled in the graduate school studying Drama at New York University and became a full-time resident at the Algonquin. That meant I wasn't simply seeing Algonquinites as guests but as neighbors. One constant presence was Maya Angelou, a towering, elegant woman, whose accomplishments were inspirational, both in their breadth and in the early tribulations she had to overcome. Maya is described on her official website as "a global renaissance woman . . . a celebrated poet, memoirist, novelist, educator, dramatist, producer, actress, historian, filmmaker, and civil rights activist." Possibly her crowning achievement was her autobiography, *I Know Why the Caged Bird Sings* (1969). Set in the South, the book poetically portrayed how she overcame racism, rape, and social isolation through self-education. She was San Francisco's first Black female cable car conductor. She danced with Alvin Ailey, and she toured as a singer in *Porgy and Bess* (1950s).[2] In other words, there wasn't anything she couldn't do when she set her mind to it.

One of the first times I saw her at the hotel was in 1973, when she appeared in the Broadway drama, *Look Away*, playing opposite Geraldine Page as the African-American confidante of the institutionalized Mary Todd Lincoln. Though the show received negative reviews and only lasted one performance, she was so impressive she received a Tony nomination as Best Supporting Actress.

Even so, she was remarkably humble and friendly when I approached her in the lobby. I remember one night she took my grandmother and me out for Cuban food, which I'd never tried before. Unfortunately, I don't recall what was said—I was just in such awe being around her.

Yet as worldly as Maya was, she sometimes had more mundane concerns. Michael Hurley, who clerked the Algonquin front desk (from 1982-1987), recounted to me a fashion emergency she faced at the hotel:

> "Early one morning, Ms. Angelou (tall, very friendly, huge smile) came to the desk wearing a beautiful white silk blouse with cuffed sleeves, but she'd forgotten to pack cuff links. She asked if I had anything that would work. I told her I'd look around the front desk. A few minutes later she came back and proudly showed me that

Maya Angelou. Photography by Lisa Pacino.

a pair of huge clip-on earrings did the trick. A good thing, too, as they looked so much better than the paper clips and rubber bands I'd come up with. She was such a nice lady."

Flash forward: years later, when I became a substitute teacher, there was a girl in one of my classes, who, probably like thousands of little girls, was named after Maya. The girl worshipped her namesake to such an extent that I contacted Maya Angelou to see if she'd write a note to the girl. Overnight, the loveliest note arrived for me to deliver. The student responded like she'd just received the Holy Grail. And I've no doubt Maya probably did the same for dozens of little girls named after her.

Maya was equally gracious when, in 2000, I contacted her about a memorial for my grandparents, held at the Algonquin. Maya sent the following note, which I read aloud at the memorial:

"Friendship and affection know no man-made barriers; age nor culture, race nor class. Ben and Mary Bodne were friends to me and we respected and cared for each other for nearly thirty years.

After Ben's death, I always found time to see, chat with, and listen to Mary Bodne. In fact, when on one of Oprah's visits to me at the Algonquin, since I knew how much Mary Bodne loved Oprah, I invited her down to my suite. She came dolled up and carrying a photograph. I think Ben had been dead two years then. She showed Oprah the photograph of Ben Bodne as a young, dashing, thirty-five year old, and said, 'Here is my buddy. We lived together in love and joy for over sixty years. Isn't he good looking?' Who wouldn't love a woman who loved love so much?

The Bodnes made our world richer. We are poorer without them. Maya Angelou"[3]

The world is infinitely poorer without Maya Angelou.

Someone else I regularly saw in the Algonquin lobby was producer/director Gordon Davidson, founder and head—until 2005—of the Mark Taper Forum in Los Angeles. He was described in *The Los Angeles Times* as "eminence grise of the regional theater movement, crusading champion of Los Angeles theater."[4] Davidson was constantly commuting between California and New York, as shows that originated at the Taper Forum were picked up for New York production, including *The Trial of the Catonsville Nine* (1971), *The Shadow Box* (1997), and *Children of a Lesser God* (1980). However, Davidson's relationship to the hotel shifted. As Algonquin employee Michael Hurley told me:

"Gordon was a frequent guest, always very friendly. When I moved to L.A. I ended up working at his Center Theater Group for several years and every time I bumped into him he'd say how much he loved the Algonquin. BUT it wasn't until 2008 that he told me the following: He said that he'd always stayed at The Royalton when he came to NYC. The day after he won the Tony for [producing] *Children [of a Lesser God]* . . . he said your grandmother called him there and said, 'Okay. Now that you have a Tony, you can surely stay at the Algonquin.'"

It took me eleven months to complete my Master's program in Drama at New York University (from Fall through Summer semesters). Enhancing my Drama studies were the plays I could see in the evening, just down the block, with some of the stars staying at the hotel. Among actors at the hotel while doing shows were Jason Robards and Colleen Dewhurst in *A Moon For the Misbegotten* (1973), Nicole Williamson in *Uncle Vanya*

(1973), and Fionnula Flanagan in *Ulysses in Nighttown* (1974). Grandma even arranged for me to conduct a breakfast interview with Ms. Flanagan, a Tony nominee, for an assignment at NYU. However, I doubt Grandma had herself attended Ms. Flanagan's show with its highly publicized nude scene. One might best describe the scene as a precursor of Sharon Stone's revelations in *Basic Instinct* (1992). I blushed through that entire interview at the Algonquin, recalling what I glimpsed in *Ulysses in Nighttown* without nightgown.

Other highlights of my program at NYU were: classes with Richard Schechner; my interviewing off-off-Broadway icon Al Carmines Jr. (*Promenade*, 1965; *In Circles*, 1968; *Peace*, 1969); and my master's thesis, a collection of recordings and material on Lorenz Hart. The influential Richard Schechner gained renown for his "radical" stagings of classical material[5]—such as *Dionysus in '69* (with audience interaction and full frontal nudity)—and as founding director of The Performance Group, the award-winning off-Broadway company specializing in environmental theatre. His classes at NYU were bold, to say the least. One night in his Political Theatre course, I was one of a group of students asked to improvise a scene from Edward Albee's *Who's Afraid of Virginia Woolf?*—as might be interpreted by the late director Antonin Artaud. Artaud specialized in "Theatre of Cruelty," incorporating violence, sadism, and garden-variety shock. Not knowing quite what to do for our interpretation of *Who's Afraid of Virginia Woolf?* (1962), my student group went around grunting, acting sloshed, and screaming at *everyone* with lines from the play, like "Hey swampy," "If you existed, I'd divorce you," and "You make me puke."[6] Nothing like this ever occurred in any of my past school experiences (though it was not unlike some nights growing up on Paine Road). Despite these verbal assaults, Professor Schechner said we weren't being cruel enough. He initiated a game of "Truth or Dare" where members of our group were asked questions by the class, and if our answers were deemed dishonest, the game became "Truth or Bare" wherein we were told to remove articles of clothing. When I was asked if I'd ever been drunk or cursed like in *Who's Afraid of Virginia Woolf?*, I said I hadn't, which no one believed. By continuing to tell the truth, I was soon down to my underwear. Shortly, this exercise in "Theatre of Cruelty" became more like "Noh Theatre" as I had noh intention of going further. Fortunately, not being as daring as Fionnula Flanagan, I was literally saved by the school bell. The class, not my modesty, came to an end just in time. I can't imagine how my family—Grandma in particular—would have responded to this illustration of college tuition expenditures.

Al Carmines. Courtesy of photographer Frederic Ohringer.

It was for a much more demure class (titled "New Theatre") that I met with off-off Broadway wunderkind, Al Carmines. I co-interviewed him alongside Susan Condos, a fellow NYU student. Carmines was, in the words of a *New York Times* tribute, "a seminal force in the rise in New York of small, experimental theatres created to challenge what many saw as the commercialization ... of Broadway."[7] Producing plays and musicals at the Judson Memorial Church, where he was also the Reverend, Carmines was a man of many talents: composer, lyricist, actor, and director at the Judson Poets' Theater located at the church. According to Carmines, in 1961 the Judson became "the first Off Off Broadway theatre to do new plays by new playwrights" (the other pioneering off-off Broadway theatre, Caffe Cino, began with revivals only).[8] Carmine's musicals—among them *Promenade*, *In Circles* and *The Faggot* (1973)—won five Obie Awards and four Drama Desk Awards for Carmines. His topics ranged from Abraham Lincoln to Gertrude Stein, Snow White to Mao Tse-tung, and gay lifestyles to Christmas. Several of his shows moved on to commercial success, though his one attempt at Broadway—the musical, *W.C.* (1971), with Mickey Rooney as W.C. Fields and Bernadette Peters—closed in tryout.

Carmines was a large, very welcoming presence during the interview, which is now part of the Judson Memorial Church website. It's intriguing to me that, in rereading that interview decades later, how often I eventually followed his example in my own shows. Carmine's musicals were produced on a shoestring, often when no one but Carmines would present them, and incorporated an all-sung format—with dialogue scenes thru-composed—that was unusual for musicals of its time. As Carmines told me, "A lot of people felt it was the first time they had seen a musical play—it wasn't an opera—move in such a way that you didn't stop everything, have an introduction, do a song, have applause. At Judson, our early musicals would go in and out of music with no break."[9]

He was fascinating company.

The third highlight of my NYU program, preparing a master thesis on Lorenz Hart, was actually a corollary of the research I began that year for Dorothy Hart's book. First off, I gathered a definitive collection of recordings of Lorenz Hart songs. At the same time, I spent countless hours at libraries pouring over manuscripts, photographs, and other paraphernalia related to Rodgers and Hart. The sources included the Lincoln Center collection, the Museum of the City of New York, and ultimately the Library of Congress (Washington DC). Going through these snapshots of Lorenz Hart's work created an exhilarating overview of a life in the theatre. There were stories on how Hart took great pride in not just being a songwriter, but in developing characters and themes through his lyrics in such shows as in *On Your Toes* (1936). There was the report of how dispirited he became when the original *New York Times* review of *Pal Joey* disparaged something so novel and adult for musical theatre. There were

Lyricist Lorenz Hart. Photo courtesy of Rodgers and Hammerstein: an Imagem Company.

newspaper clippings debunking general myths, such as the claim that Hart always wrote the lyrics *after* hearing Richard Rodgers' music. For instance, in one such interview, Hart described how he would write lyrics first on comedy songs and recitative (unlike, say, Oscar Hammerstein II, who, Hart claimed, always wrote lyrics subsequently to fit Jerome Kern's music). There were astonishing photographs, such as a double-exposed photo from *Jumbo* (1935), its circus setting looking full of apparitions. Though not used in the book, this picture haunted me, knowing that *Jumbo* was the first show my father saw and loved as a child. Spooky, too, was the fact that the show's location, the Hippodrome Theatre, had later been razed and converted into the parking garage directly across from the Algonquin Hotel.

It's Not a Formula That Makes Songs, Nor Mere Fortune

4/11/37

Rodgers and Hart Decide a Tune Must Be Found, and Get Down to Work

[Excerpt:]

For in any one of the shows that these inseparables write, it is impossible to distinguish which factor, words or music, makes the song a hit. One decides it is both.

But Rodgers cleared up all speculation as to how the team works. There is no magic formula; the process is highly methodical.

"It depends on what you're trying to do," Rodgers explained. "If the lyric is of prime importance, Larry does that first and I set it to music. On the other hand, sometimes I think of a tune and then Larry writes the words. Usually it is a question of having to write a song for a particular situation and of finding a particular tune that is appropriate."

But let not those who like to think of songs as magical gems that drop from the skies be too disappointed. There are moments when song writing seems to be a harum-scarum affair. Writing a song for a title, for instance.

"Sometimes Larry gets a title that haunts him," said Rodgers, "He has no idea what the rest of the song is going to be, but he has that title and he won't give it up. So I write a melody around the title, and Larry listens to it and gets the rest of the song. Sometimes he gets his lyrics from just one phrase in the music that seems to fit certain words."

Article on Rodgers and Hart from The New York Herald Tribune *(April 11, 1937). One of several articles in my research contradicting the notion that Hart always wrote lyrics after Rodgers composed music.*

Most intriguing of all for me was reading how Hart aimed to advance a style of all-sung, all-rhymed musicals. These musicals featured sequences with what Hart called "rhythmic dialogue" in which scenes didn't stop between songs but continued via music and lyrics that bridged events in lieu of dialogue. Such Hart sequences can be found in the movies *Love Me Tonight* (1932) and *Hallelujah I'm a Bum* (1933). Hart's intent reminded me of what Al Carmines strove to do in his musicals, as would writers of future musicals, such as *The Golden Apple* (1954; composer: Jerome Moross; lyrics: John Latouche) and my own (*Charlotte Sweet*).

My year at NYU indoctrinated me in aspects of stage writing and off-off Broadway, instrumental in my career. Fast forward: I'd be putting that knowledge to work within months as I began my first *professional* forays into the theatre world.

Chapter 19: *That Mug Is Mine*

St. Clement's Church. Photograph: Steven Schalchlin.

They all advised against it. My grandmother and grandfather didn't want me to work off-off-Broadway, especially for no money. My Uncle Andrew concurred, even though he was supportive of cabaret performers who worked for no money in far worse places. Yet I was willing to defy them all when I read about a new organization, the first of its kind, founded expressly to develop original musicals.

Stuart Ostrow, producer of *Pippin* and *1776*, announced that he was setting up "The Musical Theatre Lab" at St. Clement's Church, the building on West 46th Street off 9th Avenue. St. Clement's had its own thriving theatre program, including two stage spaces: a small cabaret theatre on the first floor; and a larger main stage on the second floor, where the musicals would be presented. While Ostrow was busy on other projects, the Lab was administered by artistic director, Stephanie Copeland, an expert on non-profit theatre, who'd been personal assistant to Nancy Hanks, chairman of the National Endowment for the Arts.

Producer Stuart Ostrow. Photo courtesy of Stuart Ostrow.

It was as if I'd been offered a wish by a genie (or was it Lucifer?). I mustered the courage to write a note to Stephanie, met with her, and talked my way into a position as her personal assistant—my apprenticeship in professional theatre. Even though I didn't expect to make a dime, I probably gained more hands-on theatre experiences in my months at the Musical Theatre Lab than in all my college years. Stephanie, who looked like Joanne Woodward dangling cigarettes like Bette Davis, taught me everything I needed to know about producing musicals in not-for-profit theatre. The Lab's first produced musical was one that would later move to Broadway, *The Robber Bridegroom* (1974 at St. Clement's). Based on Eudora Welty's novella, the show had music by Robert Waldman and a book/lyrics by Alfred Uhry. The team might have never placed the show if not for the determination of their agent, Flora Roberts (also agent to

Stephen Sondheim). In fact, Alfred was on the verge of quitting theatre after a succession of disappointments. There was no notion at the time that his stage work would lead to a Pulitzer Prize, two Tony Awards, and the Oscar. Uhry, who'd been a protégé of Frank Loesser and made a living as a high school English teacher, never forgot his first experience on Broadway. He, composer Waldman, and librettist Terrence McNally (along with Alex Gordon) collaborated on *Here's Where I Belong* (1968), a musical version of John Steinbeck's *East of Eden* (1952), produced by music-man Mitch Miller. The show was savaged by critics and closed in one night. Uhry and Waldman were devastated, but no more than Terrence McNally, who'd written *And Things Go Bump in the Night* (1965), a Broadway play that had previously bombed in the night. Fortunately, the collaborators all persevered, McNally going on to write numerous award-winning hits (both plays and musicals) such as *Master Class* (1995), *Frankie and Johnny in the Clair de Lune* (1987), *Kiss of the Spider Woman*, and *Ragtime* (1998). Uhry would write the hits, *Driving Miss Daisy* and *The Last Night of Ballyhoo*, both with incidental music by Waldman.

In the meantime, Uhry and Waldman continued to struggle. I happened to see a backer's audition of another early show of theirs, *Full Circle*. That saga about generations of one family was slated to reunite John Raitt and Jan Clayton, original stars of *Carousel*. The show never got past backer's auditions. Accordingly, Alfred Uhry and Robert Waldman seemed overjoyed having *The Robber Bridegroom* chosen as the inaugural show for the Musical Theatre Lab.

Every day I expectantly took the fifteen-minute walk from the Algonquin to St. Clement's for my professional indoctrination. Once there, I read and evaluated their submitted scripts, helped with clerical duties, and then assisted on productions. Even though the actors and staff were being paid little to nothing, this venture attracted A-talents who knew that economical sacrifices were a feasible trade-off for unpressured creativity and innovation (or so we all hoped). When auditions began, I was amazed, and sometimes saddened, by the Broadway veterans who appeared before us alongside bright, wide-eyed newcomers. On one hand, there were past-their-prime actors valiantly auditioning with songs they'd sung on original cast recordings (when their voices were stronger). Then, there were promising newcomers who weren't always the best auditioners (Kevin Kline was turned down as being "too stiff" to play the lead; he did, however, play it later on). There were performers of all ages, who, eager as they were, just weren't right for this project. Finally, an extremely talented cast was assembled, including many who'd later do the show on Broadway.

The story of *The Robber Bridegroom* is a mix of Eudora Welty whimsy, Grimm's Fairy Tale, and Mississippi folklore; half the fun is how characters try to bamboozle each other, even during the main love story, with tall tales. First choice to play Jamie Lockhart—the suitor of an heiress and secretly a bandit of the wood—was Barry Bostwick (Broadway's original "Danny Zuko" in *Grease*, 1972). When Bostwick was unavailable, the role went to someone you wouldn't usually cast as a Southern country boy, Raúl Juliá, who later appeared in the Broadway musical, *Nine* (1982) and as Gomez in the film, *The Addams Family* (1991).

There would be no real sets for the workshop, just props and minimal costumes, plus a cast of fourteen actors and five on-stage musicians. The director was Gerald Freedman, the original director of the musical, *Hair* (1967), and future artistic director of Cleveland's Great Lakes Festival (where he oversaw the George Abbott Centennial). He staged *The Robber Bridegroom* as an ongoing square dance, integrally pausing for songs and book scenes. Much of the stage business and some of the lines were improvised during rehearsals, so Alfred Uhry spent a lot of time in the Lab's second-floor office retyping pages. Supplies were limited, so I volunteered my own electric typewriter for office use. I can now brag that the Pulitzer Prize-winning Alfred Uhry rewrote part of his play on my typewriter (my earliest professional claim to theatrical immortality).

The first public performance of *The Robber Bridegroom* would be on November 4, 1974. There were three weeks of rehearsals, almost half of which were spent on the opening number, "Look At Me," in which characters would swagger, preen, and brag about themselves. The fact that everyone seemed enthusiastic rehearsing this number proves you never really know what you've got until you play in front of an audience. After the overlong first public performance, "Look At Me" was the first thing to be cut. Another scene I remember vividly from rehearsals was one in which Jamie Lockhart, disguised as the bandit, flirts with the all too willing heiress, Rosamund, while stealing her clothes. During rehearsals, it was decided that Rhonda Coullet, the blonde former beauty queen playing Rosamund, would openly doff her clothes at the end of the scene (which wasn't a big deal for Rhonda, who'd previously been in *Hair*). Rhonda had just sung "Nothin' Up," and soon afterwards, there was "Nothin' On." It was one day I was especially glad to be in a theatrical setting other than the Algonquin Hotel.

The show was presented for six evening performances, with rewrites implemented every day. Yet it wasn't until the final performance, a black-tie special event, that a producer offered to option it. Fortunately, that producer

The MUSICAL THEATRE LAB presents

The Robber Bridegroom

Musical Theatre Lab productions are works-in-progress. Consequently, we ask that this piece not be reviewed.

No smoking in the theatre, please.

The taking of pictures and the use of recording equipment is strictly prohibited.

Adapted from the story by Eudora Welty
book & lyrics   music
ALFRED UHRY   ROBERT WALDMAN

directed by
GERALD FREEDMAN

lighting   choreography
GARY PORTO   DON REDLICH

executive producer   project producer
STEPHANIE COPELAND   STEVEN WOOLF

featuring

SUSAN BERGER, WILLIAM BRENNER,
RHONDA COULLET, JOHN GETZ, CYNTHIA HERMAN,
PAUL JULIA, DANA KYLE, CAROLYN MCCURRY,
BILL NUNNERY, THOMAS OGLESBY,
TRIP PLYMALE, ERNIE SABELLA,
DAVID SUMMERS, STEVE VINOVICH

The MUSICAL THEATRE LAB at StCLEMENT'S
a joint project of
The Stuart Ostrow Foundation
and StClement's

The MUSICIANS

BOB JONES, ALAN KAUFMAN,
RICHARD SCHULBERG, STEVE TANNENBAUM,
DAVID MARKOWITZ

The PRODUCTION STAFF

Stage Manager   MARY BURNS

Prop Mistress   GAIL MCGLAUGHLIN

Assistant to Messrs. Waldman
and Uhry   JANE HARMON

Assistant to Mrs. Copeland
                                              MICHAEL COLBY

Original program from The Robber Bridegroom.

was John Houseman, representing The Acting Company. I had arranged all the seating plans that night and—like Goldilocks—must have found the seat that was "just right." *The Robber Bridegroom* toured for a year as part of The Acting Company's rotating repertory, with company members led by the young Patti Lupone and (no longer rejected) Kevin Kline. Finally, it landed on Broadway with a cast including Barry Bostwick (who won the Tony Award for Best Actor, 1977), Rhonda Coullet, and other original cast members.

I have two other special memories of *The Robber Bridegroom*. One of my ulterior motives in joining the Musical Theatre Lab was to interest them in producing my musical, *Where There's a Will*. Within a short time, it became evident that wasn't going to happen. I discussed this with Alfred Uhry, posing the possibility of my leaving the position, with its few opportunities for a writer. Alfred gave me advice: "Be patient and stay. I wish I could have worked at a place like this when I was young." He validated my job at the Lab in a way my family hadn't, and I couldn't have been more grateful.

The other memory occurred after the closing of the workshop of *The Robber Bridegroom*. The story's writer, Eudora Welty, was staying at the Algonquin. Since she'd been unable to attend the workshop, I arranged for her to be part of a cast reunion for evening cocktails in the lobby. It was the closest thing the hotel ever had to a company hoedown, as Welty had the show evoked by cast members, including Raúl Juliá, Rhonda Coullet, Ernie Sabella (the voice of "Pumbaa" in the 1994 film, *The Lion King*), and Stephen Vinovich (for whom Uhry and Waldman would later write a musical about Al Capone: *America's Sweetheart*, 1985). Incidentally, Eudora Welty did see later productions and adored the show.

The creativity seemed nonstop at the Musical Theatre Lab. Right after we wrapped up *The Robber Bridegroom*, we were packaging our next show, the Rock musical, *Joe's Opera* (1974). This show was written by Tommy Mandel and directed by Robert Allan Ackerman, whose Broadway credits would include *Bent* (1980), starring Richard Gere. The cast included Victor Garber (*Godspell* film, 1973; *Sweeney Todd*, 1979), Armelia McQueen (future Tony nominee for *Ain't Misbehavin'*), and Paul Kreppel (TV's *It's a Living*, 1980-1989). It's hard to believe now that actors of this caliber worked on the show virtually volunteering their time.

In between musicals, I became a theatre factotum, working on play productions at both St. Clement's spaces. As an expert spotter (someone who recognizes celebrities in the room), I was an attendant at the gala party marking their new theatre season. There, I served champagne to Lillian Hellman, as well as mingling with playwrights, such as Leonard Melfi (*Oh, Calcutta!*, 1969), Jean-Claude van Itallie (*America Hurrah*, 1966), and John Guare (who exuberantly recognized ME!). Months later, I house-managed the New York premiere of Tom Stoppard's *Enter a Free Man* (1974) with David Rounds, J. T. Walsh, and (as an ingénue) Swoosie Kurtz. I'd been a huge fan of Stoppard's ever since his Tony-winning *Rosencrantz and Guildenstern Are Dead*. I'll never forget how, around 6 p.m., I rushed to unlock a buzzing front door at St. Clement's. As I opened up, there was Stoppard outside. I didn't even know he was in town—staying, of course, at the Algonquin. Feeling like the official St. Clement's guide after only three months there, I led him backstage to meet with the impressive cast.

Meanwhile, I didn't dare discuss my house management gig with Grandma Mary. She would have freaked out knowing I was walking through dicey New York neighborhoods starting at 46th Street and Ninth Avenue, after locking up the theatre between 11 p.m. and midnight. It was the same neighborhood where, years later, I'd be mugged at gunpoint and

St. Clement's "family" —Stephanie Copeland, Larry Goosen, and associate Zena Shervin. Photo: E. Wolynski.

pistol-whipped. Yet, from what I heard, going out of town with a show, or facing some critics, could be even worse.

From my first day at St. Clement's, I felt like part of the family among its theatre staff. The cast of off-stage characters was headed by Executive Producer, Lawrence (Larry) Goosen. Always instructive on the ways of cutting costs, he'd previously produced Stoppard's *Inspector Hound* and *After Magritte* (1972). Protectively shadowing Larry Goosen, like a loyal secretary in a noir detective flick, was "coordinator" Jean Halbert, a willowy, silver-haired earth mother. Prominent, as well, was Artistic Director, Kevin O'Connor, a Humphrey Bogart lookalike who actually played "Bogie" in a 1980 film, when he wasn't performing at St. Clements or elsewhere off-Broadway.

Then there was the younger generation: bushy haired assistant Jeff Wachtel, now Co-President of USA Cable Network; and wiry Steve Kimball, assistant to Stuart Ostrow. At the time, Stuart Ostrow was helping Bob Fosse prepare for an upcoming musical titled *Chicago*. One day, Steve Kimball visited St. Clement's, talking about a new *Chicago* number called "Cell Block Tango." He cited some of the killer ideas being considered for the song, including one that wasn't used: a merry murderess' claim that she and her lover made a suicide pact to jump over a cliff, but—after helping him plunge—she decides to just leap for his money.

The next show presented at the Musical Theatre Lab was frameworked as a Grand Ole Opry presentation, just like *The Robber Bridegroom* was done as an ongoing square dance. This musical, *The Red Blue-Grass Western Flyer Show* (1975), was by Conn Fleming and Clint Ballard Jr. (composer of the Linda Rondstadt song "You're No Good"). I made all kinds of valuable connections on this show. The project producer, working side by side with Stephanie Copeland, was Steven Woolf. He'd held the same position on *The Robber Bridegroom* and would one day become the artistic director of The Repertory Theatre of St. Louis. A production assistant was Dan Mizell; he would later represent me as an agent at William Morris. Finally, this production marked the first time I met costumer Michele Reisch, who became my most frequent costume designer (on *Charlotte Sweet* and four other musicals).

Probably, my favorite personal memory of *The Red Blue-Grass Western Flyer Show* involved a coffee mug. The plot of the show depicted members of an ordinary family with dreams of glory days in Nashville. During a kitchen scene, the mother, played by the uproarious Barbara Coggin, grabbed a coffee mug while having a family discussion. I wanted to make sure it was just the right mug to demonstrate this family had a television mentality, susceptible to anything pitched by TV ads. I scoured the city and then I found it: a big mug with the Maxwell House logo printed on it. Every night when Barbara Coggin lifted that mug, caressing a hot cup of coffee so lovingly that she sometimes got a laugh, I felt a special pride. No matter how incidental the moment, I felt like I was creatively contributing to professional theatre at last.

Months later, I had an even more rewarding opportunity to work on a show at St. Clement's. It was a new mini-musical, independent of the Musical Theatre Lab. Presented at the theatre's cabaret space, *Olmsted!* (1975) was based on the life of landscape architect Frederick Law Olmsted, who designed New York's Central Park. It was written and directed by Jeff Wachtel in collaboration with Clark Kee (another Yale graduate). *Olmsted!*

featured two other Yalies in the cast, Steve Kimball (Stuart Ostrow's assistant) and Robert Picardo. I was asked to write lyrics to a key song composed by Clark, titled "What's the Use?" My recommendation for this project came from members of St. Clement's who'd read *Where There's a Will*, even though unproduced there. I was so glad I followed Alfred Uhry's advice, "Be patient and stay." The song was delivered by Robert Picardo, my first leading man, playing "Olmsted." He was incredibly funny and charismatic, stopping the show with the song. It was no wonder Picardo went on to originate the lead in the hit *Gemini* (1977), then played Jack Lemon's son in Broadway's *Tribute (*1978); his TV credits would include *China Beach* (1988) and *Star Trek: Voyager* (1995). It was thanks to Picardo that I felt like the toast of St. Clement's for a few days, as people congratulated me on that number. The song might have just been a small triumph during a little showcase run. Yet, for the moment, I was a validated off-off Broadway writer, not just a scion of the Algonquin Hotel.

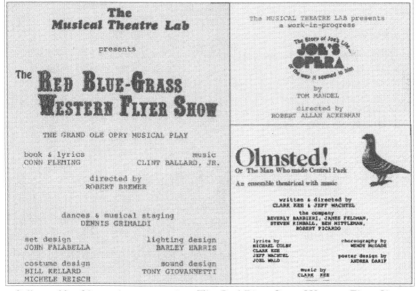

Collage of St. Clement's programs from The Red Blue-Grass Western Flyer Show, Joe's Opera, *and* Olmsted!

After *Olmsted!*, Robert Picardo got a major break in another show having its New York premiere at St. Clement's. I was asked to audition for the role he won. The play was written by a newcomer from Chicago, David Mamet. Scruffy and casual, Mamet virtually took residence at St. Clement's, frequently talking politics and world affairs with actor J. T. Walsh, who later appeared in the Mamet plays, *American Buffalo* (1975) and *Glengarry Glen Ross* (1985). Listening to the scope of their conversations, I was envious, even intimidated by how knowledgeable they were.

As for me, I was flattered but flabbergasted when asked to audition for Mamet's New York premiere: *Sexual Perversity in Chicago* (1975). Larry Goosen was presenting the non-Equity production, which needed to cast the role of Dan Shapiro, a slightly naïve Jewish fellow (for which I had many

Logo for Sexual Perversity in Chicago.

qualifications). Notwithstanding, the title of the show gave me pause about auditioning. Ditto the thought that, with limited acting skills, my audition for *Sexual Perversity in Chicago* would be more like "Theatrical Ineptitude in Manhattan." In a moment of questionable judgment, I decided the audition just wasn't worth it. Still, it was probably for the best: I never have to say those Mamet lines—like "I'm a lousy f***" and "no sh**"[1]—in front of my grandmother. As it turned out, Robert Picardo was superb in *Sexual Perversity in Chicago,* and the play received raves. Coupled with the short play, *The Duck Variations*, it moved off-Broadway in 1976 to a long and prosperous run at the Cherry Lane Theatre, as produced by Larry Goosen and Jeff Wachtel.

It was great to feel like I was now officially part of the theatre community in my own right. I now gaze at my old diaries and am astounded by some of the events happening at this time. For instance, there's the day I took a break from the Lab to visit my grandparents for lunch in the Oak Room. There I was, this rarely paid theatre assistant, eating alongside such newsmakers as Grandpa Ben, Louis Nizer, Otto Preminger, and Max Gordon (Broadway producer of *The Band Wagon,* 1931 and *Roberta,* 1933). The big surprise for me was director Otto Preminger, the bald and scary

Algonquin Round Table of the 1970s in the Oak Room. (At table) Joe DiMaggio, Harpo Marx, John Henry Faulk, Louis Nizer, Ben B. Bodne, and Otto Preminger; visitors Leonard Lyons (taking notes), Ella Fitzgerald, and the Algonquin Cat. Illustration by Dennis Porter.

Austrian Jew, who was known for playing Nazis in films and as Mr. Freeze on the 1966 *Batman* TV series. He was quite friendly to me discussing the psychology of why audiences love disaster movies: "Zay like to see UZZAH people suffah." Years later, I would have a very different meeting with him to discuss one of my shows, whereupon he rose menacingly from the shadows of his dusky office and in his stentorian voice declaimed, "VHUTT DO YOO VANT?!" In my inner mind I said to myself "I vant to be alone!"

By May, there had been some layoffs at St. Clement's and I, too, decided it was time to move on. Though I periodically continued to house-manage for their main theatre program—even getting remunerated!—I wanted to focus more on writing. In addition, I was preoccupied with my final research for Dorothy Hart's book. On my last official day at St. Clement's, they threw me a surprise party in which I was offered at least two substances I wouldn't touch, but I felt blissfully stoned anyway. Plus, I will always be thankful to Stephanie Copeland and others there for the master course they gave me in working off-off Broadway—essential to me in the next couple of years.

About two years later, on October 9, 1976, I enjoyed an especially celebratory reunion with Stephanie and her husband James when we together attended the Broadway opening night of *The Robber Bridegroom*. It was like old times as we cheered on the show and many of the actors from the Musical Theatre Lab version.

Broadway production of The Robber Bridegroom *with Barry Bostwick, Rhonda Coullet, Stephen Vinovich, and Barbara Lang. Photo courtesy of Photofest.]*

During the summer, I continued researching Dorothy Hart's book (to be published by Harper & Row) and took a whirlwind twenty-day trip to Europe (Paris, Rome, London, and Athens). The trip culminated with ten glorious days in Israel, where nobody quite understood what I was doing when I felt inspired to sing songs from Jerry Herman's musical about Israel, *Milk and Honey* (1961).

When I returned home in late August, Grandma Mary phoned me constantly to see what I'd be doing next. One morning, she phoned around 7 a.m., asking, "Are you asleep?"

I answered, "Not anymore. Why do you ask?"

Said she, "I didn't want to wake you."

Also awaiting me was another writing offer. It was from an Algonquin regular, Penny Singleton. Penny had been the voice of wife "Jane" on *The Jetsons* (1962) and was best known for playing Blondie in twenty-eight movies based on the Chic Young comic strip. Despite the ditzy characters she often played, Penny was a shrewd businesswoman who was the first female president of an AFL-CIO union, specifically the American Guild of Variety Artists (AGVA). She spearheaded the first strike of Radio City Rockettes,[2] greatly improving their working conditions (I would have loved to have watched that picket line). Penny admired my work and made many introductions for me. This eventually led to her offering me a writing assignment in Baltimore: a tribute to the AFL-CIO, the labor union, titled *A Salute To Labor*. Starring Phyllis Diller, Melba Moore, Theodore Bikel, and Penny (who also produced it), the event played September 1, 1975. It was the beginning of countless benefits for which I would write continuity. I had a wonderful weekend accompanying Penny on the train from New York, driving Penny in a car float at the Baltimore Labor Day Parade (the only time I've ever felt like a Rose Bowl attraction), and learning a new skill. You see, Penny's brother, Barney McNulty, was also there. Known as the "Cue Card King," Barney was acknowledged as "the first person to use cue cards on TV." He'd flashed—cards that is—for Milton Berle, Lucille Ball, Jack Benny, Monty Hall, and The Smothers Brothers.[3] In fact, he'd saved Bob Hope's life this way, according to *The Los Angeles Times*:

> "The bomb in the Saigon hotel, Gen. William C. Westmoreland later said, was meant to kill Bob Hope and his entertain-the-troops troupe. But Hope's motorcade arrived 10 minutes after the bomb exploded. Members of the group credited their tardiness to the cue-card man, who was delayed in moving Hope's 5,000 pounds of cardboard cheat sheets. When the comedian learned about his

Penny Singleton in her movie days. Photo courtesy of Stephen Cox.

narrow escape, Hope told the cue-card man: "Saved by the idiot cards again."[4]

Suddenly, I was there in Baltimore, jotting out—and holding up—cue cards with the man who'd virtually invented them. I was learning from a nonpareil, the forefather of the teleprompter. Our teamwork held up so well that afterwards, I stayed in touch with Barney, watching him flash at several other TV tapings. *A Salute to Labor* was one of my most unique theatrical experiences, helping create a benefit for labor unions where no one noticed that this writer was non-union.

I'd soon be writing more full-length shows; but first I concentrated on the research that would inform and refine my lyric work through my career: exploring the life and lyrics of Lorenz Hart.

Chapter 20: *Getting to the Hart of Things*

The last moments in the life of Lorenz (Larry) Hart were recounted in haunting detail by his sister-in-law, Dorothy Hart:

> "Then suddenly, at exactly nine o'clock on the evening of November 22 [1943], the lights went out. The war blackout [had] darkened the hospital corridor. And at that moment someone exited from Larry's room and shook his head. We could barely see him.
>
> "He's gone.'
>
> "This is a moment I can't forget, but also can't quite remember; I was in a merciful state of shock that remained for a long time."[1]

This is an excerpt from Mrs. Hart's book, *Thou Swell, Thou Witty: The Life and Lyrics of Lorenz Hart* (1976). The era was World War Two, when the brilliant Broadway lyricist ended his downward spiral. He passed away at the age of 47 at Doctor's Hospital, New York City. By coincidence, this is the same hospital where I was born in 1951. Few lyricists have expressed themselves with greater joy or deeper sadness than Larry Hart. As researcher for this book, I felt almost like a detective deciphering this man's life through the clues and emotions evident in his unforgettable lyrics.

Erudite, hilarious, and innovative, he was a trailblazer in his profession. He had been the epitome of enthusiasm in his youth, but gradually suffered a spiritual decline. Under five feet and self-effacing, he hit emotional bottom through alcoholism, one of several facts that struck intense chords in me. Meeting a range of his friends during my research, I sometimes felt like I knew Hart personally. Yet, it became hard to separate truth from fantasized nostalgia. Many of these friends claimed that Hart called out for them on his deathbed. If everyone who made this claim were telling the truth, Hart would still be alive calling out for them.

Then there were private issues about Hart that were not completely clear. Nowadays, it's commonly chronicled that Larry Hart was gay, and the fact seems indelible: Richard Rodgers made substantial comments about it after Hart's death. Still, for whatever reasons, Dorothy Hart in her book—and in general—insisted Hart was otherwise. Several of his friends backed up Mrs. Hart's assertion based on their personal knowledge. Though far from proof, they mentioned how he proposed marriage more than once to

Richard Rodgers and Lorenz Hart. Photo courtesy of Rodgers and Hammerstein: an Imagem Company.

his favorite leading lady, Vivienne Segal (*Pal Joey, I Married an Angel*, 1938). Another source of contradiction was Nanette Guilford, a former soprano at the Metropolitan Opera. When we spoke, she maintained Hart was deeply in love and proposed to her too. It's impossible to know the exact psychology of this very complicated man, but there's no doubt his heart was broken many times. An unquestionable nadir was the death of his doting mother Frieda, by all accounts a very sweet lady who loved him unconditionally. It can't be overlooked that he suffered inconsolable depression and died (on November 22nd) soon after Frieda herself passed away in April of the same year. Perhaps he would have had a much longer and easier life in this era of gay marriage. Perhaps, too, his depression was exacerbated by a life in the theatre where he was constantly reminded of beautiful people living happily ever after—at least on stage. With most of Hart's intimates now gone, one can only speculate.

Researching Hart was tough at times for me: his alcoholic decline reminded me of my father's bouts with alcohol. The research also reminded me, yet again, of the flukiness of show business. Hart's professional break-through was largely due to a set of lucky circumstances. His composer/collaborator, Richard Rodgers, was just about to quit show business. After years of theatrical letdowns, Rodgers seriously weighed an offer to sell babies' underwear. Then, out of the blue, Rodgers was recommended to be composer on an original revue that would benefit Broadway's presti-gious Theatre Guild. After a somewhat reluctant audition, Rodgers was offered the job, with mixed feelings, since the revue was only slated for two performances (on Sundays). Then, there was the matter that a lyricist other than Hart was supposed to work on the show. Fortunately, Rodgers convinced the presenters that they should use Hart instead. The resultant revue, *The Garrick Gaieties* (1925), was a smash beyond anyone's expecta-tions. It introduced the standard "Manhattan" and had an extended run of 211 performances. Rodgers and Hart never lacked for work after that.

There's at least one other fluke worth mentioning in regard to this team. One of their earliest credits was writing a Varsity Show at Columbia University, *Fly With Me* (1920). Though most of the songs featured lyrics by Hart, Rodgers wrote a single song with another lyricist. That lyricist was Oscar Hammerstein II, who years later would become Rodgers' other great collaborator. The title of their song: "There's Always Room For One More."

Dorothy Hart stayed at the Algonquin for long periods while the research was underway on the biography. I became acquainted with some noteworthy friends of hers. Among them was Edith Meiser, a tall, imposing actress/writer who'd been in Cole Porter's *Let's Face It!* (1941; side by side with Vivian Vance and Eve Arden) and several Rodgers and Hart shows, including *The Garrick Gaieties*. Indeed, it was Meiser who was originally slated to write the lyrics for *The Garrick Gaieties*. As recounted by Meiser:

> "We were already in rehearsal . . . Dick [Rodgers] was living with his parents . . . I went uptown across to West End Avenue to Dr. Rodger's apartment . . . There was an enormous grand piano in the living room. Dick said, 'Well, I'll play you some of the things I wrote for a Columbia University show.'
>
> ". . . I wasn't impressed . . . Then he played 'Manhattan' and I flipped. I told him I would write the lyrics. I went back to the theatre and

said to some of the youngsters who were rehearsing, 'I have found the boy!'

"Dick came down to rehearsal and played 'Manhattan' for them. They all flipped as I had. Then Dick said, 'I generally work with a guy named Larry Hart. Would you let him try a few of the ideas that we worked out?' And a few days later Dick brought in the lyrics. Well, I did have the sense to know when I was outclassed. Those lyrics were so absolutely sensational." [2]

Edith Meiser did manage to elbow out Larry Hart on one song in *The Garrick Gaieties*: she wrote lyrics to Rodger's music on "An Old-Fashioned Girl." That pluckiness remained in evidence when forty-eight years later, she and Mrs. Hart came to see *Charlotte Sweet*. She obviously had a good time, but dashed off a letter to me with recommendations on how she would rewrite the show. She zeroed in on a character based upon Mrs. Hart: Charlotte Sweet's cold-sensitive mother, sung about but never seen, who suffocates under the weight of her insulated underwear. Meiser wrote:

"May I, as an old 'China Hand,' make a few suggestions . . . Please—please don't have Charlotte lose her mother—ever—even if she froze to death. It's not only sad—it slows down the action."

She then offered some slightly convoluted ideas on what she would do with the scene, gently adding:

"Dear Michael—please don't feel these suggestions are downputting. I have in my time nudged Cole Porter, Ralph Benatsky [who wrote *The White Horse Inn*, 1931]—I translated some of his operettas for him—and darling Larry [Hart]. Not to mention the many years worth of changes I did to Conan Dolye's Sherlock Holmes, and lots & lots of others."

Reading the note, I felt like I was in excellent company.

Additional members of Mrs. Hart's circle were several of the creators of the musical, *Man of La Mancha*, not all of whom got along. Two who did get along were *Man of La Mancha's* director, Albert ("Albie") Marre and his wife, actress Joan Diener (the original Aldonza opposite Richard Kiley's Don Quixote.) Marre and Diener first met when he directed the Broadway hit, *Kismet* (1953). Only nineteen at the time, Diener was one of its original stars opposite the quintessential Broadway leading man, Alfred Drake. Diener's three and a half octave voice was as phenomenal as her buxom figure. At

Dorothy Hart and Michael.

the age of 62, she still looked toothsome—playing Aldonza again (this time opposite Raúl Juliá)—in a Broadway revival of *Man of La Mancha*. Once when I dined with Mrs. Hart and the Marres, Diener proudly described how every day she swam outdoors in the nude—to stay in shape—and had voice lessons (I presumed at separate times). The swimming was also how she retained her perpetual tan, to such an extent she could have changed the name of her role from Aldonza to "All-bronze-a."

Through Mrs. Hart, I was constantly hearing about Albie Marre's latest projects, some with Diener. His early track record as a director was enviable, including such Broadway hits as *The Chalk Garden* (1955), *Time Remembered*, and *Milk and Honey*. Still, during the time I knew the Marres, he was going through a professional slump (then again, everyone should have the kind of professional slump where they accrue royalties from *Man of La Mancha*).

Among his later-day projects were: *Winnie* (London, 1988; not about Winnie the Pooh, but a singing Winston Churchill); *The Prince of Central Park* (1989, which ran for four performances on Broadway); an ill-fated musical version of *Time Remembered* (not the unproduced version I co-wrote); and *Chu Chem*, probably the only musical ever to cover the timeless topic of Chinese Jews. Marre directed *Chu Chem twice*: once when it closed out-of-town in 1966, and a revival, twenty-three years later (1989) that also lost a fortune. You have to give Marre points for perseverance, though it's hard to fathom why anyone would revive a show with *Chu Chem*'s history. Just before the original Philadelphia tryout, actress Molly Picon quit—after her role was severely reduced—replaced by Yiddish theatre veteran, Henrietta Jacobson. On opening night in Philly, Jacobson faced the audience saying, "There was a song here, but you'll be better off without it."[3] The Marres didn't have much better luck on subsequent shows they did together. *Cry For Us All* (1970) lived up to its title, capped by the final scene with Diener. Playing the wife of a ruthless New York politician, circa 1890, Diener was supposed to break her neck falling down a flight of stairs. The fall was convincingly staged, yet her character somehow found the strength to sit up and sing a final showy aria—just before expiring. The show expired too, after nine performances. Not so fortunate was the daftly titled *Home Sweet Homer* (1976), based on Homer's *The Odyssey*, in which Diener played patient wife Penelope opposite Yul Brynner's Odysseus. That musical had the distinction of being the first show to open and close on the same Sunday matinee. Afterwards, Diener remained Marre's patient wife.

Mrs. Hart's other chum from *Man of La Mancha* was its librettist, Dale Wasserman. He based the libretto on his teleplay *I, Don Quixote*, broadcast in 1959 as part of CBS anthology *DuPont Show of the Month*. According to Mrs. Hart, when the musical was being written, the *Man of La Mancha* team first offered the role of Sancho Panza, Quixote's sidekick, to her husband, Teddy Hart. Teddy wasn't available, and the role went instead to Irving Jacobson, brother of Henrietta Jacobson (*Chu Chem*), who had a much longer run than his sister.

Dale Wasserman was like a Jewish frontiersman whom George C. Scott might have played. Orphaned at the age of nine, he was self-educated, rising from what he described as "a wayward youth, working odd jobs" like lumberjack, merchant mariner, and short order cook. He moved from place to place, riding the rails, and reading books he'd steal from one library then return to another further down the tracks. He eventually also took jobs in the Arts, finally attaining sizable success as a writer for television, movies, and theatre.[4] Along the way, he didn't mince words, sometimes feuding with the Marres and other collaborators. Among these collaborators was John Huston, who directed Wasserman's screenplay, *A Walk With Love and Death* (1969). Wasserman was appalled at the nepotism of Huston's casting the lead role with the director's teenage daughter, who happened to be future Oscar winner, Angelica Huston.[5]

Of all Mrs. Hart's friends, I got to know Wasserman best. One reason: he stayed at the Algonquin. Besides *Man of La Mancha*, he struck gold with his adaptation of Ken Kesey's novel *One Flew Over the Cuckoo's Nest* (1962).

Dale Wasserman. Photo courtesy of Martha N. Wasserman.

Giving hope to all dejected playwrights, the play version at first failed but at last succeeded six years later. David Merrick produced the 1963 Broadway premiere, starring Kirk Douglas, which garnered poor reviews and closed after eighty-two performances. In 1969, a revised version with William Devane became a smash in San Francisco and moved off-Broadway where it ran 1,025 performances: more than ten times as long as before.[6] This helped propel the movie version, produced by Kirk's son, Michael Douglas, though Wasserman didn't write the screenplay. Then in 2001, Wasserman was back at the Algonquin for the hit Broadway production (with Gary Sinese) that won the Tony Award for Best Revival.

There's another reason I got to know Wasserman so well. In all my years of meeting famous playwrights at the Algonquin, he was one of two who believed in me enough to ask me to collaborate on a show (the other playwright was Mary Chase). It was extremely fulfilling working alongside such masters and becoming part of circles I considered my theatre families.

Not so gratifying was the state of my immediate family. My mother's life was something of a mess. In the aftermath of my father's death, our

Mom and Grandma Mary in happier times.

home in Hewlett had been sold, never to be revisited—it was too painful being there. My mother moved to an apartment on East 79th Street and Madison Avenue and, by 1975, had remarried. The less said about that marriage, the bitter—I mean the better. At that time, most of my father's estate was depleted, and the one happy ending for everyone involved was the divorce in 1977.

Nonetheless, there were ample compensations in my own life. Through recommendations, I received new and diversified theatre opportunities, such as general managing the Elizabeth Keen Dance Company at the Roundabout Theatre. It was during this time that I started collaborating with Gerald Jay Markoe on musicals, the first being the *Time Remembered* adaptation. Visting his apartment, where he harbored tropical birds and reptiles, I'd met an eccentric match for my writing skills while ducking flying cockatoos.

What's more, even if it was a difficult time to visit my mother, there was plenty of family to see at the Algonquin. My grandmother frequently hung out with her siblings and their families. She had an enormous walk-in closet where she horded gifts for everyone. For instance, it was there that you'd find a dozen billowy housedresses, which she snapped up while

Cable Address: ASCAP New York
TWX 710.581/0084

American Society of Composers, Authors and Publishers
ASCAP Building—One Lincoln Plaza, New York, N.Y. 10023 Area Code (212) 595-3050

Walter Wager   September 15, 1976
Director of Public Relations   For Immediate Release

ASCAP TOASTS NEW BOOK ON LORENZ HART

A celebrity-packed audience of Broadway and Hollywood star performers and songwriters gathered at Sardi's Belasco Room today (5:30 P.M.) for a cocktail party at which the American Society of Composers, Authors and Publishers honored the late Lorenz Hart, and the new book about his life and lyrics titled "Thou Swell, Thou Witty." ASCAP President Stanley Adams, himself a noted lyricist, was the host at the gathering which attracted such major songwriters as Arthur Schwartz and Howard Dietz, Burton Lane, Yip Harburg, Harold Rome and Lorenz Hart's distinguished collaborator, Mr. Richard Rodgers.

Luminaries such as Debbie Reynolds, Tammy Grimes, Myrna Loy, Constance Carpenter, Ray Heatherton, Tamara Geva, Joan Bennett, Jack Weston, Linda Hopkins, Christine Andreas and others who appeared in some of the magnificent Rodgers and Hart musicals gathered to toast publication of the handsomely illustrated Harper & Row volume by Dorothy Hart - sister-in-law of the late "little giant" of theatre lyrics.

Excerpt from invitation to ASCAP party for the book, Thou Swell, Thou Witty: The Life and Lyrics of Lorenz Hart.

the supply lasted. That way, she'd have extras for her sisters and spares for herself. She also stocked up on designer purses that she gave to friends, family, and celebrities. Recipients sometimes had to remind Grandma she had given them the same purse two or three times before.

The greatest gift I received during this period was to be associated with Dorothy Hart's beautiful book, as edited by Joan Kahn, when it was finally published in 1976. Chockfull of lyrics, recollections, and illuminating photographs, it was a godsend for musical theatre devotees. Greeted by excellent reviews, it sold well for Harper & Row and was given one helluva publication party by ASCAP at Sardi's. In attendance that night were many legends of Broadway and cabaret. It was also one of the last big gatherings of Rodgers and Hart alumni.

As if this weren't enough icing on the cake, I was overcome by emotions, when I read this sentence in the acknowledgments of the book:

> "And last, very special thanks to Michael Colby, whose enthusiasm and dedication to the theatre are so reminiscent of the young Larry Hart's."[7]

As if cued by Mrs. Hart's words, just around this time, an off-off-Broadway theatre made me an offer to write lyrics and libretto for a full-length new musical they would produce. This would be my first major stepping-stone as a writer of musical theatre.

ACKNOWLEDGMENTS

My thanks are due to Mel Shauer, Sig Herzig, Gene Zukor, Dick Leonard, Bob Gersten, Bob Lewine, Fred Nolen, Florence Weingart, Max Wilk, Barbara Kennedy and ASCAP.

[Edited section: Mrs. Hart acknowledges other people, including her son, Lorenz Hart II, Edith Meiser, Richard Rodgers, Vivienne Segal, Josh Logan, and Nanette Guilford.]

And lastly, very special thanks to Michael Colby, whose enthusiasm and dedication to the theatre are so reminiscent of the young Larry Hart's.

Edited acknowledgments in Dorothy Hart's Thou Swell, Thou Witty: The Life and Lyrics of Lorenz Hart *(1976).*

Chapter 21: *Somet'ing Special*

Was I being misled? That's what I wondered during my meeting after contacting Jim Payne, the administrative director of the Thirteenth Street Repertory Theatre. Among the hits produced by this off-off-Broadway company were: *Line* (1974), a long-running Israel Horovitz play; and the musical, *Boy Meets Boy* (1957), a Fred Astaire/Ginger Rogers type musical where both sweethearts happened to be male. Jim Payne made me believe the company was seriously interested in producing not one but *two* of my musicals: *Where There's a Will*; and *Golden Dreams,* composed Gerald Jay Markoe, based on a Washington Irving story. I was ecstastic!

Then Payne did a complete about-face. Rejecting those shows, he asked if I'd instead work on another musical. He claimed he'd definitely produce this other show, except it had to be completely rewritten. I answered, "Ahhh . . . sure." The show was *North Atlantic*, a spoof of Rodgers and Hammerstein musicals set in Eskimo land, the other side of the world from *South Pacific* (1949). The project was the brainchild of composer James Fradrich, who'd done musical arrangements for *Boy Meets Boy.*

Within two months, I got together with James Fradrich, overhauled the extant material, and wrote a new libretto, incorporating every Rodgers and Hammerstein cliché I could summon. The heroine was a cockeyed optimist named Honey Snodgrass who'd come to the frigid North Atlantic region to teach cute illiterate Eskimo students through a song. Numbers such as "Someting Special" were takeoffs of Rodgers and Hammerstein standards—e.g. "Something Wonderful" (1951) and "Bali Ha'" (1949)—with Fradrich's evocative tunes and my lyrics such as: "Mos' persons float in a sinking kayak off in da centah of a los' lagoon."[1] There would be an Agnes de Mille-type ballet with strangers falling in love across a crowded room, a hoedown with a prize pig, and a nun dancing over mountaintops. Everything seemed to fall into place fast. Jim Payne gave a tentative green light. Then, he and James Fradrich had an unexpected falling out, and plans were off. I learned to always expect the unexpected, especially *after* getting an offer to have a musical produced.

Still, by this time, I was too excited to allow *chorus interruptus*. With the skills I'd learned at the Ostrow Musical Theatre Lab, I determined to present *North Atlantic* myself. I swiftly contacted various theatres and agreed on a co-production with the Gene Frankel Media Center. I raised half the capitalization from the number one source used by many people starting out in the Arts: family. My grandparents, the Bodnes, established a fund to be matched by the Frankel Media Center, headed by Gene Frankel. Frankel arranged an Actors Equity-approved showcase run, which meant a shoestring budget, rehearsing three weeks, and playing twelve performances.

Gene Frankel. Photo courtesy of Gail Thacker, Gene Frankel Theatre.

Frankel was the chain-smoking, ground-breaking teacher/director/producer, whose credits included the Tony-Award nominated *Indians* (1969, with Stacey Keach) and *The Blacks* (1961), the longest-running off-Broadway play of its time, which featured James Earl Jones, Louis Gossett, Jr., Cicely Tyson, and Maya Angelou. Dapperly dressed in a jacket and tie, like a grizzled James Mason, Frankel's presence could be heard down the hall; he was a percussion section of throat-clearing and hacking cough. Yet he was a gently guiding force, never imposing on the creative process, while instructive and supportive when consulted. It was a fortuitous beginning; I would learn, not all producers are so unobtrusive.

Auditions commenced at the Frankel Center on East 63rd Street. First there was an Equity general call, open to anyone and anything, union, non-union, animal, vegetable, or alien—all of which seemed to turn up. The judging panel were James Fradrich and I, director Clinton Atkinson (a veteran of off-Broadway musicals), and choreographer Dennis Dennehy (whose show, *The Lieutenant*, 1975, had been Tony Award-nominated for Best Musical). I was about to meet some actors who would become lifetime friends, and others who were like oddballs out of a Mel Brooks movie.

One girl belted out "There's a Kind of Hush All Over the World" (1967) like Ethel Merman on acid. A Jack LaLanne type, whose chief credit was posing for *Playgirl*, warbled—ever so wobbly—all seven-minutes of the "Soliloquy" (1945) from *Carousel*; listeners understood why Billy Bigelow commits suicide shortly after the number. Moments later, a fellow resembling a derelict walked in and began to recite, not sing, an original composition: "I am George Washington Adams Jefferson Jackson Lincoln

Roosevelt Truman Kennedy ...." That was enough. We politely interjected that we needed to move on to the next audition. Yet, several auditions later, he snuck back in, saying, "I must inform you I'm on a break from Bellevue but didn't want to miss this opportunity. Do you think there's a chance I'll be cast, because I have to let them know?"

My succinct response was, "Well, please don't plan around our show."

Through all these wacky auditions, our panel managed to keep respectful faces. Yet toward the end of the process, someone did us in. A statuesque, slickly dressed girl handed us her glossy, then confidently took stage center. She proceeded to do an imitation of Chita Rivera performing "All That Jazz" (1975) with her eyes batting like fly swats and her hips practically swiveling into outer space. Still, we tried desperately to keep a straight face. Then, Clint pointed out a typo on her resumé, and we all lost it. It said that in the musical *Cabaret,* this undulating wind-up doll had played "Sally *Bowels.*" We imagined her auditioning around town and having everyone notice her prominent "Bowels" credit. After she gave us an exit look like "How dare you not offer me a role immediately," we were giddy for the rest of the afternoon.

Having sorted out the mixed nuts, our final callbacks were at the Algonquin Hotel. *North Atlantic* was the first among many shows to use the Algonquin annex for callbacks and as a rehearsal space. The annex was a two-floor townhouse-like structure appended to the hotel with its own exit to the street. For decades before, it had been used to store family and hotel belongings, including pileups of furniture. An unconfirmed rumor is that, during the Prohibition, the annex was the setting of an Algonquin speakeasy. What I can confirm is that the annex was thoroughly overhauled on the occasion of *North Atlantic.* The second floor was largely cleared away, with some furniture stacked on the sidelines. That left two main rehearsal rooms, including a large room with a solid floor for dance. People crossed a narrow hall abutting offices and the resident tailor's workplace, and then climbed up a stairway to the dual space.

It was in the annex that I met the actress we would cast as Honey Snodgrass. She had made a trip from Washington DC at the request of Clinton Atkinson, who'd directed her before and thought she was "someting special." Yet when she walked in, that windy cold day, what I saw was a disheveled, lanky brunette with prominent eyeglasses, like on a secretary from the Algonquin office. She wasn't the Shirley Jones type I envisioned to play the quintessential Rodgers and Hammerstein heroine. But then Susan Bigelow pulled off her glasses and sang, and it was a revelation, like watching an American equivalent of Julie Andrews. That audition

Lori Tan Chinn, Susan Bigelow, and Debra Moreno in North Atlantic *(1977). Photo: Mike Zetter.*

was one of my two favorite kinds, either: (1) where someone is exactly what you had in mind for a role; or (2) as in Susan's case, when someone arrives and redefines the role in their own wondrous ways. Subsequently, she would go on to play Nellie Forbush in the Lincoln Centre revival of *South Pacific* (1987). Plus, Susan's sidekick in the show—Lori Tan Chinn, as the All American soubrette, Melanie Fong—went on to play Bloody Mary opposite Glenn Close in TV's *South Pacific* (2001).

Rehearsals at the Algonquin became a love-fest, not only because the show was fun and the rehearsal locale a historical one, but—bottom line—everyone was well-fed. Supervised by Grandma Mary and the Algonquin chef, sumptuous Algonquin meals were served to the show's cast and staff during our lunch break. Nobody missed a single day of rehearsal. This would become a tradition when my shows rehearsed at the hotel. Even well-known actors who weren't in my shows would show up at lunchtime.

Adding to the cheer, we rehearsed during the Christmas season. Thereupon, the Algonquin was decked with boughs of holly and the lobby populated with the season's stage stars, such as John Gielgud (*No Man's Land*, 1976), Jonathan Pryce (*Comedians*, 1977), and George C. Scott (*Sly Fox*, 1976). To augment the holiday spirit, I pulled out an artificial Christmas tree and decorated it, helped by cast member Julie Kurnitz (*Minnie's Boys*, 1970), naturally one of the few other Jews on the production.

Scenes from North Atlantic *(1977): with Susan Bigelow, Stratton Walling, Mark Manley, Lori Tan Chinn, Rick Emery, James Clark, Ted Williams, Marilyn Hiratzka, and Mary Ann Taylor. Photos: Mike Zetter.*

What practically no one at rehearsals knew was that, outside of the show, I was beset by strife, in particular a very troubled mother in the middle of divorce proceedings. I often rushed to her side to help placate her through this rough period. There was corollary upheaval throughout my family, with my grandparents taking care of all the complicated and costly legal matters. What a welcome respite it was to enter the carefree world of working on *North Atlantic*, where all I needed to worry about were rewrites, providing an optimum production on a minimum budget, and occasional cutthroat critics.

The buzz on the show must have been good because, as we began performances at the Frankel Media Center, we were jam-packed. The reception was excellent, too. *Show Business* gave us an award as Outstanding Theatre Production of 1977. John Madden of *Variety* wanted to break the paper's policy of not reviewing showcases—and write a glowing notice—but he couldn't get permission. Henry Hewes, then President of the New York Drama Critics Circle, sent a note stating, "It was not only the best of the three musicals I saw last week, it was the best of the year" (it helped that the hits, *Annie* and *Side by Side by Sondheim,* hadn't yet opened: both in April 1997). Consequently, I met with quite a number of Broadway producers who were seriously interested. One producer, David Klein, actually optioned the show for Broadway. Not that there weren't some naysayers (it's the smattering of bad reviews that will forever weigh on my brain, like an anvil). In any case, *North Atlantic's* prospects proved transitory—announced

North Atlantic *Company and cast: (first row) Ted Williams, Mark Manley, Mary Ann Taylor, Marilyn Hiratzka, and Rick Emery. (second row) James Fradrich, Lori Tan Chinn, Dennis Hearn, Susan Bigelow, Debra Moreno, stage manger Rena Rockoff, and Stratton Walling. (back row) Michael C., Svetlana McLee, Dennis Dennehy, William Brohn, Julie Kurnitz, Alvin Lum, and pianist Robert Plowman. Photo: Mike Zetter.*

several times as heading for Broadway, but fading into the sunset instead. Moreover, this would be the first of several musicals for me where treasured memories and lasting friendships have been the lifelong compensation when other plans never panned out.

The post-closing blues of such productions can be something fierce. I visited the empty, once-again darkened Algonquin annex, fighting spans of melancholy. Fortunately, I was soon busy again. When I worked at St. Clement's, I met director Allan Albert, who'd heard of my research for Dorothy Hart and my encyclopedic knowledge of musical theatre history. Albert became the artistic director of the esteemed Berkshire Theatre Festival, in Stockbridge, Massachusetts, from 1977-1979. He hired me as his musical theatre consultant for two seasons there. His ambitious summer seasons included plays by William Inge, Saul Bellow, Lillian Helman, and Sinclair Lewis, plus original shows developed by the Proposition, an acclaimed improvisational group he directed with such alumni as Jane Curtin and Henry Winkler.

As musical theatre consultant, I helped clear the rights to the first revivals in decades of two major musicals. One was Rodgers and Hart's original version of *I Married An Angel* with Phyllis Newman. The other musical revival was *Let 'Em Eat Cake* (1933)— the sequel to *Of Thee I Sing* (1931)— starring Tony Roberts and Arnold Stang, with a score by George and Ira Gershwin and book by George S. Kaufman and Morrie Ryskind. Little did

Anna McNeeley and Brenda O'Brien sing "The Social Ladder" in Animal Crackers *at Goodspeed. Photo: Diane Sobolewsky.*

I know then that I myself would collaborate, in a sense, with Kaufman and Ryskind. It happened when composer Albin Konopka and I wrote a new song, "The Social Ladder," for a revival of *Animal Crackers* (supplementing a score by Bert Kalmar and Harry Ruby). This vintage (1928) Marx Brothers' musical, with a Kaufman/Ryskind libretto, played the Goodspeed Opera House and later transferred to the Paper Mill Playhouse. It was in the Paper Mill version that future Tony-winner, Kristin Chenoweth, got her Equity card.

Finally, I felt like I was coming into my own. It started with contributing a Maxwell House mug as a prop for one musical, and then I was being sought for what I could bring to the table. Though there were always people who only thought of me as a grandchild of the former owners of the Algonquin, it was uplifting to feel like I was something more than just the "Algonquin Kid."

Chapter 22: *Presents From the Past*

Producer Harry Rigby with Alice Faye of Good News *revival (1974). Photo courtesy of Photofest.*

It is said that musicals of the past had more "hummable" music. I'm not sure about that. Still, you didn't have to worry about playing their original cast albums in front of the kids, as you might today with *The Book of Mormon* (2011) or *Hedwig and the Angry Inch* (1998; revived 2014). Musicals of the past were a more innocent breed that nonetheless included some of the most timeless material ever created. One frequent visitor at the Algonquin specialized in musicals of the past: producer Harry Rigby.

Rigby, who looked like an aging sprite, sort of a Peter Pan back from Shangri La, produced such nostalgic shows as *Sugar Babies* (1979) and revivals of *No, No, Nanette* and *Irene* (1973). Often the stars of his shows would stay at the Algonquin during runs, among them Mickey Rooney, Ruby Keeler, John Payne, and Alice Faye. Rigby liked my work and met with me several times about writing a show for him. In particular, he wanted to develop a musical thriller based on Fu Manchu, the evil genius created by writer Sax Rohmer (borrowing the title of a hit song from *No, No, Nanette*, I dubbed the show, "Tea For Fu"). One night, Rigby invited me to join him at Joe Allen's, a favorite theatre hangout. I arrived to discover his other guests included his stars, Debbie Reynolds and tap dancer extraordinaire Ann Miller. I felt like I'd been conveyed to an MGM commissary. While Debbie Reynolds was gracious, it was Ann Miller who monopolized the dinner conversation. I'd heard stories about Miller's saying unintentional punchlines. For instance, when asked what she was doing for Passover, she reportedly answered, "Sorry, I don't do game shows." Harry wanted me to hear another of her ripostes, announcing, "Ann, tell Michael your big complaint about the show *Cats*." She responded, "Oh, just that it has too many pussies." She went on to add, "What I really want to try is a Stephen Sondheim show. Nobody would believe what I could do with *Sweeney Todd*." Immediately I envisioned her as Mrs. Lovett executing shuffles and double wings to assist Sweeney slicing throats. Actually, a few years later she got her wish, praiseworthily playing Carlotta Champion in a Paper Mill Playhouse revival of Sondheim's *Follies*.

Like Harry Rigby, I, too, participated in the resurrection of vintage musicals. I'd already begun through my work on the Lorenz Hart biography and revivals at the Berkshire Theatre Festival. Then, from the late 1970s onward, I assisted at several non-profit organizations geared to restore past musicals. At times, this was like Don Quixote tilting against amplified windmills in an advancing age of Rock music.

The first of these organizations was the National Musical Theatre in 1978, headed by elegant actress/singer Paulette Attie, who stated, "This city has magnificent repertory companies, when it comes to ballet and opera, but there is absolutely nothing to keep alive the art of the American musical theatre."[1] Paulette's dream was to first present a revival of the Gershwins' *Strike Up the Band*, till she struck out at raising money. The most successful of Paulette's fundraisers was a party at Sardi's, with a sale of memorabilia signed by such greats as Eartha Kitt, E. Y. Harburg, and Imogene Coca (who attended) and Ethel Merman and Fred Astaire (who were otherwise occupied). Unfortunately, Paulette's organization never got much farther than presenting Sardi's parties.

Michael hawking souvenirs at Paulette Attie's fundraiser at Sardi's; old sheet music from Floradora.

Next, I became a member of the Board of Directors for The Bandwagon, a similar organization spearheaded by Jerry Bell, an ebullient dancer/singer/bartender. The company's first planned revival was *Floradora*, a musical that had been the rage of London and New York back in 1899, spotlighting the beauteous Floradora Sextette of dancers.[2]

One might question the modern appeal of such a choice. One might also wonder how to squeeze what was originally an elephantine production into a peanut-size showcase theatre. Nevertheless, topnotch rising artists were attracted to the organization and its goals. It was through the Bandwagon I met the likes of Stuart Ross (who later created *Forever Plaid*, 1990), Evans Haile (a musical director who became a major regional artistic director), Sam Rudy (the Broadway press agent), and Glen Kelly (the musical arranger who later helped Mel Brooks develop the score to *The Producers*, 2005).

Yet most of these names parted ways with the Bandwagon for various reasons. I, along with several founding members, resigned in 1980 because we felt the quality of casting and production values might be *too* compromised by financial issues. To his credit, artistic director Jerry Bell and the Bandwagon Company did ultimately mount *Floradora* and other showcase revivals. Plus, they presented first-rate fundraisers with Broadways luminaries like Helen Gallagher, Jerry Herman, Nancy Dussault, and newcomer Nell Carter (Nell arrived between rehearsals of a new musical being workshopped called *Dreamgirls*).

Perhaps the best outcome of the Bandwagon was that it motivated musician Bill Tynes, a former member, to gather many of the same people and found his own company. This new organization, The New Amsterdam Theatre Company (NATC), would indeed achieve the goal to revitalize

Bill Tynes, founder of the New Amsterdam Theatre Company. From Ethan Mordden's obituary in The New York Native, *January 1987. Courtesy of Clairee Tynes.*

vintage American musicals and operettas as an ongoing series. Bill named the organization after the theatre on 42nd Street, once operated by Florenz Ziegfeld (and now owned by the Disney Company). Bill planned to have NATC present past shows as staged readings with Broadway actors, a full ensemble, and a complete orchestra playing the original orchestrations (or reconstruction thereof). In fact, NATC was acknowledged as a model for future such companies, including Lost Musicals (London), 42nd Street Moon (San Francisco), and Encores! (New York).

Prior to the NATC, there were only semblances of this format. There were individual concerts; and there was a short-lived series at Manhattan's Town Hall, with stars and a small band, that closed before its third scheduled show due to insufficient box office sales. Yet, NATC really set the style. As Greg MacKellan, co-founder of 42nd Street Moon has affirmed, citing NATC as his model:

> "They did these concerts at Town Hall and they staged them—everyone in tuxes and evening gowns, everyone holding books, and I think of that as the first time that some of these old shows actually existed in a form that could finally be presented . . . This really is a new genre . . . The basic reason why we do a concert musical…is in not having to finance some enormous production."[3]

On May 25-26, 1981, my grandparents donated the use of the Stratford Suite (connected rooms 307 and 306) at the Algonquin for the New Amsterdam's Theatre Company's first major fundraiser. The SRO audience spilled into the hallways.

The Algonquin was the perfect setting, as visitors felt idyllically transported back in time via tunes from 1926's *Peggy-Ann* (by Rodgers and Hart), 1927's *Show Boat* (by Kern and Hammerstein), and 1943's *One Touch of Venus* (Kurt Weill and Ogden Nash). The exceptional Evans Haile musical directed at the piano, with Bill Tynes on violin, accompanying a delightful small cast singing in close harmony. Narrating was Broadway veteran Paula Laurence, who'd played opposite Mary Martin in *One Touch of Venus* and Ethel Merman in *Something For the Boys* (1943, a Cole Porter show). Recreating her songs from *One Touch of Venus,* Paula was so spectacular that I apprised Ben Bagley the next day; he signed her to record the songs for the first time on his *Kurt Weill Revisited* album (1981).

Within several months, Bill Tynes had made his dream a reality. On Monday, November 23, 1981, with a budget of $5,000, the New Amsterdam Theatre Company originated at Town Hall with a one-performance event: a concert version of the operetta, *The New Moon* (1928), by Sigmund

Holiday card from Paula Laurence, pictured with her husband, producer Charles Bowden.

Romberg and Oscar Hammerstein II. Unlike at Encores!, where some old scripts were tweaked, the decision was made—for most shows—just to abbreviate, bridging script gaps and scenic changes with a short narration delivered by stars. For *The New Moon*, the narrators were Oscar-winner Estelle Parson and Alan Jones, who sang leads in such films as *Show Boat* (1936) and *A Night at the Opera* (1935). Performers included Broadway's John Reardon, Meg Bussert, and Debbie Gravitte, a large chorus (the New York Choral Society), and The Riverside Symphony Orchestra. Given such a deluxe treatment, it was no wonder that songs "Stouthearted Men," "Lover, Come Back to Me," and "Softly, as in a Morning Sunrise" received rapturous applause. Prices were kept reasonable so we had a fairly full house.

It also helped that many of the colleagues I met through the Bandwagon were involved. Evans Haile was NATC's other prime mover, as well as its primary musical director. Stuart Ross directed the first show. Sam Rudy, whose numerous later credits would included *Avenue Q* (2003), was the ongoing publicist.

The Algonquin Hotel figured prominently, too, conveniently located, around the corner from Town Hall. The Saturday before the performance, the Algonquin annex was re-opened so that Glen Kelly could rehearse singers there. My grandparents' generously donated the space because I was involved; they had no notion of how impacting this company would be.

The night after *The New Moon* rose, I picked up the early reviews and phoned Bill. Stephen Holden of *The New York Times* wrote supportively but with reserve: "It was the opportunity to hear Romberg's melodies well-sung . . . that constituted the chief pleasures of the work's first professional

New York presentation since its 1944 revival at the City Center."[4] What put us on the map though was the *Daily News* review by Bill Zakariasen:

> "Because the Minskoff Theater was dark Monday and *The Pirates of Penzance* couldn't play there, the best musical heard that night on Broadway was Sigmund Romberg's *The New Moon*. The performance took off with enviable spontaneity and style. Even though the concert performance of it didn't have the accoutrements of sophisticated staging, it had no trouble in reminding us that the present has a lot to learn from the past in producing a string of immortal songs. The performance took off with enviable spontaneity and style."[5]

Quoting Bill's mother, Clairee Tynes, from a book she'd write about him:

> "The management of Town Hall, that great old theater . . . built in 1914 and seating 1500, was so impressed with the quality and artistry of *The New Moon* . . . they promptly signed the company to a contract to perform a series of the vintage musicals for the next season—and then the next season—and then the next.

> "Bill was twenty four years old. He had hocked his grandfather's heirloom watch, I found out later, to augment the funding for *The New Moon*. It took him years to pay off the loan."[6]

Bill's sacrifice paid off, at least artistically. Subsequent seasons brought a succession of acclaimed concerts presented by NATC. To name just a few:

Jubilee (1935: score by Cole Porter with Carole Shelley, Paula Laurence, Davis Gaines, Rebecca Luker, and Alyson Reed.)

Music In the Air (1932: Kern and Hammerstein, with E. G. Marshall, Patrice Munsel, John Reardon, and Rebecca Luker.)

One Touch of Venus (Weill and Nash, with Paige O'Hara [later the voice of Belle in Disney's 1991 film version of *Beauty and the Beast*], Susan Lucci, Lee Roy Reams, Ron Raines, Peggy Cass, and—recreating her original role—Paula Laurence.)

Roberta (1933: Kern and Harbach, with Arlene Francis, David Carroll, Russ Thacker, Judith Blazer, Jeff Keller, and Loni Ackerman.)

Sweethearts (1913: Victor Herbert and Robert B. Smith, with Jane
Powell, Judy Kaye, Brent Barrett, and Christopher Hewett.)

Collage of New Amsterdam Theatre Company logos.

The quiet, unassuming Bill Tynes poured into the organization his own
money, earned from his bread-and-butter job as a violinist in Broadway
shows, such as *Strider* (1979) and *Show Boat* (1983 revival).   Another
major artistic contributor was frequent director Jason Buzas. Tall and com-
manding, Jason was also instrumental in guiding the career of playwright
David Ives, meticulously helming Ives' breakthrough show *All In the Timing*
*(*1993). Ives would later make a niche for himself adapting scripts for the
Encores! series. Jason Buzas, on the other hand, engaged two different writers to devise the narration for NATC scripts: alternately, Michael Neville
and me.

By the next year, the number of NATC shows per season had grown to
three: *Eileen* (1917: Victor Herbert and Henry Blossom), *The Firefly* (1913:
Friml and Harbach), and *Rosalie* (1928: G. Gershwin and Romberg/ I.
Gershwin and Wodehouse).   During this time, the Algonquin's annex was

occasionally donated for rehearsals. The hotel, likewise, became an unoffi-
cial hangout for participants before and after the shows. Rather than "Let's
put on a show," there was the constant atmosphere of "Let's save endangered
shows from extinction!" Orchestrator Larry Moore, who later served in
the same capacity for Encores!, pieced together and supplemented scores
scattered through the years. Other reconstruction work was accomplished
by rehearsal pianist Paul Ford, who later was the pianist on such original
productions as *Sunday in the Park With George* (1984), *Into the Woods* (1989),
Falsettos (1992), and *Passion* (1994).

My grandparents gave the group a special rate for a gala after-theatre
dinner in the Chinese Room following the second season opener, *Eileen*.
To commemorate the musical's Irish theme and composer (Victor Herbert),
the room was festooned with green carnations, and Bailey's Irish Cream was
served. Gracing the table were the concert's stars, including E. G. Marshall,
Maureen O'Sullivan, Judy Kaye, Frances Sternhagen, and—as Eileen—
Jeanne Lehman (she would one day be my leading lady in *Mrs. McThing*).
This show was so well received that it was presented the following year at
the Shubert Performing Arts Center in New Haven, Connecticut.

The NATC became a cause célèbre, winning a special Drama Desk
Award for Bill Tynes "for bringing back the Golden Age of the American
musical in distinguished concern productions."[7] On occasions where the
annex was donated for rehearsals, I visited and saw the likes of Susan Lucci
(on a break from *All My Children*), singer Connie Coit (who would later
appear in *Charlotte Sweet*), Alfred Drake, and a non-Equity actress who—
recommended by Judy Kaye—would make her New York debut as the
ingénue in *Music In the Air*. Her name: Rebecca Luker, later a three-time
Tony Award nominee. Among participants in NATC presentations were
lots of the same people who later worked on the Encores! series, such as
Luker, Judy Kaye, Karen Ziemba, Debbie Gravitte, Charles Repole, choreographer Randy Skinner, and musical director Robert Fisher.

I had the privilege of writing continuity that was delivered by such
guest narrators as Arlene Frances (*Roberta*), Jane Powell (*Sweethearts*), and
Dina Merrill alongside Cliff Robertson (*Rosalie*). The audiences and public
profile of the company were booming. In *The New York Times*, Stephen
Holden enthusiastically wrote of *Rosalie*:

> "*Rosalie* proves to be the giddiest of period operetta confec-
> tions, buoyed by half a dozen memorable tunes. Affectionately
> tongue-in-cheek. A 30-member chorus and the New Amsterdam
> Theatre Company orchestral, directed by Evans Haile, executed

the score's large, bubbly ensemble numbers with a crisp sense of coordination."[8]

As voluntary treasurer and writer for the group, I wasn't paid but was given complimentary tickets per show, which I usually offered my brother, Douglas, and my friends, singer Bobbie Baird and her husband, Maurice Levine. For years, I subscribed to Maurice's monumental "Lyrics and Lyricists" series at the 92nd Street Y, where lyricists from Alan Jay Lerner

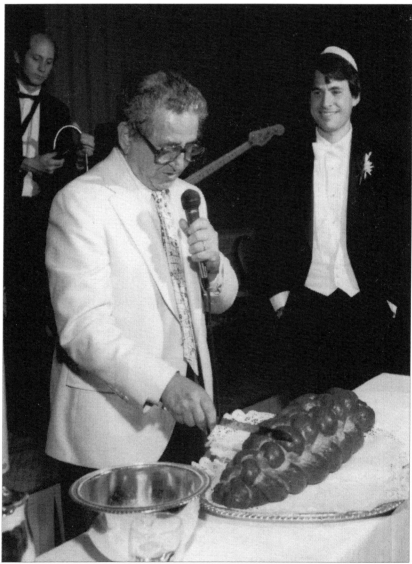

Maurice Levine, when he said the motzi (blessing over bread) at Michael's wedding.

to Stephen Sondheim spoke as their songs were presented. I felt like I was reciprocating for all the years of enjoyment—and inspiration—I derived from his series.

Sadly, two factors caused the ultimate demise of this important company. Typically for a theatre institution, as the company grew, so did the considerable costs. Matters were particularly burdensome for Bill Tynes, who didn't always have musician's earnings to pump into the company. The financial strain was further exacerbated by the pre-production costs of a proposed showcase production of Rodgers and Hart's *Peggy-Ann*, which had to be canceled. The more serious reason for the company's demise was the same calamity limiting Bill's efforts on *Peggy-Ann*: he was suffering from AIDS, which made it increasingly difficult for him to raise money and run the company. Bill was one of several of my closest colleagues to become victims of this horrible epidemic during this nightmarish period.

By 1986, Bill had to entrust the leadership of NATC to another producing director, who unfortunately alienated members and compounded the financial problems. Adhering to a strict macrobiotic diet, Bill persevered, doing what he could for *I Married An Angel* in May 1986. I stood by Bill and arranged for rehearsals at the Algonquin. After the performances, Bill's spirit skyrocketed when he received a substantial check from Dorothy Rodgers, Richard Rodgers' widow, with a letter stating:

> "I had a great time yesterday at *I Married An Angel* and so did the entire audience. You did a really beautiful job.
>
> "I hope the enclosed contribution will encourage you to continue with the same enthusiasm."[9]

However, the continuation of the company would not last long. On January 9, 1987, Bill died peacefully at home. Even though we knew he was sick, his friends and alumni were still in great shock. He was only thirty. On February 16, there was a memorial for him at the Helen Hayes Theatre, where an impressive array of his alumni spoke and sang. I gave a keynote speech, declaring:

> "Even though musical preservation societies have risen and fallen in New York like paper airplanes, Bill decided to found his *own* company. And against all odds, this strong little man succeeded where so many had failed. Nothing could distract him from his goal. Not the round-the-clock, grueling effort it took. Not illness. Not the financial worries of a non-profit group. Nothing, except

the stolen hour he took every day to watch Susan Lucci on *All My Children*."

Bill Tynes' successor tried to keep the company afloat. The company's next show was *Sally* (1922: Kern/Bolton/Grey) in January 1988, for which I wrote program notes. However, I couldn't just go along when reliable sources shared increasingly alarming stories of production misconduct, denied by Bill's successor. Reluctantly, I handed in my resignation. As much as the company meant to me, the decision was astute. Not long after, authorities investigated the claims and contacted me as a witness on the history of the company. I tried my best to simply state facts as I knew them without being incriminating. Still, this was not a story that could be tweaked.

Regrettably, the New Amsterdam Theatre Company folded soon after. Bill's triumph had for the moment become tragic. Yet the memories of those early days, leading to a remarkable organization will prevail. Moreover, Bill's legacy continues in companies like Encores! that are now found throughout the United States and beyond. Humbly, I take great pride in having been part of it. And the phenomenon had its delicious launch at the Algonquin.

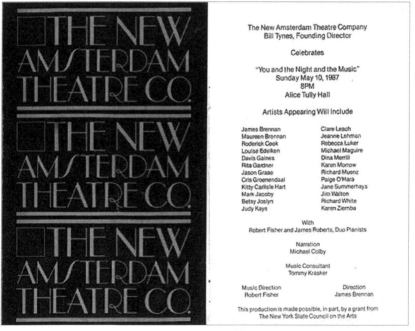

Program for special NATC all-star presentation, You and the Night and the Music, *1987.*

Chapter 23: *Days and Algonquinites*

Donald Smith (photo courtesy of Mabel Mercer Foundation); Michael Feinstein (photo courtesy of Michael Feinstein).

The Algonquin abounded with musical activity during the early 1980s, including my own. Most notably, at 9 p.m. on Wednesday, January 14, 1981, the Algonquin Oak Room inaugurated its new supper club series with a sensational performance by singer/pianist Steve Ross—on a roll with Cole (Porter), Noel (Coward), Hart (Lorenz) and soul (Fats Waller). My Uncle

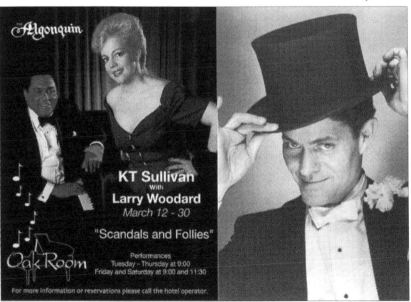

K. T. Sullivan and Larry Woodard (photo courtesy of Mabel Mercer Foundation), and Steve Ross (photo courtesy of Steve Ross).

Andrew and his cabaret comrade, Donald Smith, had converted the room into a source of new renown and business for the Algonquin. Now all they needed to do was prove it to skeptical Grandpa Ben.

And prosper it did. For visitors and performers alike, the room would become the center of countless enchanted memories. In coming years, the Oak Room would become a launching pad for the careers of Michael Feinstein, Harry Connick Jr., and Diana Krall, among others. It likewise became the Manhattan home for top cabaret performers, such as Julie Wilson, Andrea Marcovicci, and K. T. Sullivan, whose shows were not only entertaining but lessons in the art of the American songbook. I spent countless nights there with Grandma Mary, as seated by stately manager Arthur Pomposello, who always looked like he was about to pop open some champagne. One particularly grand night, we socialized with Francis Gershwin Godowsky (singer/sister of George and Ira) and chanteuse Mary Cleere Haran, after Mary's fabulous tribute to the Gershwins. Occasionally, someone like Michael Feinstein even sang one of my songs.

Michael and Grandma Mary in the Oak Room.

A visit to the Algonquin cabaret was a time machine to the past. You'd enter the oblong, darkly romantic Oak Room dotted with flickering sconces and candlelit tables. You practically felt the presence of the ghosts of Dorothy Parker and original Round-Tablers, as performers shared witty

Andrea Marcovicci (photo courtesy of Andrea Marcovicci), and Julie Wilson (photo courtesy of Mabel Mercer Foundation).

repartee and sang winsome standards by Jerome Kern, Richard Rodgers, Harold Arlen, and other timeless songwriters.

Yet the magnitude of what would follow is not the full thrust of my diary entry on the night of Steve Ross's smashing opening. The entry mentions the heavy press turnout, the general excitement, and the overflowing crowd; but it also focuses on the deep concern my family had about my mother. My mother was accompanied to the pre-show dinner by Bernie Chubet, who would become her third husband (when asked at the time if my mother was a widow or a divorcée, I said, "You name it.") On that night, she was in a very unhappy state, and the family was afraid she would be disruptive. She wound up leaving before the performance, angry at some comments that she perceived as hurtful. When I think back on this momentous night, I can't help lamenting how such a celebratory event couldn't be wholly enjoyed because of such circumstances.

Beyond the newly opened Algonquin nightclub, I was making my own kind of music. Through the week, I was having project meetings galore. There was a round of talks with Broadway producers seriously interested in *North Atlantic*, even if—apt for a show about Eskimos!—they later got cold feet. Meanwhile, I was writing lyrics for composer Jack Urbont (Emmy Award winner; credits including *General Hospital*) and book-writers, Mary

Chase and Henry Ephron, on the musical version of *Mrs. McThing* (when Mary passed away in 1981, I took over the libretto, going on another merry chase seeking producers). In addition, I collaborated with Jack and librettist Dale Wasserman (*Man of La Mancha*) on *Great Big River*, a musical version of Mark Twain's *The Adventures of Tom Sawyer* (1876). It was produced in exotic Dubuque, Iowa in 1981. That was the first and last time I've done a show there.

Program for Great Big River *(1981). I supplemented the work of the late Bruce Geller, writer and TV producer.*

Lots was happening for *Ludlow Ladd*, too. WBAI Radio produced a radio version with most of the cast from the Lyric Theatre of New York. The New American Theater in Rockford, Illinois presented it two years in a row. There were two concert versions directed by the marvelous Sara Louise Lazarus, and New York's Circle In the Square almost produced it in 1985. Equally gratifying, based on regional enthusiasm for *Ludlow Ladd*, I was recommended for inclusion in *The National Playwrights Directory* (1981), published by the O'Neill Theater Center. My page could be found somewhere between those for Woody Allen and Dale Wasserman. This was very consoling during my long periods of having shows rejected. It would become clear—through the years—that my work, often whimsical and stylized, wasn't for everyone.

On the other hand, during the early 1980s, I kept busy with projects that did reach fruition. Gerald Jay Markoe recommended me for two assignments on which he was the composer. One was a country musical titled *C & W* at the American Theatre of Actors (ATA). The ATA would later be the venue for the original productions of shows like *Urinetown* (2001) and *Charlotte Sweet*. *C & W* featured a book and direction by James Jennings, a jovial guy, who looked like one of the sons from the Ponderosa on *Bonanza* (1959). He has been the artistic director of the ATA since its outset in 1976. James had a simple request for me: rewrite all the lyrics to *C & W* before opening night the next week. I finished in a matter of days. James was so impressed that he welcomed me to work at the ATA any time. All I needed were the shows, producers, and capitalization.

The other assignment I received through Gerald was with Lee Frank, she the artistic director of the children's theatre program at Hartley House, a social center on West 46th Street. For several years, I became resident lyricist for their children's shows, gaining a rare commodity for me in theatre: a little money. Not long after, I became a founding member of another theatre devoted to children's musicals, TADA! Youth Theater. Unlike Hartley

TADA!. Among those pictured, Jordan Peele would one day have his own award-winning TV series (Key and Peele, 2012 on Comedy Central), Mizo Peck would play Sacajawea in Night at the Museum *(2006), and Sean Nelson would appear in many TV episodes and movies.*

House, which presented shows with small casts of adults often playing children, TADA! featured large casts of real kids—from pre-school to high school years—offering them an invaluable training program in the Arts. Founded in 1984, TADA! was the brainchild of Janine Nina Trevens, who'd worked for a similar past organization, the First All Children's Theater. I knew Nina through her mom, Francine Trevens, a short dynamo who'd been a publicist on the original production of Harvey Fierstein's *Torch Song Trilogy* (off-Broadway, 1982) and represented me on several shows.

Nina inherited her mother's high-octane genes and has produced, directed, and taught at TADA! for the last thirty years. Today TADA! remains a model youth theatre, winning a special Drama Desk Award and serving as a training ground for such future stars as Ricki Lake, Kerry Washington, and Josh Peck, as well as an early employer of such writing talents as Jeanine Tesori (*Violet*, 1997), Winnie Holzman (*Wicked*), and Jason Robert Brown (*The Last 5 Years*, 2002).[1]

I've served TADA! in several capacities. Throughout its history, I've been on its Artistic Advisory Board, humbly sharing that honor with far more recognizable names including Sheldon Harnick, Chita Rivera, and Stephen Schwartz. In 2006, they commissioned me and composer Ned Paul Ginsburg to write a musical about adoption—*They Chose Me!*—which was well reviewed and subsequently received many regional productions. Yet my biggest challenge at TADA! was singing at one of their benefits in 1986. Thereupon, I—along with Mara Beckerman (*Charlotte Sweet*) and composer Paul Katz—previewed songs from *Tales of Tinseltown* (then titled *Tinseltown Tattletale*). I'm always a bundle of raw nerves when I sing in public, but that afternoon I was a basket case. I had to immediately follow one of the all-time great singers, Margaret Whiting. I don't remember exactly what she sang, perhaps "My Shining Hour" (1943: Harold Arlen/ Johnny Mercer). She truly shone. I followed her with what might be subtitled "My Semi-Luminous Three Minutes."

Of course, all of my shows until 1986 (when I married), were written at the Algonquin, and most—including *Tales of Tinseltown*—rehearsed there. My grandparents also occasionally allowed me to donate the annex to companies with which I was associated, such as the Goodspeed Opera House and the Berkshire Theatre Festival. At auditions for my musicals, I witnessed future stage stars, such as Victoria Clark, J. K. Simmons, and Faith Prince. Other visitors included Mark Hamill (*Star Wars*, 1977), working on the Goodspeed musical, *Harrigan 'n' Hart* (1985); and Peter Bergman (of TV soaps, *All My Children*, 1979, and *The Young and the Restless*,

Tales of Tinseltown *(1985) rehearses in the Annex (pictured: assistant musical director Steve Alper, Bob Arnold, Nat Chandler, Jason Graae, Alison Fraser, Jason Graae, Rick Lombardo, Nora Mae Lyng, Greg Mowry; scenic designer Alexander Okun works in the Stratford Suite).*

1990-present), there to see his pal Edward Stone, director of *Charlotte Sweet* (they'd met as waiters at O'Neal's Restaurant).

Occasionally, after a long day of rehearsing in the annex, I topped things with a terrific nightcap. For me, that meant a cabaret show and a Coca Cola in the Oak Room. Even before the Oak Room opened, I became good friends with Sylvia Syms, a singer, who fervently wanted to perform there but didn't for years. As a child, I saw her as Bloody Mary in a summer tent production of *South Pacific* (and still think she was the best Jewish jazz-bird I've ever seen playing a Polynesian huckster). I first met her through LaVerne Gunton, an Algonquin regular. LaVerne was secretary to Frank Sinatra's attorney, Mickey Rudin, and part of Sinatra's fulltime entourage, assisting and traveling across the globe with him.[2] LaVerne, a towering, always sunny redhead with big hair, was likewise responsible for my meeting Sinatra at one of his concerts in Atlantic City. After his concert, my grandparents and I climbed onto the stage in an experience that can only be described as Living Surrealism. Pushing aside the stage curtain, I suddenly found Sinatra, with an outstretched hand, saying "Hello." Yes, Frank Sinatra—whose music my father played religiously, Hollywood's "Pal Joey," and as famous a legend as I ever faced—greeted me and my grandparents like a new next-door neighbor.

I'd love to say that was just the beginning with Sinatra, but the thrill of that moment and words he exchanged with my family would have to suffice. In contrast, my relationship with LaVerne's friend, Sylvia Syms, who *was* close to Sinatra, grew and blossomed. After an introduction in the lobby, I frequented her appearances at Jazz clubs around New York and—dazzled by the depth and nuance she gave to a song—understood why Sinatra acknowledged her as his mentor in lyrical phrasing. He called her "The best saloon singer in the business" and nicknamed her "Buddha" based on her short, round physicality.[3] He also conducted her popular album, "Syms by Sinatra (1982)." My own favorite performance of Sylvia's was when she sang "It Amazes Me (1958)," a standard about how an average woman is elevated by someone's adoration of her, written by lyricist Carolyn Leigh and composer Cy Coleman. The sentiment of the song mirrored what the adoration of an audience meant to her. As she said in an interview:

> "I can live without a lot of things, but I can't live without singing. This is the most glamorous I'll ever be, the most loved I'll ever be. It's the most love I can give. I'm down to the bottom of my sound, but I'm up to the clearest understanding of my life."[4]

At first my friendship with Sylvia was based on talking theatre, with perhaps a touch of Sylvia's pitching to play the Algonquin (early on, she believed that her outspokenness had rubbed talent-booker Donald Smith the wrong way, undermining her chances for an engagement at the hotel). Still, she was always upfront with me. When I asked her to be my guest at the opening of the showcase production of *Charlotte Sweet*, she replied, "Well, tell me the honest truth—is it any good?" I'm pleased to say, after the show, she gave me the ultimate compliment: on her own, she invested in the commercial move of the show.

Moreover, she taught me volumes about resilience. A true survivor, Sylvia had soldiered on despite bouts of lung cancer and a serious car accident that put her in a wheelchair for a year. That fortitude was in evidence when she performed at Resorts International in Atlantic City around Autumn 1985. Sinatra had arranged the engagement at one of the hotel's smaller venues, just before he was to appear at the hotel. I attended her opening night, midweek, to cheer Sylvia on. Yet other than me, her accompanist Mike Renzi, and bassist Steve La Spina, there might have been six other people there. Nonetheless, after an initial look of disappointment,

Sylvia Syms with Michael and Andrea Colby. Photo: E. Wolynski.

she psyched herself up and gave the show her all, as if to say, "I'm going to give you seven people the best private concert you've ever had!"

On the night of April 28, 1992, Sylvia fulfilled one of her dreams: she finally began an engagement at the Algonquin, as arranged by Donald Smith. Yet, despite an enthusiastic reception, there were nights when Sylvia played to small crowds. She phoned me quite a bit during this period, worrying about the size of her audiences and concerned that her allergies were acting up. She told me she was having serious trouble breathing and thought she might be allergic to the current Algonquin Cat. Sylvia had already told a reporter she suspected her Algonquin engagement "may be my last time on the pike."[5] Paradoxically, she was busy planning her next album, to be called *Sylvia Sets New Standards*, with songs by new writers, and she wanted to feature at least one of mine. I couldn't have been more excited, even if recording material by a Bodne grandson was apt for Sylvia, whose biggest hit single, "I Could Have Danced All Night (1956)," was a song written at the Algonquin.

It has been widely reported what happened to Sylvia at her closing performance at the Algonquin on May 10, 1992. As Bob Harrington of *Back Stage*, eloquently wrote:

> "By now, you probably know that Sylvia Syms left us last Saturday night. For those of us who knew and loved Sylvia Syms, the fact

that she was doing what she loved to do eases the sadness of her sudden passing. Sylvia always said she wanted to die on stage, and she did. There in the Algonquin's venerable *Oak Room*, between the closing number and first encore of a show that had garnered the best reviews of her career, that great heart just gave out. It was quite an exit, and totally in keeping with the way Sylvia lived and worked.

"She'd done two shows that night. Cy Coleman was at the second show, sitting right up front. As she came off stage after singing 'Blues in the Night' to an enormous ovation, she bent over as if to say something to him and collapsed. Moments later, the Queen of the Saloon singers was gone."[6]

Sylvia's engagement at the Algonquin is now part of show business legend. Her exit is probably the most famous moment in the history of the entire Oak Room series. It made the front page headline of *The New York Post*, which would have delighted Sylvia. How perfect it was that Sylvia was surrounded by applause and love in her last moments. Her memory has become inseparable from the Algonquin. As well, the entire cabaret series of the Algonquin is but a memory now. Fortunately, Sylvia's voice lives on in all its glory through her ever-vibrant recordings. And the Oak Room series has become a major chapter in the history of New York cabaret.

Chapter 24: *It Could Only Happen in the Theatre*

Charlotte Sweet *logo by Frederic Marvin.*

Despite rosy reviews and high hopes, *Charlotte Sweet* closed off-Broadway after only 102 performances. I sat in the Algonquin, discussing our fate with Edward Stone, the long, lanky director, who looked like a blond version of Plastic Man. The conversation became typical of show-biz types: delusional. Ed referred to *Little Shop of Horrors* (1982), a musical that opened around the same time and was often reviewed alongside us—in most cases, favorably for both shows. We both started off-off Broadway (*Charlotte Sweet* at the American Theatre of Actors, *Little Shop of Horrors* at the WPA Theatre). We even had the same original press agent, Fred Hoot, who promised us he would promote the shows together, but couldn't. In a gesture of camaraderie, I was the person who got an advance review of *Little Shop of Horrors*, reporting to Fred a rave in *The New York Times* from Mel Gussow. Fred was hugely relieved, concerned that the audience had been on the "quiet" side when Gussow attended. A half a year later, Ed and I mulled the fates of both shows: "Years from now when people talk about the two shows, which one do you think people will remember?" said Ed, as if to imply *Charlotte Sweet* would have the edge.

We all know the answer: *Little Shop of Horrors* is now considered a classic, *Charlotte Sweet* a relative footnote in musical theatre history. Yet, despite the ironies of Ed's statement, the show was a glorious experience we cherished.

I originally wrote *Charlotte Sweet* to be the hour-long Act Two of the short musical predating it, *Ludlow Ladd*. The framework I used was partly inspired by my St. Clement's/Musical Theatre Lab days. I recalled how *The Robber Bridegroom* unfolded as a square dance and *The Red Blue-Grass Western Show* was framed by Grand Ole Opry type songs. Indeed, many of my shows were frameworked with specific genres of music, which I played all day in my Algonquin room (#408), imbuing myself with their style. When I wrote *Ludlow Ladd*, I played Christmas carols during the long, hot summer. On *Tales of Tinseltown*, it was 1930s Hollywood songs. For *Charlotte Sweet*, it was Gilbert & Sullivan, as well as British Music Hall recordings.

The idea of setting *Charlotte Sweet* in the British Music Hall was a stroke of luck. It was suggested to me by Elizabeth Wolynski, a British photographer/comedienne I met at the Berkshire Theatre Festival. I'd hired her as a photographer on *Ludlow Ladd*, when one night, she asked I see her in a British Music Hall style evening at a New York pub, David Copperfield's. It was there that we brainstormed about following the Christmas carol framework of *Ludlow Ladd* with music hall turns for *Charlotte Sweet*.

Within three weeks, I handed to composer Gerald Jay Markoe a first draft of *Charlotte Sweet*, with *dialogue* carefully rhymed, as well as the songs. Sometimes, it's easier for me to write scenes as rhythmic dialogue in the Larry Hart tradition than choose between the myriad options for spoken dialogue.

Having a fully rhymed libretto—intended to be all-sung—meant a huge amount of work for Gerry, who became flustered. Before I began the libretto, he'd requested I at least set a few songs to old trunk tunes (i.e. melodies he'd already written). While composing, Gerry complained there was one lyric that was impossible to set; the title was "Bubbles In Me Bonnet." I reassured Gerry not to fret—it was already done. It was a lyric I wrote to one of his trunk tunes; he just hadn't realized.

Once *Charlotte Sweet* was completed, I encountered the typical rounds of rejection pandemic to musical theatre writers. When I've been interviewed by media and asked what I thought of other people's musicals, I've always said I won't publicly criticize other shows: it's a miracle anything gets on these days and I'm not going to knock someone battling the staggering odds. Ulitmately, I asked my family for help, feeling half ashamed, half comforted to know they'd stand by me.

With a tax write-off donation from my grandparents, before tax reforms prevented such donations, I had sufficient funding to myself produce a low-cost showcase of *Charlotte Sweet*, off-off Broadway. By now, owing to my co-producing experiences at the Musical Theatre Lab and *North Atlantic*, I was prepared to fly solo. What's more, it was time to cash in some chips. As a result of my volunteering to revamp the lyrics to his musical, *C & W*, I negotiated a sweetheart deal from James Jennings to present the show at his space, the American Theatre of Actors. Of course, I also required a creative team. It wasn't easy to find the right director for an all-sung, all-rhymed musical, set in Victorian England, about a troupe of freaky Music Hall performers whose chief attraction is a helium-addicted high soprano. On a whim, I grabbed a phone book and contacted a director whose work I had strongly admired that year, Murray Horwitz, associate director and co-creator of the Tony-winning revue *Ain't Misbehavin'*. I suspected there was scant chance he'd be available, after working on the season's biggest musical hit, but in the theatre one must be bold. It turned out I was right—he wasn't available. Even so, Murray saw the potential and recommended two directors, one of whom was his relative through marriage. Edward Stone was the relative. Ed's chief credits were writing and directing a nightclub act for Christine Ebersole—with whom he grew up in Winnetka, Illinois—and writing material for her on TV's *Saturday Night Live* (1981-1982). He'd also directed a one-night tribute to Mabel Mercer, produced by Donald Smith, and served as a non-union writer for the TV soap opera, *Ryan's Hope*, during a writers' strike (1981). Some friends called him "Eddy." Business colleagues often called him "Ed." I called him *frequently* in the next few days. He had some reservations about the show, but said that since Murray liked it, he would do it.

I myself had some reservations about Ed and considered other options. My first inclination was Raymond Benson, who'd directed *Ludlow Ladd*; but he was busy working on another project (he later became a best-selling novelist and the fourth official writer for the James Bond series, from 1996-2003). Several other interested directors had schedule conflicts. Still, I had to decide soon—auditions would begin two days after I met Ed. Cornered by circumstances, I offered Ed the job. It turned out to be among the best decisions I would make in my career. It also helped that our choreographer was the ever-resourceful Dennis Dennehy of *North Atlantic*

Edward Stone and Polly Pen outside Westside Arts Center.

Nevertheless, I clashed with Ed during the first weeks of production, which took place within the Algonquin annex. Though I wrote the musical for Mara Beckerman (who could hit stratospheric high notes), Ed had a close friend he wanted to cast instead; he and Polly Pen had attended Ithica College together. Polly auditioned and—though impressed—Gerry Markoe and I just thought she was wrong for the part of Charlotte. Ed put his foot down, but I prevailed as producer. To make peace, I agreed to give Polly a role in the show, as well. Again, luck was in our favor. She garnered kudos in the role of Skitzy Scofield, the "half-man, half-woman" dual personality, who duets with herself. People thought we'd done a massive search to find the right actress for this role, but it was another case of lucky circumstance.

A role that was more difficult to fill was "Ludlow Ladd," the boy born on Christmas who becomes the romantic lead in *Charlotte Sweet*. We offered it to Charles Michael Wright, who originated the role in the pre-quel. However, he was doing *Master Harold and the Boys* opposite James Earl Jones (not a gig he'd desert for an off-off Broadway showcase). We were just about to compromise on a so-so choice but held one more set of auditions. Then, an actor walked in who was the physical embodiment of the thin Dickensian juvenile I'd always envisioned. It was one of those cases of perfect casting—if he could only sing. I actually cried when Christopher Seppe, the longest running "Boy" in in *The Fantasticks*, sang like an angel.

The first week of rehearsals at the Algonquin, free food aside, was not easy. Typical for a showcase, one actor got other work and needed to be replaced. Then, Ed Stone became feverishly ill during the first week of rehearsal. He had to rest in my Algonquin room, while Dennis Dennehy and I reassured the actors. To play safe, I secretly phoned two other directors about possibly supplanting Ed. Dennis saved the day, staging a show-stopping number aptly titled "Quartet Agonistes," in which the show's villain, theatre impresario Barnaby Bugaboo, cajoles the high-voiced Charlotte into joining his freaky troupe, the Circus of Voices. After that, everyone was elated. Ed took over and did an ingenious, hilarious job of staging the show. Thank heavens no additional replacement was necessary. Ed's background as a writer was invaluable as he guided just the right changes, additions, and edits.

The previews were wobbly, as usually happens when you're refining new material. Yet, by opening night April 13, 1982, it was evident we'd created a show beloved by many. I particularly remember my sense of pride observing three people rolling with laughter: Sylvia Syms, singer Bobbi Baird, and her husband, Maurice Levine, (of "Lyrics and Lyricists" at the 92nd Street Y). As the cherry on top, we learned that critic Michael Sommers of *Backstage* would be writing a valentine to the show. Our company felt like we'd struck oil and were on our way to a major payoff. However, the next performance sat there like an exhausted gazelle and a critic left at intermission. As I paced in the lobby, sighing something like "We're doomed!," Ed Stone reassured me that we had a winner on our hands. Apparently, he was right. For the rest of the run, extended by a week by popular demand, we obtained good to exceptional reviews, played to packed houses, and received offers for a commercial transfer. I was particularly pleased by John Corry's review in *The New York Times*:

> "*Charlotte Sweet*' mixes the adorable and the strange, and it is delec-table. It is done in the style of the British music hall, more or less as if the Crummles from *Nicholas Nickleby* had stumbled onto the

set of *Sweeney Todd*. In large part, it is delectable because Michael Colby, the librettist, and Gerald Jay Markoe, the composer, know what they are about: a parody that rises above parody and stands by itself . . . The glory, however, is Mr. Colby's lyrics."[2]

Another audience member who went wild about the show was Geraldine Stutz, president of Henri Bendel's, the chic women's specialty store on Fifth Avenue. That night after the show, I visited a restaurant with my Uncle Andrew and Aunt Barbara Anspach. At some point, we heard a woman at the next table raving about a musical she'd just seen. Aunt Barbara excitedly pointed out, "That's Geraldine Stutz."

I, even more excitedly pointed out, "She's talking about *Charlotte Sweet!*"

While Aunt Barbara insisted on introducing me to her, I tried to act nonchalant, dizzy with delight at this self-validating coincidence. Like Al Hirschfeld, Geraldine recommended the show to all her friends when it ultimately moved (her close friends included Harold Prince and Stephen Sondheim). Generously, she put up a *Charlotte Sweet* display in the windows of Henri Bendel's. I did a lot of window-shopping there during that month.

When I worked at the Musical Theatre Lab, there was one producer all the writers wanted at their new musical in hopes he might option their show. That producer was Kenneth Waissman, at the time presenting one of the biggest hits on Broadway, *Grease*. He regularly attended the Lab shows but never made an offer. However, like a fantasy come true, he was one of the three producers who wanted to option *Charlotte Sweet* after seeing the showcase. I visited his office, where he asserted our production was one of the best showcases he'd ever seen. There was one rub. As in the case of *Grease*, which he saw in Chicago (Polly Pen had been an original cast member), he proposed presenting an entirely new production—staff and cast. It was his modus operandi to present his own version.

There were two other offers on the table: one from Elliot Martin (*Never Too Late, Glengarry Glen Ross*), who wasn't sure when he'd be available to present it; the other from Stan Raiff, who would produce it right away with the showcase company. There was no way, given the choice, that I could turn my back on the showcase company, whom I considered a vital reason for the success of the showcase.

Gerry Markoe and I chose to go with Stan Raiff, a producer of limited background who attended the show solely to see his ex-office assistant, Mara Beckerman, and flipped. After we signed with Stan, the show was booked at the Cheryl Crawford Theatre (Westbeth Arts Center) on West

43rd Street, opening shortly after *Little Shop of Horrors*. *Little Shop of Horrors*—whose tryout version received excellent reviews a month after our showcase—had been optioned not by one, but by two theatre heavyweights: the Shubert Organization and Cameron Macintosh (producer of *Cats*, 1982). Stan Raiff could never match their clout.

Almost everyone from the *Charlotte Sweet* showcase was retained for the move. The exception was the unavailable Virginia Seidel, a Tony Award nominee for *Very Good Eddie* (1975). She'd been hysterical as our "bubble-voiced" Cecily Macintosh, a character patterned on Billie Burke's Glinda the Good Witch in *The Wizard of Oz* (1939). Our initial disappointment soon turned to delirious excitement. Our casting director, Roger Sturteyvant, had called in Merle Louise, the original Beggar Woman from *Sweeney Todd*, who had originated more roles in Stephen Sondheim musicals than practically anyone.

I owed an apology to other auditioners, whom I practically ignored in my euphoria that Merle Louise was auditioning for us. Merle was immediately offered the role, and she was sublime in the show. By the end of the run, she, Polly Pen, and some other cast members had a virtual

Opening night party for Charlotte Sweet *(1982) at Algonquin. Pictured: Gerald Jay Markoe, Merle Louise, Michael, Peter Bergman, Celeste Holm, Vincent the doorman, Edward Stone, Steve Ross, Mara Beckerman, Nicholas Wyman, Polly Pen, Christopher Seppe, Hermoine Gingold, Ben Bodne, Liliane Montivecchi, and Mary Bodne. Photos: E. Wolynski.*

competition as to who'd steal the show on consecutive nights. Furthermore, there was immense satisfaction, after *The New York Times* compared the show to *Sweeney Todd*, that Merle's character in *Charlotte Sweet* would be presumed dead toward the end, then spring back to life—as if to suggest "The Beggar Woman rises again!"

Our week of previews generally went well. Seeing my name on the marquee of the Westside Arts Theatre was like reaching Camelot. Our opening night on August 12, 1982, was a middling performance compared to the showcase opening. Still, we had a wingding opening night party. In Victorian style, horse-drawn carriages delivered first-nighters to the Algonquin, where they proceeded to the Oak Room. Covering the event was radio host Casper Citron (for WQXR), who would open and close his radio show announcing the address of all his broadcasts: "This is Casper Citron from the Algonquin Hotel, legendary rendezvous for people in the Arts."[3]

Vincent, the Algonquin's doorman (a Danny DeVito type), waited at the Algonquin entrance to greet everyone. Throughout the show's run, he would tell Algonquin guests not to miss the musical. As Steve Ross played a medley of tunes from *Charlotte Sweet*, the crowd included Celeste Holm, Hermoine Gingold, Eli Wallach and Anne Jackson, Charles Strouse, and the Algonquin Cat.

There was a lot to celebrate, with one exception. I had begged Stan Raiff not to invite Mel Gussow of *The New York Times* to review our Broadway transfer. We already had a rave in the *Times* and didn't need Gussow, who I predicted—based on my knowledge of Gussow's preference for gritty shows and aversion to whimsy—wouldn't like us. I recommended waiting for Walter Kerr, who loved whimsy and at the time wrote follow-up reviews in Sunday editions of *The New York Times*. Kerr would have been a no-risk situation. True, he famously gave lukewarm reviews to such classic musicals as *Fiddler On the Roof* and *Man of La Mancha*. But he was a good friend of my grandparents and wouldn't have filed a review if he didn't like us. Stan couldn't imagine anyone disliking *Charlotte Sweet*. He hadn't attended the showcase performance when the critic left at intermission or heard from the show's occasional naysayers, who were bothered by its all-rhyme style and other eccentricities. Sure enough, I soon heard Gussow planned to file a mediocre to negative review. Fortunately, our publicist, Fred Hoot, was able to have the review pulled. Yet, as a result, it was difficult to get *The New York Times* to give us serious coverage. It was quite a while before their illustrator, Al Hirschfeld, would turn things around with his advocacy for the show.

Without much publicity and advance sale, Stan stated it might be too tough to keep *Charlotte Sweet* afloat, even though our overall reviews and audience reaction just got better and better. Still, I wasn't going to take the situation sitting down. I figured if *Charlotte Sweet* could be rescued from her helium addiction by the show's close, there was no reason I couldn't overcome a little hot air. Often flanked by others (Edward Stone, Gerald Jay Markoe, and my brother Douglas), I became a fixture at TKTS half-price booths at 47th Street and Duffy Square, talking people into coming to our show. I, alongside my occasional team, could sell out what was available at the booth, then distribute discount coupons for future performances. At the time, a survey was taken of customer satisfaction at the booth and *Charlotte Sweet* and *Torch Song Trilogy* were the two highest-rated offerings. There were even a few *Charlotte Sweet* groupies who visited several times; by the end of the run, some of them would quietly sing along at sections.

The show benefited, as well, from some rental fees when designer Holmes Easley's scenery was used in a movie being filmed at our theatre space. That's why, during scenes in *Tootsie* (1982) where Dustin Hoffman is auditioning for plays, you'll find the pastel backdrop of *Charlotte Sweet* as the setting. In addition, our weekly grosses were steadily improving, to the point where, in accordance with union rules, the cast received a raise. Most of the company finally felt secure about the show. Yet I knew otherwise: our financial reserve was still very small.

Then, the bottom dropped out. During the weeks of Halloween and Election Day, theatre grosses were down everywhere. I was told if business didn't improve, the show would be forced to close. I remember being at a sparse half-price line, when some waiters from Serendipity restaurant were specifically there to see *Charlotte Sweet*. They were amazed to find the writer at the line, and they declared that *Charlotte Sweet* and *Cats* were the musicals everyone was recommending at Serendipity. I churned with mixed emotions, bedazzled that we were so well regarded, bewildered that we were probably closing, befuddled we were being compared to *Cats*.

The waiters asked me if I thought they'd be able to get tickets for that night's performance.

I insisted, "Don't worry, I'll see that you get in!"

Later, someone else on the line asked if he could use a discount ticket for Thanksgiving Day in a few weeks.

I insisted, "Buy now!"

It was a Saturday night, in which we had two performances, at 7 and at 10. I knew that the 7 p.m. performance had only sold thirty or so tickets and didn't think I had the emotional strength to look in as I usually did.

But I forced myself. I poked my head inside to see what was probably our sparsest audience in weeks, knowing that was the death knell for the show. Yet suddenly, I realized that this very tiny audience was also one of the most responsive we'd ever had, laughing and clapping louder than some full houses. A sense of gratified acceptance came over me.

Charlotte Sweet closed on the Sunday matinee of November 7th to a sold-out house, including some of the groupies. "Quartet Agonistes"—the number that Dennis Dennehy had staged when the cast was dispirited and Ed Stone ill—received a two-minute ovation. Other numbers, group and solo, likewise stopped the show. That was a performance I'll always remember and prize.

So Ed's prediction about which show would be remembered was wrong. *Little Shop of Horrors* became an all-time smash. It has certainly enjoyed more success and longevity, plus won a Drama Desk Award for Best Musical that we did not. Maybe in some parallel universe, Walter Kerr (or some equally influential figure) raved about *Charlotte Sweet*, more audiences came sooner, and we were established as a bona fide hit; but that wasn't the case in reality. Still, I cannot discount how fortunate we were at everything that went right for *Charlotte Sweet*: from its fluky inspirations to its perfect creative team, splendid cast, and the magic it meant to so

Charlotte Sweet *casts (opening and closing). (top) Christopher Seppe, Mara Beckerman, Polly Pen, Merle Louise, Timothy Landfield, and Michael McCormick. (bottom) Alan Brasington, Beckerman, Nicholas Wyman, Sandra Wheeler, Jeff Keller, Beckerman, and Lynn Eldredge. Photos: Elizabeth Wolynski and Edward Stone.*

many audience members. In addition, the show does get done occasionally and will live on through its cast album, even if Ed, Christopher Seppe, and Gerald Jay Markoe are no longer with us. Christopher and Ed left us in their young thirties, early victims of AIDS (we later learned AIDS was the cause of Ed's illness the first week of rehearsals). Nonetheless, in that precious period, we and our company were having the time of our lives, a wonderful musical theatre family, working side by side on *Charlotte Sweet*. Quoting a song title from the show, "It Could Only Happen in the Theatre."

Chapter 25: *End of an Era*

A Celebration of Mary and Ben. *Pictured: Christine Andreas, Mary Cleere Haran, Steve Ross, and Julie Wilson. Photos: Rosalind Jacobs.*

Flash forward. On May 22, 2000, friends and family gathered at the Algonquin Oak Room to pay tribute to my grandparents, Mary and Ben B. Bodne. We reminisced about their illustrious lives and once-upon-a-time years as owners of the Algonquin Hotel, from 1946-1987. My grandmother had passed away in late February of 2000. My grandfather had predeceased her in May of 1992.

It was the end of an era. We had previously planned a memorial for Grandpa Ben in 1992; yet the grief was too much for Grandma Mary, and we canceled at the last moment. After Grandma left us, too, the family felt the need to present *A Celebration of Mary and Ben.*

Algonquin alumni performed in their honor. Christine Andreas, who played Eliza Doolittle in *My Fair Lady* (1976), sang "I Could Have Danced All Night." Steve Ross delivered "There's a Small Hotel" (1936). Mary Cleere Haran and Sir Richard Rodney Bennett offered George Gershwin's "I'd Rather Charleston" (1926; lyric: Desmond Carter). Julie Wilson and David Lewis presented "In My Dreams," (2000) a song I wrote with

Gerald Jay Markoe. Letters were read, written by Maya Angelou, Liliane Montivecchi, Joseph P. Riley (the Mayor of Charleston), and Senator Ernest Hollings. I was Master of Ceremonies, and speeches were given by other Bodne grandchildren, my brothers, Douglas and David, as well as the Anspach daughters, Elizabeth Carlson and Roxanna Devlin. It was probably the last time we Algonquin kids felt entirely at home there.

There are numerous events and people encountered at the Algonquin of which I could write additional chapters. In fact, that would probably take a separate book. Herein, I'll try to cover the ones that most relate to my years at the hotel. The last musicals I wrote and rehearsed there were *Mrs. McThing* (music by Jack Urbont)—which I've already detailed—and *Tales of Tinseltown* (music by Paul Katz). The time I spent working on *Tales of Tinseltown* was enormously rewarding for me, with a fantastic collaborator (and best friend) Paul Katz, and highly imaginative co-workers, including choreographer Dennis Dennehy and director Rick Lombardo. In addition, the show was powered by a cast of all-stars including Alison Fraser, Jason Graee, Bethe Austin, and Nora Mae Lyng.

Tales of Tinseltown *[1985]. Pictured: Olga Talyn, Jason Graee, Greg Mowry, Nat Chandler, Bethe Austin, Nora Mae Lyng, Bob Arnold, Alison Fraser; Bethe Austin as Ellie, and Jason Graee as Elmo on the Hollywood sign; Paul Katz and Michael. Photos: E. Wolynski.*

Tales of Tinseltown was a musical farce with a 1930s Hollywood Babylon backdrop about the desperate roads traveled, side by side, by a musical movie star and an idealistic screenwriter, along with other talents seeking film success. It ends with the star and the writer about to jump off the Hollywood Sign, then deciding to live instead for a worthier goal: the Broadway stage.

What few people realized was, despite the old-time Hollywood setting, it was probably the most autobiographical musical I wrote. The character of Elmo Green, an aspiring writer surrounded by glamour and screen legends, feels that he has failed by comparison. Elmo mirrored the times I've felt my efforts paled by comparison to those I've known.

Tales of Tinseltown was my first of several experiences co-producing a show with the off-off Broadway group, The Directors' Company, producers of *Bat Boy* (2001) and *Irena's Vow* (2009). Its artistic director, the excellent director Michael Parva, had always been supportive of my work and, indeed, encouraged me to write the "Algonquin Kid" series. He tirelessly promoted *Tales of Tinseltown*, frequently visiting rehearsals at the Algonquin.

Nowadays, I often miss my old rehearsal space at the Algonquin annex. There was always a sense of unique theatricality and New York history in that compact, isolated space at the far end of the Algonquin. I believe it has been converted into office and event spaces. I moved out of the hotel permanently in 1986 for the best of reasons: I got married. I was thirty-four, my fiancée was about to turn thirty, and we found each other at just the right moment. We met through a dating service and proved to be such

Betty Loshin; Bernice Cohen (photo courtesy of ASCAP).

a convincing ad for the service, several of our acquaintances signed up and married through that service. Andrea Lee Loshin looked just like Andrea Leeds, the actress (of *Stage Door*, 1937) for whom she was named by her musical loving mother, Betty. Beyond beautiful, she was a brainy attorney and a fan of Broadway. Her first note through the dating service included the statement, "When I read you loved Rodgers and Hart, my heart stood still." We had several other common bonds, such as losing young fathers and having two brothers, the youngest of whom was named David.

Something else we had in common was Bernice Cohen. Bernice was the head of the musical theatre department of American Society of Composers, Authors, and Publishers (ASCAP) and founded its musical workshop program. I'd known Bernice, a nurturing Mother Goose to young musical theatre writers, since my days at the Musical Theatre Lab. She had recruited me as a member of ASCAP (years later, I switched to BMI). It turned out that Bernice was my mother-in-law's best friend in school and her maid of honor. However, Betty Loshin (my dream of a mother-in-law—she even loved *my* musicals) hadn't seen Bernice in years. My relationship with Andrea led to a rekindling of the ladies' lifelong friendship. Sadly, both ladies died of cancer in subsequent years.

Some time in months that followed, I mustered up the courage to ask Andrea a big question: "Would you help me make a demo recording of a song?" (Andrea is also an excellent pianist). Visiting her apartment, I took out a recording device, setting before her the sheet music to a song I wrote with Jack Urbont, "Better Late Than Never [Finding Your True Love]." I sang it to her, dropped to my knees and pulled out an album of Wagner's "The Ring," asking if it would do till I could buy a formal engagement ring. Andrea said, "Yes."

Before our engagement, Grandma Mary had given Andrea a hard time, as she did every girl I dated. She dispensed comments such as "What an interesting dress—did your mother make it?" and "Don't worry about Michael—I have someone else lined up for him." Regardless, my grandparents arranged a gala engagement party for us in the Stratford Suite of the Algonquin. It took place on Valentine's Day, a.k.a. Charlotte Sweet's birthday. For me, it was like an episode of *This Is Your Life*, featuring Andrea's friends along with representatives from entire lifetime: family, Sylvia Syms, Maurice Levine, as well as alumni of Woodmere Academy, St. Clement's, *North Atlantic*, *Charlotte Sweet*, *Mrs. McThing*, and *Tales of Tinseltown*. Everyone but my wet nurse.

Andrea and I married in July 1986, feeling somewhat like a Jewish Donna Reed and James Stewart from *It's a Wonderful Life* (1946), very

Engagement party at Stratford Suite. From Charlotte Sweet*: Timothy Landfield, Gerald Jay Markoe, Mara Beckerman, Christopher Seppe, Merle Louise, Alan Brasington, Polly Pen, Virginia Seidel, assistant director Donna Jacobson, stage manager Peter Weickert, and lighting designer Jason Kantrowitz. From* North Atlantic*: Marilyn Hiratzka, Debra Moreno, James Fradrich, Susan Bigelow, baby Emma Jerome (Susan Bigelow's daughter), and Lori Tan Chinn. From* Tales of Tinseltown*: Rick Lombardo, Olga Talyn, musical director Steven Alper, casting director Mark Teschner, Alison Fraser, production associate Ethelda Tabackman, Paul Katz, Jason Graae, Jason Kantrowitz, Bob Arnold. From* Mrs. McThing*: Jack Urbont, Jeanne Lehman. Plus: the future Andrea Loshin Colby, Janine Nina Tevens, Francine Trevens, Maurice Levine, Sylvia Syms, photographer Elizabeth Wolynski.*

fortunate that Fate brought us together. By the time our son Steven was born, the Algonquin had been sold. There would not be another Algonquin Kid in my family. The hotel was purchased in June 1987 by Caesar Park Hotels of Brazil, a subsidiary of the Aoki Corporation, a real estate company based in Japan[1] (it has subsequently changed ownership several times). The hotel's employees were somewhat surprised because, some months earlier, my grandfather had stated, "This is my home. I love it here. And it's not for sale." Upon the contradictory development, my Uncle Andrew Anspach announced, "People change their minds, and circumstances change."[2]

The truth was that there were some internal conflicts, financial dilemmas, and serious fears about the hotel's future profitability without needed alterations. With U.S. tax laws about to be overhauled by the Tax Reform Act of 1986, the decision was made to sell while it was most advantageous. *The New York Times* reported that, "Mr. and Mrs. Bodne had been

Michael and Andrea Colby wedding day.

influenced by the fact that no younger relatives had shown great interest in taking over the business."³ I cherished the hotel and might well have been interested in "taking over," even if theatre was my preference. However, I knew that Grandpa Ben and Uncle Andrew, among others, clashed on how to best maintain the place. Moreover, I saw what such dissension had done to my father. Above all, even though Grandpa Ben seesawed till the last minute, it was foremost his decision to make.

Finally, the deal was concluded. A dual-edge proviso was that, no matter who owned the hotel, the Bodnes would be allowed to continue living in their apartment—receiving meals and other niceties—for the rest of the lives. Yet from the day of the sale onward, my grandparents wavered from feeling like honorary rulers in their rightful realm to outsiders in their former country. Other family members had a kind of vestigial foothold there, visiting my grandparents; but it would be bittersweet.

On October 3, 1989, many Colbys and Anspachs were present at a party billed as the "Algonquin Restoration Gala." Actor Jack Gilford was toastmaster, and Al Hirschfeld cut a symbolic ribbon, as the party launched the redesigned hotel, most notably the lobby and the Rose Room. The alterations cost a reported $20 million—"on improvements"[4]—though much of what we saw reminded the family that this wasn't quite the Algonquin that the Bodnes had owned. In fact, the hotel had been so reconfigured, I barely knew my way around some sections. Another reminder that the Bodnes had lost charge occurred when any of their grandchildren visited Grandma at lunchtime. Self-conscious that she no longer could treat the family to meals, Grandma pretended to be exceedingly hungry. She'd order double portions and extra courses (all gratis), then tell the waiter they were too much for her, letting her company finish the food at no extra charge. It was around this time that I got some sobering advice from Sophie Globerman, the kindly Algonquin disburser, who remained as my grandparents' personal money manager. Sophie sat me down and candidly stated that, henceforth, funds would be limited; I, who had no worries about money before, needed to seriously look for work to supplement my income, meaning, theatre would have to be a sideline.

In many ways, this was actually a blessing. It set me on a course of independence taking jobs in office work, advertising, and teaching that broadened my scope, even in my writing. It also prepared me for the inevitable time when I could no more rely on my grandparents.

We lost Grandpa Ben first in May 1992. Weak and ill, he'd recently been admitted to a hospital for testing. This was around the same time that Sylvia Syms passed away. Ironically, she phoned me that week, concerned not about her own health, but about my grandparents (From her taped message):

"I'm calling to find out how Grandpa is. I'm hoping he'll be better. I'm hoping they'll take care of him. I'm just worried about Grandma. So let me know, Michael, okay?"

On May 12, two days after Sylvia left us, Grandpa Ben died of heart failure. Our paterfamilias, who'd risen from poor Chattanooga paperboy to big news in New York, was gone. The true-life Jewish version of a Horatio Alger story was over. Grandpa had saved a hotel that was on the edge of extinction and guided it to a decade in which it became a landmark. In 1987, the hotel was designated a "New York City landmark;" then, in 1996, it was cited as a "Literary landmark."[5] What's more, even though Grandpa's childhood was underprivileged, he made certain his family had the best of everything possible, from education to social advantages. He may not have fully understood us—and sometimes lashed out when of a different mind—but he always tried his best to look out for us.

Also missed was Grandpa's wicked sense of humor. Notwithstanding, he managed to conjure an uproarious laugh even posthumously. Right after both of the Bodnes were gone, my Aunt Barbara Anspach was sorting through Grandpa's old drawers at the Algonquin and found a large movie reel. By that time, I had pretty much become the family custodian of home movies and other memorabilia. Accordingly, Aunt Barbara phoned me, "Michael, I've come across an old home movie of Grandpa's and thought you might like it." I was extremely pleased, having previously found old movies—in our basement in Hewlett—of the Bodnes and family members when they were youthful and vibrant. These included movies of Grandpa with celebrities like Marcel Cerdan, the boxing champion he promoted. When I arrived to pick up the reel from Aunt Barbara, we agreed it was a good idea to have the reel preserved in video format. Directly from that meeting, I ventured over to a video service and dotingly presented them with the reel, saying, "Please be careful. These are home movies of my family and I wouldn't want anything to be lost." Days later, I received a call that the videotape was ready and rushed over to pick it up. I had no idea why, but I got a strange look when I expressed, "Thanks so much. I can't wait to see these home movies."

When I returned to my own home, it was fortunate that I waited until the family was asleep before I checked the video. I slipped it into our player and began watching on our TV screen. I expected to see a nostalgic gathering of cheerful and much younger family faces. Instead, within a grainy black and white silent movie, a zaftig woman entered in the nude, about to get down to business with a mustachioed gentleman. It was definitely not a *family* movie that Grandpa Ben had kept through the years. I was just relieved it hadn't been in Grandma's drawer. In any case, I then knew why I had gotten that funny look from the video salesperson. I chuckled for the next ten minutes, quietly so as not to wake up the house.

Not so funny was looking in on Grandma. Widowed and fighting depression, she clung to her family—and sense of purpose at the Algonquin—more than ever. She established herself as a doyenne of the Algonquin, often greeting guests and recalling memories and history of the hotel. On occasion, she sat with actress Madeline Gilford and her husband Jack, the incomparable comic star of such Broadway musicals as *Cabaret* and *No, No Nanette.* Another bonding factor between my family and the Gilfords was the McCarthy era. Both Madeline and Jack had been blacklisted and knew the Algonquin represented a safe harbor for victims of the Red Scare.

Even outside of the Algonquin, the Gilfords had become like mishpocha to me. I'd been hired to write two all-star benefits, in 1987 and a follow-up in 1988, for their daughter Lisa Gilford. These benefits were to raise funds for a musical theatre program in Aspen, Colorado, that was planned by Lisa. They were directed by yet another Gilford, their son, Joe; and one of the benefits featured Joe's future wife, Algonquin singer Mary Cleere Haran.

Madeline was like a talent yenta: if she liked you, she constantly tried to fix you up with the right theatre match to produce beautiful creative offspring. Through her and the benefits, I was able to write material for

The Night of 20,000 Stars *benefit (1988 edition) for the Gilfords. (fourth row Martin Vidnovic, Wilford Brimley, Evan Bell, Ron Richardson, Ellen Hanley, and Joe Bousard. (third row) John McCallum, Mary Cleere Haran, Sue Anne Gershenson, Gretchen Wyler, Jo Sullivan Loesser, Nancy Dussault, Kim Criswell, Annie-Jo, Thelma Lee, Edie Adams, Patrice Munsel, Judy Blazer, Nikki Sahagan Siretta, Lisa Gilford-Smerling, and Madeline Gilford. (second row) Michael Colby (bearded writer), Joe Gilford Gregg Edelman, Jack Gilford, Tim Jerome, Kevin Daly, P. J. Benjamin, and Savion Glover. (first row) Nora Mae Lyng and Susan Bigelow.*

such top performers as Edie Adams (star of the first musical I ever saw, *L'il Abner*), Vivian Blaine, Patrice Munsel, Savion Glover, and Harve Presnell. Best of all was writing speeches for Jack Gilford, whose unforgettable performance as Herr Shultz I saw many times in my all-time favorite musical, *Cabaret*. A treasured memory is my sharing a taxi with the Gilfords from the Aspen airport as Jack rehearsed the lines I'd written him. He repeated the lines until he captured every nuance. If I never did another day's work in theatre, I would still have the priceless memory of one of my theatre idols practicing material I had created for him.

While I was busy with assignments, Grandma Mary was feeling at loose ends. In 1998, she was interviewed by *The New York Times,* when the Algonquin's lobby was re-designed once more. This time, "hotel design Guru"[6] Alexandra Champalimaud oversaw a $5.5 million "facelift" commissioned by the latest owners, the Atlanta-based Camberly Hotel Company. The interview reported:

> "Mary Bodne . . . is of two minds. She has lived on the 10th floor on the hotel for 52 years, presiding over the lobby from her won chair. Last Friday night, she came down to tryout out a new, velvet one that is awaiting its sags. 'What I've seen looks very nice, but it will never look like my old Algonquin again,' she said. 'No, darling, I know it will never be the same.'"[7]

The new designs may have been what the hotel needed to bridge into the contemporary world, but they were very different.

Grandma's discomfort with the renovations had been further reflected in a 1997 article, printed in *The New Yorker,* in which she was assuaged by actress Billie Whitelaw (the definitive interpreter of Samuel Beckett plays):

> "Mary Bodne, whose late husband owned the Algonquin from 1946 to 1987, came over to greet the actress. 'Look what they've done to my dear, dear hotel,' she said, dabbing her eyes with a tissue. 'They've closed the Oak Room doors. The Oak Room doors were never once closed! I can't dance anymore.' The great Beckettian [Whitelaw] rose, put her arm around the older woman's waist, and twirled her gently. 'Of course you can dance,' Billie Whitelaw said."[8]

Change was a keynote in all our lives. By August 1994, I—with Andrea and our young son Steven—had moved to New Jersey to ease Andrea's commute to her job as an attorney at Johnson & Johnson (in New Brunswick,

New Jersey.) Grandma occasionally talked about also moving, back to Charleston. She was thinking of purchasing a home there. She had in fact helped buy a small house in Ridgeville, South Carolina, near Charleston, as a gift for Louise Brown, the housekeeper who had worked at various times for the Bodnes, the Anspachs, and—longest of all—the Colbys. I had the loveliest trip flying to South Carolina to join Louise on her 75th birthday. It was an occasion for the most delicious Southern fried chicken and ice tea since the Friday meals Louise cooked during my childhood. The popular Louise was surrounded by family members, but insisted that her only child Leonard and I sit directly at her sides, as her "two sons." I was deeply touched for, in many ways, Louise had indeed raised me. She'd certainly protected me, as much as she could, during the often-tumultuous years on Paine Road. Unhappily, that splendid day was the last time I could enjoy Louise's company in person; she too passed away soon after.

Young Louise Brown, who raised my mother; older Louise, who raised me. Photo courtesy of Elizabeth Linning and the Haigood Family.

Grandma Mary never did move. She continued being a tremendously supportive figure in my life, even if—by this point—I needed other main sources to finance my musicals. *Slay It With Music*, a show I wrote with Paul Katz, was largely financed through the settlement I won after being hit by a car (I like to say it almost killed me to get that show on, but I had a terrific time working on it). The musical, *Delphi or Bust* (1998), my last

Colby musicals. (top) Slay It With Music *(1989: Jill Bernstein, J. P. Dougherty, Louisa Flaningam, Janet Metz, Virginia Sandifur, and Barry Williams, photo courtesy of William Gibson/Martha Swope Associates). Theatre by the Blind's production of* Whattaya Blind? *(1993: Peter Seymour, Susan Stevens, Rosalind Scheer, George Ashiotis, and Tom DeRosa, photo courtesy of Carol Rosegg). (bottom)* Delphi or Bust *(1998: John Simeone, Tia Riebling, Jill Geddes, Ken Prymus, Kimberly Harris, Colleen Hawks, Darren Lee Frazier, and Jody Ashworth, photo courtesy of Elaine Criscione);* They Chose Me! *(2006: Katie Welles, Sam Levin, Dea Julien, and original cast, photo courtesy Henry Chen).*

collaboration with Gerald Jay Markoe, was financed when I sold one of my most beloved possessions, my childhood comic collection.

Grandma Mary was fond of both shows, attending on several occasions. She even arranged for a special opening night party for *Delphi or Bust* and its sponsor, Amas Musical Theatre, at the Algonquin. I was particularly thrilled to work for Amas, whose members, including founder Rosetta LeNoire, and Artistic Director Donna Trinkoff, had broken boundaries in championing non-traditional, color-blind casting.

Nowadays, most of my work each week encompasses substitute teaching in areas around Central New Jersey, where I love working with kids. In my New York days, especially the months when *Charlotte Sweet* played, I was sometimes recognized in theatre circles, whereupon someone might warmly call out, "Look, there's *Michael* Colby." These days, I walk down the streets of my town and frequently students will warmly call out, "Look, there's *Mister* Colby!"

I no longer take on any writing projects for which I personally must shoulder the finances. Nonetheless, there have been various assignments of which I'm especially proud. One was writing revues, composed by Steven Silverstein, for the Theatre By the Blind (now renamed Theatre Breaking Through Barriers), a company directed by Ike Schambelan that casts actors with disabilities. Another was creating *They Chose Me!*, the musical about adoption commissioned by TADA! (Several of its subsequent productions have, in fact, been supported by adoption institutes). I also collaborated with Steven Silverstein and Pat Hoag Simon on *The Human Heart* (1998), a musical about adolescent depression that received a Billy Rose Foundation grant, then was produced at Marymount Manhattan College. Finally, there have been several benefits I've penned for Amas, writing speeches for the likes of Cecily Tyson, Celeste Holm, Ossie Davis, and Ruby Dee.

Caption: Cast of Quel Fromage *(2002).*

Amas also presented a sold-out benefit commemorating my 50th birthday, *Quel Fromage: 50 Years of Colby* (2002). It was another of the best events of my life, spotlighting alumni from all my shows. I just regret that my grandparents and father had all passed away by then. Yet I could feel their spirits—my father's love of music, my grandparents' constant support—impacting the entire occasion.

My most enduring booster, Grandma Mary, barely made it to the year 2000. She suffered a stroke a year and a half earlier and had never really recovered. She left us on February 28th. Still, the Mary Mazo who was almost silenced in infancy when Cossacks stormed Odessa had survived to the ripe age of ninety-three—making an indelible difference in the lives of countless friends and family members.

A Celebration of Mary and Ben *(2000)*. *Pictured: Michael, Elizabeth Anspach Carlson, Douglas Colby, David Colby, and Roxanna Anspach Devlin. Photo: Rosalind Jacobs.*

Relatives and friends came from far and wide to attend *A Celebration of Mary and Ben* (2000). They included family from Charleston, Algonquin regulars, and my mother and her third husband Bernie. You could feel the sense that we were not only celebrating Mary and Ben but a bygone period in which the Bodne family was at the center of a cultural institution. On that night, we knew that time and our lives must move past that point, yet we would always recall our magnificent times at the Algonquin. We closed the festivities with everyone singing "Our Love Is Here to Stay," a standard by the Bodnes' friend from their Charleston days, George Gershwin, and his brother, Ira. Abiding love was evident all evening. Still earlier, my own feelings were expressed when Julie Wilson performed "In My Dreams," a song I wrote from the heart with Gerald Jay Markoe to commemorate those I most missed. The lyric was dedicated to my grandparents:

> "When you're not here
> You still appear
> Playing the happiest scene,
> Somewhere that's warm and serene
> In my dreams.
> Lively and bright,
> Joking all night,
> Nothing can keep us apart,

Having that old heart to heart
In my dreams.
When I yearn to
See you once again,
I return to
That special place and then . . .
Laughter and joy
None can destroy
Shine through the night on and on
As we catch up till the dawn
In my dreams.
You are there in
So much that I do
As I share in
The things I've learned from you.
Let sunrise break,
As I awake,
I know that you'll somehow stay
Guiding me through ev'ry day
Through my dreams."[9]

Photos of the Bodnes through the years.

Other Books About the Algonquin Hotel Include:

The Algonquin Cat by Val Schaffner. Drawings by Hilary Knight. New York NY: Wings Book © 1980.

The Algonquin Round Table New York: A Historical Guide by Kevin C. Fitzpatrick. Guilford CT: Lyons Press © 2005.

The Algonquin Wits. Edited by Robert E. Drennan. Secaucus NJ: The Citadel Press © 1968.

Do Not Disturb by Frank Case. New York NY: Frederick A. Stokes Company © 1940.

Feeding the Lions: An Algonquin Cook Book by Frank Case. Garden City NY: The Greystone Press © 1942.

A Friendly Game of Murder: An Algonquin Round Table Mystery by J.J. Murphy. New York NY: Signet @ 2012.

A Journey into Dorothy Parker's New York by Kevin C. Fitzpatrick. Berkeley CA: Roaring Forties Press © 2005.

The Lost Algonquin Round Table by Frank Case. Edited by Nat Benchley & Kevin C. Fitzpatrick. New York NY: Donald Brooks © 2009.

Merry Gentlemen (and One Lady) by Joseph Bryan III. New York NY: Atheneum © 1986.

Murder Your Darlings: An Algonquin Round Table Mystery by J.J. Murphy. New York NY: Signet @ 2011.

Tales of a Wayward Inn by Frank Case. New York NY: Frederick A. Stokes Company © 1938.

Under the Table: A Dorothy Parker Cocktail Guide by Kevin C. Fitzpatrick. Guilford CT: Lyons Press © 2013.

The Vicious Circle: The Story of the Algonquin Round Table by Margaret Case Harriman; Illustrated by Al Hirschfeld. New York NY: Rinehart & Co, Inc. © 1951.

Wit's End: Day and Nights of the Algonquin Round Table by James R. Gaines. New York NY: Brown © 1959.

You Might As Well Die: An Algonquin Round Table Mystery by J.J. Murphy. New York NY: Signet @ 2011.

And One Video:

The Ten-Year Lunch: The Wit and Legend of The Algonquin Round Table Produced and directed by Aviva Slesin. Winner of the 1987 Academy Award for Best Documentary.

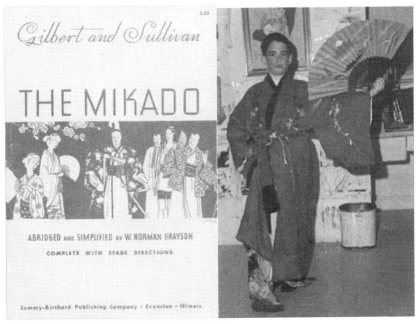

From 1961 Woodmere Academy production of The Mikado: *script and Michael in costume.*

Bibliography

Chapter 1: *Way Back When*

[1] Reside, Doug (Lewis and Dorothy Cullman Curator for the Billy Rose Theatre Division, Library for the Performing Arts). "Musical of the Month: Fiddler on the Roof." Blog for New York Public Library. Steptember 29, 2014: http://www.nypl.org/blog/2014/09/29/musical-month-fiddler-roof

Chapter 2: *Algonquin Renaissance*

[1] Reynolds, Quentin. "The Hotel That Refused to Die" in *Esquire* (New York NY). February 1950.

[2] Lyons, Leonard. "The Lyons Den," *NY Post* (New York NY). November 30, 1961.

[3] Reynolds, Quentin. Ibid.

[4] Poe, Randall. "The Unicorn of Big-City Hotels…With Thurber, Parker, Benchley, Ross and company."Travel and Leisure, New York. No date given.

[5] Newspaper clipping. Source unidentified.

Chapter 3: *Screaming At Agnes Moorehead and Other Adventures*

[1] Dalton, James. *James Dean: The Mutant King: A Biography*. Chicago IL: Chicago Review Press © 1974.

[2] Davis, Charles, "Nancy Carroll" obituary in *Los Angeles Times* (Los Angeles CA). August 8, 1965.

[3] *West Side Story—The Broadway Classic* website: BB Promotion GmBH in cooperation with Sundance Productions, Inc.: http://www.westsidestory.de/index.php/en/show/historie

[4] Dennis, Patrick. *Auntie Mame: An Irreverent Escapade*. New York NY: Vanguard Press, 1955.

[5] Lawrence, Jerome, Lee, Robert E., Herman, Jerry. *Mame*. New York NY: Random House, 1967.

[6] Anderson, Susan Heller. "City Makes It Official: Algonquin Is Landmark" in *The New York Times* (New York NY). September 30, 1987.

Chapter 4: *Dreams of Camelot*

[1] Canby, Vincent. "When Irish Eyes Are Smiling, It's Norman Mailer" in *The New York Times* (New York NY). October 27, 1958.

[2] McGrath, Douglas. "The Seven Wonders of Preston Sturges" in *Vanity Fair* (New York, NY). May 2010.

[3] Sturges, Sandy. "Preston Sturges Biography" on *The Official Preston Sturges Site*. http://www.prestonsturges.net/biography.html.

[4] McGrath, Douglas. "The Seven Wonders of Preston Sturges" in *Vanity Fair* (New York NY). May 2010.

[5] McGrath, Douglas. Ibid.

[6] Bodne, Ben. "Broadway: Inn of Distinction" ("Substituting for vacationing Jack O'Brian") in *New York Daily Column* (New York NY). August 12, 1969.

[7] Keats, John. *You Might As Well Live: The Life and Times of Dorothy Parker*. New York: Paragon House Publishers, September 1970.

[8] "Interesting Facts," Algonquin Hotel website. http://www.algonquinhotel.com/interesting-facts.

[9] Lyons. Jeffrey. *Stories My Father Told Me: Notes From "The Lyons Den,"* New York NY: Abbeville Press, June 2011.

[10] "admin." *Writers Club: Brendan Behan (1923-1964)* from Writers Tears Irish Whiskey. 2010: http://www.writerstears.com/?p=216.

Chapter 5: *Somewhere Between Marilyn Monroe and Liz Taylor*

[1] Seymour, Gene. Special to CNN: "Elizabeth Taylor: 'The Last Star'". March 23, 2011: http://www.cnn.com/2011/OPINION/03/23/seymour.elizabeth.liz.taylor/.

[2] "Butterfield Eight (1960)" from *The Hollywood Review*, July 7, 2010: http://hollywoodrevue. wordpress.com/2010/07/07/butterfield-8-1960/.

[3] Van Gelder, Lawrence. "Theater Review; A Poignant Slice of Lives Restarted" in *NY Times* (New York NY). December 16, 2000: http://www.nytimes.com/2000/12/16/theater/theater-review-a-poignant-slice-of-lives-restarted.html.

[4] LaPorte, Nicole. "Staff in flight as the Algonquin Gets New Owners" in *New York Observer* (New York NY). July 15, 2002.

[5] Kerr, Jean. *Mary, Mary*. New York: Dramatists Play Service Inc., 1961.

[6] Smith, Howard. "Glittering Technique: Music by Gershwin for piano and orchestra" from CD SPOTLIGHT / Music & Vision Homepage (Masterton, New Zealand). October 14, 2009: http://www.mvdaily.com/articles/2009/10/gershwin.htm.

[7] Lyons. Jeffrey. *Stories My Father Told Me: Notes From "The Lyons Den."* New York NY: Abbeville Press, June 2011.

[8] Lyons. Jeffrey. *Ibid.*

[9] Hagan, Agnes. "Canton Women's Club hosts illustrious author Hallie Ephron." *Wicked Local Canton* (Canton OH). October 30, 2013: http://www.wickedlocal.com/canton/news/x1275637358/Canton-Womens-Club-hosts-illustrious-author-Hallie-Ephron?zc_p=0.

Chapter 6: *Could Jed Clampett be Jewish?*

[1] Paul Henning Interview: EMMYTVLEGENDS.ORG. Interviewed by Bob Claster, Toluca Lake, CA, 1997. Archive of American Television: http://www.emmytvlegends.org/interviews/people/paul-henning#

[2] Paul Henning Interview. Ibid.

[3] Paul Henning Interview. Ibid.

[4] Haranis, Chrys. "BLIMEY! THE WHOLE BLOOMIN' BUNCH HAS BEEN BITTEN BY THE BLOOD BUG!" in *Photoplay* magazine. New York NY: Macfadden Publications, August 1962.

[5] Haranis, Chrys. Ibid.

[6] Beckett, Francis. *Laurence Olivier*. London, Great Britain: Haus Publishing Limited, 2005.

[7] Signoret, Simone. *Nostalgia Isn't What It Used to Be* (English translation). New York NY: Harper & Row, 1978.

Chapter 7: *A Mazel Tov from Robert F. Kennedy*

[1] Sullivan, Patricia. "Earl Mazo obituary" for *The Washington Post* (Washington DC). February 18, 2007.

[2] Sullivan, Patricia. Ibid.

[3] Sullivan, Patricia. Ibid.

[4] Portfolio, 1969. Woodmere NY. June 1969.

[5] Hollings, Ernest. *Congressional Record: Proceedings and Debates of the 102^d Congress, Second Session*, Vol. 138, No. 83 (Washington DC). June 11, 1992

[6] Sharland, Elizabeth. *The British on Broadway: Backstage and Beyond—The Early Years*. Lancaster England: Barbican Press, 1999.

Chapter 8: *As William Faulkner Wrote at the Algonquin...*

[1] Faulkner, William. "Interviews: Gore Vidal, The Arts of Fiction No. 50," Interviewed by Gerald Clarke. *The Paris Review*, No. 59 (Paris, France) Fall 1974.

[2] Vidal, Gore. *Nobel Lectures, Literature 1901-1967*, Editor Horst Frenz, Amsterdam, Netherlands: Elsevier Publishing Company, 1969.

[3] Marrs, Suzanne. *Eudora Welty: A Biography*. Orlando FL: Harcourt Books, 2005.

[4] Frail, T.A. "Eudora Welty as Photographer" in *Smithsonian* magazine, Arts & Culture section (Washington DC). April 2009.

[5] "Biography: James Thurber." Thurber House (Columbus OH): http://thurberhouse.org/james-thurber.html © 2014.

[6] "Arthur Miller Biography." Bio. TRUE STORY: http://www.biography.com/people/arthur-miller-9408335? © 2014 A+E Networks.

[7] Doolittle, Leslie (attributing story to Joely Fisher). "Playboy Helps Faye Resnick Find Joy" in *Orlando Sentinel* (Orlando FL). February 5, 1997.

[8] Levy, Arthur. Biography: Joan Baez. July 2008: www.joanbaez.com/officialbio08.html.

[9] Rabe, W.T. "The Tru Historie of Mary Morstan's Companions" from the Shoso-in Bulletin" (Japan) © 1991: http://shoso.ninja-web.net/Shoso-inBulletin/vol2Rabe.html

[10] Bay, Cody. "The Story Behind the Styles" from *On This Day In Fashion*. June 16, 2010: http://onthisdayinfashion.com/?tag=history-of-the-bathing-suit&paged=2.

[11] Nauta, Antoinette Gerarda. "Rudi Gernreich, Misunderstood Fashion Profit" in *A.G. Nauta Couture*. November 25, 2012: http://agnautacouture.com/2012/11/25/rudi-gernreich-misunderstood-fashion-prophet

Chapter 9: *The British Are Staying!*

[1] Sharland, Elizabeth. *The British on Broadway: Backstage and Beyond—The Early Years*. Lancaster England: Barbican Press, 1999.

[2] O'Connor, Gary. *Ralph Richardson: An Actor's Life*. New York: Applause Books. March 1, 2001.

[3] Walters, Barbara. On *20/20* (ABC-TV), first broadcast November 19, 1999: http://www.pspinformation.com/voices/other/dudley_moore_interview.shtml.

[4] Ustinov, Peter. "Quotations by Author" @ http://www.quotationspage.com/quotes/Peter_Ustinov/.

[5] Edwin McDowell, Alec Waugh obituary in *The New York Times* (New York NY). September 4, 1981.

[6] Uncredited. "BELLHOP" from "Talk of the Town" in *The New Yorker* (New York NY). September 20, 1993.

[7] Murgatroyd, Simon. "How the Other Half Loves: Background" from Alan Ayckbourn's Official Website, 2014: http://howtheotherhalfloves.alanayckbourn.net/styled/index.html.

[8] "Tommy Steele Biography & Filmography" on Matinee Classics LLC © 2014: http://matineeclassics.com/celebrities/actors/tommy_steele/details/.

[9] Barker, Dennis, Harold Fielding obituary in *The Guardian* (London UK). September 30, 2003: http://matineeclassics.com/celebrities/actors/tommy_steele/details/.

[10] "Harold Fielding Biography" on ALLMUSIC Website © 2014: http://www.allmusic.com/artist/harold-fielding-mn0000995528/biography.

[11] Moir, Jan. "Still swinging at 77! Mary Quant put the swing into the 60s, gave us that iconic bob cut and – hallelujah! - invented waterproof mascara" from *Mail Online*. February 3, 2012: http://www.dailymail.co.uk/femail/article-2096184/Mary-Quant-swing-60s-gave-iconic-bob-cut--hallelujah--invented-waterproof-mascara.html.

[12] "Mary Quant" Biography. Lifetime TV © 2014 AETN UK: http://www.thebiographychannel.co.uk/biographies/mary-quant.html.

[13] Cooke, Rachel. "Edna O'Brien: 'A writer's imaginative life commences in childhood'" from *The Guardian / The Observer* (London UK). February 5, 20011: http://www.theguardian.com/books/2011/feb/06/edna-obrien-ireland-interview.

Chapter 10: *Musicals "R" Us*

[1] Darien, Joe. Lyric to "Aldonza" from the musical *Man of La Mancha* (music: Mitch Leigh; libretto: Dale Wasserman) © 1965.

[2] From the song "Frank Kiley": lyric by Michael Colby, music by Peter Millrose, © 2013.

[3] Williams, Tennessee. *The Selected Letters of Tennessee Williams, Volume II: 1945-1947*. Edited by Albert J. Devlin, co-edited by Nancy M. Tischler. New York NY: New Directions, 2004.

[4] Lees, Gene. *Inventing Champagne: The Musical Worlds of Lerner and Loewe*. New York NY: St. Martin's Press, 1960.

[5] Hart, Lorenz. Lyric to "Ten Cents a Dance" from the musical *Simple Simon* (music: Richard Rodgers; book: Ed Wynn & Guy Bolton) © 1930.

[6] Lerner, Alan Jay. *The Street Where I Live*. New York: W. W. Norton & Company, 1978.

[7] Lees, Gene. *Ibid*.

[8] Zollo, Paul. "American Icons: Irving Caesar" in *American Songwriter Magazine*. June 23, 2010: http://www.americansongwriter.com/2010/06/american-icons-irving-caesar/.

[9] Steyn, Mark. *Broadway Babies Say Goodnight: Musicals Then & Now*. London: Faber and Faber Limited, 1997.

[10] Caesar, Irving & Hart, Lorenz. Lyric to "Stonewall Moskowitz March" from the musical *Betsy* (music: Richard Rodgers; book: Irving Caesar & David Freedman, revised by William Anthony McGuire) © 1926.

[11] Harburg, Yip. "An Atom a Day Keeps the Doctor Away" in *Rhymes for the Irreverent*. Illustrated by Seymour Chwast. New York NY: Grossman, 1965.

Chapter 11: *Learning the Ropes*

[1] "Helen Thurber Obituary" in *The New York Times* (New York NY). December 26, 1986.

[2] Romine, Dannye. "Wife Not a 'Thurber Woman'" in *Lakeland Ledger* (Lakeland FL). August 17, 1980.

[3] "Helen Thurber Obituary" in *The Hour* (Norwalk, CT), December 24, 1986.

[4] "Biography: E. B. White." Scholastic Inc.© 2013.: http://www.scholastic.com/teachers/contributor/e-b-white#top..

[5] Schuller, Gunther, McGlohan, Loonis, & Levy, Robert (supplied by Ron Prather). Biography of Alec (Alexander) Wilder in *Classical Net™: The Internet's Premier Classical Music Source*. 2014: http://www.classical.net/music/comp.lst/acc/wilder.php

[6] Lambert, Philip. *Alec Wilder*. Champaign, IL: University of Illinois Press, 2013.

[7] Notes for the album "Alec Wilder: Music for Winds and Brass" (TROY763), Albany Records (Albany, NY). 20014: http://www.albanyrecords.com/mm5/merchant.mvc?Screen=PROD&Store_Code=AR&Product_Code=TROY763&Category_Code=a-Orch.

[8] "About 'While We're Young'" on "The Interactive Tony Bennett Discography: a project from The Year of Tony Bennett" © 2014: http://discography.bloggingtonybennett.com/composer/alec-wilder/

[9] Uncredited. "BELLHOP" from "Talk of the Town" in *The New Yorker* (New York NY). September 20, 1993.

[10] Cleveland Amory. "Dana Andrews was Lucky" in *Spokane Daily Chronicle* (Spokane WA). December 8, 1976.

[11] DeVeaux, Scott & Giddins. *Jazz*. New York NY: W.W. Norton & Company, January 30, 2009.

[12] Kelley, Robin D.G. "Biography of Thelonious Sphere Monk" from *The Monk Zone* © Thelonious Records, 2001-2009. http://www.monkzone.com/silent/biographyHTML.htm.

[13] Uncredited. "BELLHOP" from "Talk of the Town" in *The New Yorker* (New York NY).

Chapter 12: *This Doesn't Happen at the Holiday Inn*

[1] Severo, Richard, "Jules Dassin, Filmmaker on Blacklist, Dies at 96," obituary in *The New York Times* (New York NY). April 1, 2008.

[2] Dowling, Colette. "Chronicle of a Closing Night" in *Playbill Magazine*. As reported in http://www.theatreaficionado.com/tag/flops.

[3] "Norman Krasna, 74, Is Dead; Playwright and Screen Writer," obituary in *The New York Times* (New York NY). November 7, 1984.

[4] Rice, Charlie. "45 Seconds from Broadway" / "Charlie Rice's Punchbowl" in *The Spokesman-Review* (Spokane WA). January 14, 1967.

[5] Gottfried, Martin. *Jed Harris, The Curse of Genius*. New York: Little, Brown, and Company, 1984.

[6] Coleman, Terry. *Olivier*. New York: MacMillan Publishers, January 1, 2005.

[7] Gottfried, Martin. *Jed Harris, The Curse of Genius*. New York NY: Little, Brown, and Company, 1984.

[8] Lyons, Leonard. "The Lyons Den" in *New York Post* [various editions] (New York NY). 1968-1969.

Chapter 13: *Who Knew?*

[1] Glover, William. "Drama critics goof: Wrong 'best play' announced." *Associated Press / Eugene Register-Guard* (Eugene OR). May 24, 1972.

[2] Halbfinger, David M. "Jack Valenti, 85, Confidant of a President and Stars, Dies" in "Movies" section of *The New York Times* (New York NY). April 27, 2007.

[3] Halbfinger, David M. Ibid.

[4] Valenti, Jack. This Time, This Place: My Life in War, the White House, and Hollywood. New York NY: Harmony Books, 2007.

[5] Calder, John. Obituary: William Targ. *The Independent* (London UK). August 27, 1999.

[6] Calder, John. Ibid.

[7] Neyfakh, Leon. "Glamour, Amour: A Grande Dame of Publishing Looks Back" in *New York Observer* / News (New York NY). February 26, 2008.

[8] Audrey Wood: An Inventory of Her Collection at the Harry Ransom Humanities Research Center." RLIN Record # TXRC01-A0. The University of Texas at Austin. 1984: *http://www.lib.utexas.edu/taro/uthrc/00247/hrc-00247.html*

[9] Barranger, Millie S. Audrey Wood and the Playwrights. New York NY: Palgrave Macmillan, January 2013.

[10] Sullivan, Dan. "Laughter Important to Late Playwright" in *Los Angeles Times / Washington Post News* Service (c/o *The Victoria Advocate*, Victoria TX). February 28, 1983.

[11] Coe, Marian. "Victor Buono was a natural for the role" in "Suncoasting, *St. Petersburg Times* (St. Petersburg FL). March 19, 1977.

[12] Prial, Dunstan. *The Producer: John Hammond and the Soul of American Music*. New York NY: Farrar, Straus and Giroux, June 2007.

[13] de Lisle, Tim. "Hallelujah: 70 Things About Leonard Cohen at 70" in *The Guardian* (London UK). September 27, 2004.

[14] Nadel, Ira B. Various Positions: A Life of Leonard Cohen. Toronto, Canada: Random House, August 1, 1994.

[15] Baneshik, Percie. "Taubie Kushlick" from *They Shaped Our Century: The Most Influential South Africans of the Twentieth Century*. Cape Town SA: Human and Rousseau, 1999.

[16] Baneshik, Percy. "Showbiz: The PERCY BANESHIK column" in *The Star* (Johannesburg SA). February 24, 1982.

[17] Schwartz, Pat. "Travels With Taubie" in *Mail and Guardian* (Johannesburg SA). 1981.

[18] Baneshik, Percy. "Taubie Kushlick" from *They Shaped Our Century: The Most Influential South Africans of the Twentieth Century*. Cape Town SA: Human and Rousseau, 1999. February 24, 1982.

Chapter 14: *Moving Days*

[1] Hart, Larry. Lyric to "The Most Beautiful Girl in the World" from the musical *Jumbo* (music: Richard Rodgers) © 1935.

[2] Sondheim, Stephen. Lyric to "Uptown, Downtown" cut from the musical *Follies* (music: Stephen Sondheim) © 1971; used in *Marry Me a Little* (1980).

[3] Browning, Robert. "The Glove" (1845) in *The Literature of England: An Anthology and a History*. Volume Two, Fifth Edition. Ed. George K. Anderson and William E. Buckler. Glenview IL: Scott, Forseman and Company, 1968.

[4] Browning, Robert. "Rabbi Ben Ezra" (1864) in *The Literature of England: An Anthology and a History*. *Ibid.*

[5] Browning, Robert. "Porphyria's Lover" (1834; 1836) in *The Literature of England: An Anthology and a History*. *Ibid.*

[6] Fletcher, Lucille. *Sorry, Wrong Number* (screenplay) based on the radio play by Lucille Fletcher. Paramount Pictures, United States. September 1, 1948 (release date).

[7] "Maude Chasen Dies at 97; Fed the Legends of Hollywood" from Obituary section, L.A. Online, December 12, 2001: https://groups.google.com/forum/#!topic/alt.obituaries/MQRCWD1fNio

[8] Brown, David. "Chasen's Fadeout" in *The New Yorker* (New York NY). February 20, 1995.

[9] Edwards, Bobb. "Dave Chasen" from "Find a Grave" website. March 4, 2000: http://www.findagrave.com/cgi-bin/fg.cgi?page=gr&GRid=8696.

Chapter 15: *Excelsior*

[1] Lyons. Jeffrey. *Stories My Father Told Me: Notes From "The Lyons Den."* New York NY: Abbeville Press, June 2011.

[2] Guare, John. *Rich and Famous*. New York NY: Dramatists Play Service Inc. 1977.

[3] Guare, John. *Ibid.*

[4] Liukkonen, Petri. "Leon (Marcus) Uris (1924-2003)" from Books and Writers, rights reserved by Petri Liukkonen (author) & Ari Pesonen. Kuusankosken kaupunginkirjasto, 2008: http://www.kirjasto.sci.fi/uris.htm.

[5] Nadel, Ira B. *Leon Uris: Life of a Best Seller*. Austin, TX: University of Texas Press. September 24, 2010.

[6] Nadel, Ira B. *Ibid.*

Chapter 16: *Coming Attractions*

[1] Hammerstein, Oscar II. Lyric to "It Might As Well Be Spring" from the musical movie *State Fair* (music: Richard Rodgers), produced by 20th Century Fox © 1945.

[2] "Ben Bagley Biography" c/o Painted Smiles Records: https://www.facebook.com/pages/Painted-Smiles-Records/7100242179?sk=info. 2008.

[3] Holden, Stephen, Ben Bagley obituary in *The New York Times* (New York, NY). March 27, 1998.

[4] Colby, Michael. Lyric to "The Cemetery Social Set" from the musical *Where There's a Will* (music: Douglas Colby) © 1971.

[5] Bagley, Ben. Notes on "Ben Bagley's Alan Jay Lerner Revisited." Jackson Heights NY: Painted Smiles Records, 1992.

[6] Bagley, Ben. Notes on "Ben Bagley's Ira Gershwin Revisited." Jackson Heights NY: Painted Smiles Records, 1992.

[7] Holden, Stephen. "Donald F. Smith, Champion of Cabaret, Dies at 79," obituary in *The New York Times* (New York NY). March 13, 2012.

[8] Monahan, Patrick. "To Bricktop, on Her Belated Birthday" from "Arts & Culture" section of The Daily" c/o *the Paris Review* (New York, NY). August 15, 2011.

[9] From "Celebrity Beat—New York to Hollywood" in *Jet* Magazine, A Johnson Publication (Chicago, IL). September 26, 1983.

[10] Leichner, Helen. "Smith, Ada 'Bricktop' (1894-1984)" in BlackPast.org™ Blog: Remembered & Reclaimed © 2007: http://www.blackpast.org/aah/smith-ada-bricktop-1894-1984

[11] Hart, Lorenz. Lyric to "Where Or When" from the musical *Babes In Arms* (music: Richard Rodgers) © 1937.

Chapter 17: *You Mean, That Arnold Schwarzenegger?*

[1] Gaines, Charles. "The Arnold Schwarzenegger I Knew" in *Men's Journal*, New York NY: Wenner Media. January 2004: http://www.mensjournal.com/magazine/the-arnold-schwarzenegger-i-knew-20130727Wenner media.

[2] Gaines, Charles. Ibid.

[3] Grody, Ray. "Just a Minute" in *Milwaukee Sentinal* (Milwaukee WI). August 8, 1948.

[4] Editor. "George Spelvin" in Encyclopaedia Britannica © 2014: www.britannica.com/EBchecked/topic/559232/George-Spelvin.

[5] Lerman, Leo. *The Grand Surprise: The Journals of Leo Lerman.* New York NY: Random House LLC, February 19, 2009.

[6] Grinstead, David. "Ghosts" in *New York Magazine* (New York NY). October 19, 1992.

Chapter 18: *Fast Forward*

[1] Arias, Ron. "Marking His First Century, George Abbott Once Again Brings Broadway to Broadway" in *People Magazine* (New York NY). July 6, 1987 (Vol. 28, No. 1).

[2] Johnson, Guy B. Biography from "Dr. Maya Angelou, The Official Website" © 2014: http://mayaangelou.com/bio/

[3] Angelo, Maya. A letter spoken at *A Celebration of Mary and Ben*, May 22, 2000.

[4] McNulty, Charles. Gordon Davidson is till giving to theater" in *The Los Angeles Times* (Los Angeles CA). February 09, 2013.

[5] Richard Schechner biography for "The 10th Annual BURIAN LECTURE ("The Relationship of Practice and Theory"). New York State Writers Institute, State University of New York. February 28, 2006.

[6] Albee, Edward. *Who's Afraid of Virginia Woolf?*, New York NY: Scribner © 1962.

[7] Martin, Douglas. Al Carmines obituary in *The New York Times* (New York NY). August 13, 2005.

[8] Colby, Michael & Condos, Susan. "Al Carmines and the Judson Poets' Theater." 1974: http://www.judson.org/images/AlCarminesandtheJPT.pdf.

[9] Colby, Michael & Condos, Susan. "Ibid."

Chapter 19: *That Mug Is Mine*

[1] Mamet, David. *Sexual Perversity in Chicago & The Duck Variations.* New York NY: Samuel French © 1974.

[2] Bergan, Ronald. Penny Singleton obituary in *The Guardian* (London England). November 15, 2003.

[3] Martin, Douglas. Barney McNulty obituary in *The New York Times* (New York NY). December 26, 2000.

[4] Oliver, Myrna. Barney McNulty obituary in *Los Angeles Times* (Los Angeles CA). December 22, 2000.

Chapter 20: *Getting to the Hart of Things*

[1] Hart, Dorothy. *Thou Swell, Thou Witty: The Life and Lyrics of Lorenz Hart*. New York NY: Harper & Row, Publishers © 1976.

[2] Edith Meiser recollections in Dorothy Hart's *Thou Swell, Thou Witty: The Life and Lyrics of Lorenz Hart*. Ibid.

[3] Mandelbaum, Ken. *Not Since Carrie: 40 Years of Broadway Musical Flops*. New York NY: St. Martin's Press, October 1991.

[4] Webber, Bruce. Dale Wasserman obituary in *The New York Times* (New York, NY). December 27, 2008.

[5] Webber, Bruce. Ibid.

[6] Leeds, Barry H. Essay on *One Flew Over the Cuckoo's Nest* in Take Two: Adapting the Contemporary American Novel to Film. Barbara Tepa Lupack, editor. Bowling Green OH: Bowling Green State University Popular Press © 1994.

[7] Hart, Dorothy. "ACKNOWLEDGMENTS" in *Thou Swell, Thou Witty: The Life and Lyrics of Lorenz Hart*. New York NY: Harper & Row, Publishers © 1976.

Chapter 21: *Somet'ing Special*

[1] Colby, Michael & Fradrich, James. Lyric to "Someting Special" from the musical *North Atlantic* (music: James Fradrich; book by Michael Colby) © 1977.

Chapter 22: *Presents From the Past*

[1] Silverman, Stephen M. "The Post reviews New York/Musical heritage for sale" in *New York Post* (New York NY). May 22, 1978.

[2] Green, Stanley. Encyclopedia of the American Musical. New York NY: Dodd, Mead Company, November 1, 1976.

[3] Jacobs, Leonard. "Working in Concert: How Neglected Musicals Come Back to Life" in *Backstage* (NY edition). February 11, 2004.

[4] Holden, Stephen. "Music: New Amsterdam's 'New Moon'" in *The New York Times* (New York NY). November 25, 1981.

[5] Zakariasen, Bill. "Stouthearted revival of 'The New Moon'" in *Daily News* (New York NY). November 25, 1981.

[6] Tynes, Clairee. The Miracle of Bill: A Family Confronts AIDS. Cincinnati OH: Forward Movement Publications, May 1989.

[7] Tynes, Clairee. Ibid.

[8] Holden, Stephen. "Music/Note in Brief/ 1928 Musical 'Rosalie' In Concert at Town Hall" in *The New York Times* (New York NY). April 21, 1983.

[9] Tynes, Clairee. The Miracle of Bill: A Family Confronts AIDS. Cincinnati OH: Forward Movement Publications, May 1989.

Chapter 23: *Days and Algonquinites*

[1] "About TADA!" from website for TADA! Youth Theater. New York, NY © 2008: http://www.tadatheater.com/historyoftada.asp

[2] Obituary for LaVerne Gunton in *The Modesto Bee* (Modesto CA). May 21, 2014,

[3] Gavin, James. Sylvia Syms obituary in *The New York Times* (New York, NY). May 17, 1992.

[4] Gavin, James. Ibid.

[5] Gavin, James. Ibid.

[6] Harrington, Bob. "Eulogy for Sylvia" / "Bistro Bits" in *Back Stage* (New York, NY). May 15, 1992.

Chapter 24: *It Could Only Happen in the Theatre*

[1] Benson, Raymond. "James Bond 007" section of RaymondBenson.com: http://www.raymondbenson.com/jamesbond007/

[2] Corry, John. Review of *Charlotte Sweet* in *The New York Times* (New York NY). May 3, 1982.

[3] Martin, Douglas. Casper Citron obituary in *The New York Times* (New York NY). February 10, 1997.

Chapter 25: *End of an Era*

[1] Horsley, Carter. "Going, Going, Algonquin!" in *New York Post* (New York NY). June 12, 1987, 1998.

[2] Isère, Esther. "Archives: The Algonquin Sold to Japanese Hotelier" in *The New York Times* (New York NY). June 12, 1987.

[3] Iverem, Esther. Ibid.

[4] Iovline, Julie V. "Algonquin, at Wit's End, Retrofits" in *The New York Times* (New York NY). May 28, 1998.

[5] "The History and Traditions of The Algonquin Hotel" from www.algonquinhotel.com © 2014: http://www.algonquinhotel.com/newsroom/article/history-and-traditions-algonqun-hotel

[6] Ayrton, Kate, "Interview: Hotel Design Guru Alexandra Clampalimaud" in *Wandermelon:* The ultimate travel companion featuring news you can use by travel writers. Australia: April 7, 2011: http://wandermelon.com/2011/04/07/interview-hotel-design-guru-alexandra-champalimaud/

[7] Iovline, Julie V. "Algonquin, at Wit's End, Retrofits" in *The New York Times* (New York NY). May 28, 1998.

[8] Samuels, David. "Play It Again, Sam" In *The New Yorker* (New York NY). February 10, 1997.

[9] Colby, Michael. Lyric to "In My Dreams" (music: Gerald Jay Markoe) © 2000.

Index

Made in the USA
Columbia, SC
17 March 2018